What you do speaks so loud that
I cannot hear what you say.

RALPH WALDO EMERSON (1803–1882)

I Hear What You Say, But What Are You Telling Me?

I Hear What You Say, But What Are You Telling Me?

The Strategic Use of
Nonverbal Communication
in Mediation

Barbara G. Madonik

JOSSEY-BASS
A Wiley Company
San Francisco

Published by

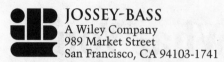

JOSSEY-BASS
A Wiley Company
989 Market Street
San Francisco, CA 94103-1741

www.josseybass.com

Jossey-Bass books and products are available through most bookstores. To contact Jossey-Bass directly, call (888) 378-2537, fax to (800) 605-2665, or visit our website at www.josseybass.com.

Substantial discounts on bulk quantities of Jossey-Bass books are available to corporations, professional associations, and other organizations. For details and discount information, contact the special sales department at Jossey-Bass.

We at Jossey-Bass strive to use the most environmentally sensitive paper stocks available to us. Our publications are printed on acid-free recycled stock whenever possible, and our paper always meets or exceeds minimum GPO and EPA requirements.

Library of Congress Cataloging-in-Publication Data
Madonik, Barbara G.
  I hear what you say, but what are you telling me?: the
strategic use of nonverbal communication in mediation / Barbara G. Madonik.—1st ed.
    p. cm.
Includes bibliographical references and index.
  ISBN 0-7879-5709-7 (alk. paper)
1. Body language. 2. Nonverbal communication.
3. Interpersonal communication. 4. Negotiation. I. Title.
  BF637.N66 M34 2001
  153.6'9—dc21

2001003015

FIRST EDITION
HB Printing

10 9 8 7 6 5 4 3 2 1

Contents

Preface

As a child I attended public schools. In those days we had to stand beside our desks to answer questions. Sometimes we knew the answers. Sometimes not. Silent students often lifted their heads and stared upward. Even years later I can hear one teacher mock, "Do you think that the answer is written on the ceiling?" Oddly enough, for many it often was. They just had to know where to look.

What I did not know then, but do now, is how these students were making sense of communication and looking for information. I did know that most students were not cheating when they raised their heads from test papers to stare into space or look in different directions. I sensed they were intuitively locating answers in their minds. My instinct told me this. I just could not prove it.

Learning That Some Answers *Are* Written on the Ceiling

Over the next years I continued to be curious, but the answers still evaded me. So I turned to what I thought would be a different area. Because I had always craved a way to understand people on their own terms, I pursued foreign languages. By the end of my university studies, I had acquired six foreign languages, and I went into the adult world believing that I could approach people on their terms. I understood their languages.

Yet questions still niggled at me. I became a French teacher. One summer I traveled to Europe and the Middle East. In Venice I saw two people needing train timetables. They were yelling at a man in an information kiosk. The couple spoke only English. He spoke only Italian. As the couple's frustration increased, they used more words. That did not help. The man never did understand. In Istanbul I needed directions to two landmarks. I did not speak Turkish. Instead I simply gestured and drew on bits of papers. I found my destinations. During that summer I kept wondering what I was missing about the way communication works. I began to sense that I would not find my answers in words. I also had a hunch that those answers had something to do with things written on the ceiling.

I began working in corporations in areas that involved communication. Around the same time, my hunches received a major boost. I met Paul Klein, a therapist who had been studying radically new concepts and was using communication systems based on nonverbal communication patterns. These patterns, he stated, existed outside people's awareness. Some of the concepts he disclosed to me related to the physical patterns and eye positions people displayed. Finally, I discovered what was written on the ceiling! People were looking up as they accessed visual information in their minds. Those who looked from side to side during examinations were listening for internal sounds. My friend even explained how test papers placed on the left side of the desk could be troublesome for some. When they looked down and to the left, an eye position generally associated with listening to internal dialogues, the position itself could cause them to hear such internal dialogues and distract them.

These explanations sounded farfetched, but my curiosity was piqued. Then my associate delivered the one-two punch. He said that less than 20 percent of all communication related to words. I realized that if he were correct, all my foreign languages would fetch were frequent chances to miscommunicate. I believed that I had to disprove his contention. So over the next eighteen months, I tested my associate's theories with my clients. I observed, listened to, and used their nonverbal communication patterns. Then I looked at my results. As much as I tried to ignore them, they were astounding. When I re-created the patterns that people used, I built rapport. I was able to predict how they would make their decisions. I could model and master just about any communication situation. At this point, however, I could do it only mechanically.

Discovering How to Use This Knowledge

I had not met the man who could teach me how to make nonverbal communication strategies work elegantly. The next year I came to know and study with Dave Dobson, the psychologist who named and taught about *other-than-conscious communication*. Among other things, he demonstrated to me that a knowledge of communication patterns is ineffectual when it is not accompanied by respect for other people. He and his senior trainer, Eric Oliver, insisted that those who are aware of nonverbal communication patterns must develop communication flexibility to accommodate the communication needs of people who do not recognize these patterns.

Now that I had my answers, I just needed to know where to use them. In 1986, I started applying this information as I worked with clients at corporations, associations, and community colleges. Soon after, I talked to a few lawyers. Some were fascinated by the subject. Others were scared or skeptical. I could not blame them. I had been pretty leery myself at first. However, I kept knocking on legal doors and writing for law journals. I was asked to speak in legal forums, and I became a program consultant for The Advocates' Society Institute. The information was seeping into the staid legal community; however, I was not satisfied yet. Eventually, I began doing some work as a jury consultant. Overall, though, lawyers remained resistant to ideas about nonverbal communication.

It was around this time that I found myself watching the live, daily broadcasts of an inquiry into the use of anabolic steroids by athletes at the Seoul Olympics. I only glanced at the witnesses at first. Then I looked and listened more carefully. I sensed some were credible and others were not. At first, I had no basis on which to justify my impressions. Then I made a breakthrough discovery. Credible witnesses ran through a predictable set of two or three movements just before they said yes. They executed a different set of movements just before saying no. Noncredible witnesses mixed up these signals. Soon I could predict yes and no answers before the words were out of witnesses' mouths. Finally, I turned off the sound. The nonverbal cues were more reliable than the words.

This knowledge reignited my drive to bring my information into the legal system. Years before, Justice Rosalie Silberman Abella (currently a judge of the Court of Appeal for Ontario) had encouraged me to explore alternative dispute resolution, a new field at the time. Now Cliff Hendler, a veteran mediator (and current president of the International Academy of Mediators), graciously agreed to let me observe him. Next I was invited to guest lecture at Osgoode Hall Law School's Graduate Program in Alternative Dispute Resolution. A little later, Kathleen Kelly, a seasoned mediator and arbitrator (and current Chair of the Canadian Bar Association National Dispute Resolution Section), became my mentor. I was committed.

Improving Your Mediation Processes and Outcomes

Mediation has proven just the spot to use nonverbal communication strategically. It is a winning situation for everyone. I had already been identifying nonverbal communication patterns in order to profile judges, lawyers, and witnesses and also in my work as a jury consultant. I had been profiling people before and during trials. Now, as a mediator and as a resource for other mediators, I track parties' nonverbal communication patterns and profile their lawyers' patterns too. I use nonverbal strategies to investigate disputes within organizations and take advantage of the same mechanisms to create solutions for those organizations. The results have been remarkable.

The benefits of recognizing and understanding nonverbal communication are enjoyed by both conflict resolution professionals and the parties at the table. During mediation, in caucus, or at the time of offer, the foremost benefit to the mediator of knowing about nonverbal patterns is the ability to distinguish between stalls caused by the terms and those caused merely by clashing communication structures. By tracking nonverbal communication, mediators can focus on the component that needs adjustment and leave what is working alone. That way, they work on the troublesome issues and avoid the risk of neutralizing the elements that are leaning in their favor.

Benefits, however, begin well before the time of offer. Mediators who track parties from the first telephone call can prepare themselves, the mediation environment, and the parties in the most productive manner. For example, through tracking, mediators can pick up nuances of information about things that often have an influence during mediation, such as health conditions or ethnicity. The mediator's ability to detect and prepare for what he or she has learned about these things allows the mediator to maximize the session. As a result of the advance knowledge, parties function effectively from the outset of the process. The mediator's knowledge eliminates surprises that can stall or derail the process completely. Knowing about nonverbal communication and being able to track communication structures minimizes surprises for mediators and increases their control of the dispute resolution environment. As a result of tracking, mediators can anticipate and diffuse potential outbursts. They can capitalize on their ability to use different communication structures with different parties and counsel to clarify issues and present information in more compelling ways. Recognition of patterns assists mediators to head off or neutralize power imbalances or inadvertent cultural offenses. They can lay a path for parties to heal themselves. Overall, the ability to recognize and use nonverbal patterns assists mediators and parties at the same time.

The parties to a mediation are the ones who ultimately benefit from mediators' knowledge of nonverbal communication patterns. The result of mediators' using these strategies is faster, more respectful resolution. Clients feel the mediation experience has been a positive one even though they may not consciously know why. Time is saved. Money is saved. Face is saved. People feel acknowledged. Closure is reached. The ultimate result for the mediator is not only a statistical success and the feeling of success but actual success as determined by the real decision makers—the parties.

Although I have written this book specifically to address the needs of professional mediators, I invite others to take advantage of it also. The more aware people are of all forms of communication, the more flexible and fluid a mediation will be. Mediators, lawyers, arbitrators, and judges—and also educators, parents, counselors, and anyone else who at times has a role to play in conflict resolution—can use any of these techniques strategically in assisting others to reach satisfactory, enduring agreements.

August 2001   BARBARA G. MADONIK
                                                                  Toronto, Canada

To Watson
Who said he would be there when I called
—and always was.

Acknowledgments

I have come to learn that the people who support an author are as much the fabric of the book as the fibers from which the pages are woven. Without them the book would never exist. This is particularly true in my case.

My unending gratitude goes to my best friend, biggest fan, and *covivant*, Eric Posner. Every day he has always been there, supporting my dreams, cheering me on, being my sounding board, doing my research, making my meals, calming my fears, raising my spirits, and keeping me level. His faith in me has never wavered. He has been my compass.

As a communication consultant and mediator I have benefited from many colleagues who unselfishly shared their time and experience. I would like to thank them. Psychologist Dave Dobson allowed me to stay in his home while I attended one of his workshops. His generosity both inspired me and gave me a window into how elegant communication could really work. Lucy LaGrassa, communication consultant and president of Lucy LaGrassa Inc., was the first person to encourage me to write a book and gently prod me to keep at it. Anne Grant, principal of Mediated Solutions Inc. and former chair of the Canadian Bar Association (Ontario) Dispute Resolution Section, loaned me the two Jossey-Bass books that first piqued my curiosity about mediation. Cliff Handler, president of DRS Dispute Resolution Services and current president of the International Academy of Mediators, kindly allowed me attend my first mediations and discover for myself what this "mediation stuff" was all about. Finally, my heartfelt thanks go to Kathleen Kelly, president of Kelly International Settlement Services Inc. and current chair of the Canadian Bar Association National Dispute Resolution Section. As my colleague, friend, mentor, and constant adviser, she has continued to provide me with unending challenges and has generously shared her wisdom.

I would also like to express my gratitude to those people who worked to make this book materialize. My deepest thanks go to Alan Rinzler, executive editor at Jossey-Bass, who had the vision to see how this information would benefit mediators. I would also like to acknowledge the dedication of Amy Scott, assistant editor, and Dawn Walker, associate production editor, both at Jossey-Bass, who have been infinitely patient, good natured, and thorough about answering my endless questions and assisting me. I would like to express my appreciation to Elspeth MacHattie, a superb editor, who demonstrated an uncanny ability to climb into my mind. Finally, words of encouragement from established writers Spider Robinson and Knowlton Nash have given me the courage to persevere.

I am grateful to my friends and family who endured my cave dweller mentality for all the months I have been writing. My nieces Megan and Melissa kept pushing me forward with daily quizzing about how many words I had written. Michelle reminded me about the "magic button," and Jessica's perseverance inspired me. My nephew, Matthew, kept my brain alive with his fascinating questions. Finally, I want especially to thank my sister, physician Bonnie Madonik. She has given me peace of mind by reminding me that my family is always there waiting for me.

B.G.M.

Introduction

When I first started working with attorneys, I met a trial lawyer who fancied herself an expert at reading nonverbal communication. After we had chatted for five minutes she suddenly said, "I know why you are wearing those glasses. They are generally fashionable but understated. You've also picked them because they have a slightly horn-rimmed look that gives you an educated appearance." This was an interesting fantasy. I was wearing them because I earned very little money in those days. The frames had come free with the lenses.

Such unfounded interpretation of nonverbal communication serves only to create great fictions in some people's minds. In fact, the accurate interpretation of nonverbal communication requires recognizing specific, repeated patterns.

Communication Realities

To begin to understand these patterns and the strategic uses of nonverbal communication, it is first important to appreciate some communication realities.

Attention Limits

Our conscious awareness is limited to being cognizant of approximately seven things concurrently. Many people learning of this limitation think that it applies to remembering sets of things, names or dates perhaps. But it has much broader applications. A seminar participant, for example, once asked me whether car accidents might result from this limitation. She was curious about people who said they "didn't notice the other car," and she wondered whether the other car might sometimes be the "eighth piece of information" for a driver. In fact many car accidents are a result of pieces of missed communication. People do not see the other car reflected in the rearview mirror. The radio is playing and the driver does not hear another car's horn. Cell phone conversation can require holding the phone and pushing buttons. Even if the driver simply listens and talks, he is doing two things that are unrelated to driving, and he has less capacity to attend consciously to the things that do matter.

The number of pieces of consciously available information we can work with at one time in any situation is flexible but usually limited to five to seven. That seems to be average. Beyond that number, items of information tend to be deposited into an area outside conscious awareness.

Methods of Communication

Before 1933, people commonly believed that words were the primary conveyors of human communication. In 1933, Alfred Korzybski published a seminal work, *Science and Sanity: An Introduction to Non-Aristotelian Systems and General Semantics*. In it, he identified how people used words as "maps." These maps helped people understand what a communication meant. Until that time people believed that they connected words with things. Korzybski, however, discovered that this concept was incorrect. In people's minds, words actually *became* the things they represented. For example, people did not think of the word *chair* as *the word chair*. If they heard the word *chair,* that sound represented the actual piece of furniture and not the word that represented the furniture. From this discovery the famous concept "the map is not the territory" evolved. Korzybski's discovery about this differentiation was pivotal. It was the beginning of our modern understanding of the ways people hear language and make sense of it.

In 1957, Noam Chomsky published his doctoral thesis on transformational grammar. The work, from which many successors developed profiling techniques, examined language and people's experiences. It showed that people use words to record their experiences. To do this, they store the words in their personal set of fixed linguistic structures. Later when they talk about their experiences, their language structure is organized in exactly the same way as it was when the experience was stored. Moreover, this activity happens without people's conscious knowledge. The discovery was profound. If communicators could track and replicate these unique linguistic models, they could reach people at a level below their conscious awareness.

While Chomsky was doing his work, most people interested in communication were still missing significant and powerful information: nonverbal communication patterns. Then, in the 1970s, John Grinder and Richard Bandler teamed up to study the communication patterns of accomplished communicators. The two men worked together to isolate the linguistic patterns of these people. Grinder and Bandler reviewed the work of people like renowned therapists Fritz Perls, Virginia Satir, and Milton Erickson. Their distilled results pinpointed how people clearly demonstrate personal communication patterns. Their research established that individuals prefer to communicate through language that evokes a specific sense: sight, sound, touch, taste, or smell. Bandler and Grinder came up with more than linguistic patterns. Their results identified communication patterns that included specific language and nonverbal communication cues too. At that point Bandler and Grinder created the core concepts of a communication system that explained how people organize and communicate their experiences. They called this system *neuro-linguistic programming,* or NLP. People using NLP techniques can simplify communication, and they find it easier to give and get information.

In examining communication patterns, Bandler, Grinder, and other professionals, like psychologist and hypnotherapist Dave Dobson, discovered that most communication behavior is automatic. Dobson began to teach about a mode of communication he had used when treating patients: *other-than-conscious communication.* He called it this rather than subconscious or unconscious communication after recognizing that it happens *concurrently* with conscious communication. Yet it occurs without the communicators themselves being aware of it.

These discoveries of Bandler, Grinder, and Dobson, might seem to suggest that people have little choice in their communication because these important patterns are functioning outside their awareness. There is a choice, however. People can ignore or pay attention to their communication and that of others. If they focus on the patterns, if they become aware of what ordinarily functions outside their awareness, they can communicate and respond more effectively. They can do this through verbal and nonverbal communication. When they do, the results are exceptional. Their messages become streamlined. They develop rapport more quickly. They are understood more easily. They understand others instantly. Using their knowledge about linguistic and physical patterns in communication, they can create flexible, fluid communication. These positive effects can reach into areas ranging from interpersonal relationships to business to the practice of law and dispute resolution.

A Blueprint for Nonverbal Strategies

If you are wondering how you can profit from these discoveries, you will find your answers in this book. It is a kind of tool kit, loaded with practical information, tips, and ideas you can use in mediation. It is structured as a step-by-step guide so you can be creative about preparing for mediation and facilitating the mediation process. The material starts where "Communication 101" leaves off. It tells you how to tune all your senses into what is happening with all parties. It describes how you can gather information about the ways individuals communicate and what to do with it once you have it.

This book is a two-part blueprint for strategic nonverbal communication. Part One gives you a solid foundation by defining the features and applications of nonverbal communication. Part Two guides you through a methodical process of applying this knowledge to create and use nonverbal communication strategies in mediation.

Part One prepares you to understand the techniques that follow. This comprehensive set of definitions and explanations of basic applications will make you comfortable with the concepts and materials of nonverbal communication. You will develop new levels of awareness about information passed from person to person, especially about methods of communication that have nothing to do with words. Part One also teaches you to identify patterns of eye movement and the significance of these patterns. You will become aware of additional physical patterns and how these patterns precede verbal responses. You will learn to spot inconsistent signals and know which ones deserve attention. You will gain awareness of aspects of nonverbal communication such as space, touch, and time. In this part of the book, I also show you how to track and profile the communication patterns of the parties at the mediating table. You will learn about communication that triggers action and about identifying the frameworks in which each party operates most productively. From there you will progress to techniques to create rapport, gather information, and clear mediation hurdles.

At this point, you are ready to use the ideas and techniques in Part One to get the results you want. Part Two describes how to do this in seven steps.

In Step One you undertake practical ways to ready yourself for the mediation and to set up your work space to maximize your effectiveness. This chapter describes how to prepare written forms to track verbal and nonverbal communication patterns from the time of the first telephone call and suggests an exercise for developing a vocabulary to fit each person's pattern. Because your office equipment and its placement significantly affect communication, this chapter explains equipment pitfalls and strategies too. It also suggests specific methods of gathering nonverbal communication clues and alerts you to potential biases and the advantages of preliminary inquiries.

In Step Two you make the initial telephone contact, and this chapter tells you how to make the most of it. First, it discusses how to improve attentiveness to critical information by doing small things like closing your eyes. Then it explains other strategies such as finding common interests and matching the other person's language structure. This chapter teaches you how to deescalate conversations, to gather information by listening to sounds that accompany words, to isolate and deal with a party's fear, and to use questions to elicit vital information.

In Step Three you focus on managing the mediation environment so you can control it. Here, I explain the importance of recognizing both perceived and real levels of power among the parties. Then this chapter takes you through techniques to provide for parties' safety and make them feel comfortable. This chapter also considers dealing with the meeting location as a strategic issue; attending to small details that can make a difference, like chair height or position; using props and objects to control communication; and using space, time, and symbols to convey respect.

In Step Four you assess the parties to the mediation. After helping you recognize your own preferences and biases, I suggest methods to use, first, to gauge the parties at arm's length and, second,
to build a close-up profile of each party. This chapter leads you,
step-by-step, through isolating the unique clues that form each profile. Among these clues are parties' patterns relating to eyes, bodies, language, and paralanguage; their ways of indicating yes or no
without saying a word; their action triggers and working frameworks; and their methods of making decisions. All this prepares
you for working with the parties during mediation and in finalizing an agreement.

In Step Five, you engage each party to create powerful rapport.
This chapter shows you how to get nonverbal permission to begin
the mediation process, what strategies to use to welcome parties
verbally and nonverbally, and how these strategies empower the
parties. You learn how to adjust your responsiveness by mirroring
communication and by responding directly to each person's nonverbal communication. You also learn how to use different questioning styles, like the Columbo technique and the onionskinning
approach. I demonstrate how you can capitalize on metaphors,
analogies, and humor and how you can change the communication in the room to encourage more productive mentalities and
change people's focus. Finally, I help you become comfortable with
guiding parties to communicate with each other and with creating
work units in which everyone works most effectively.

In Step Six you create an environment that triggers action. I
show you how to deal with underlying issues by exploring specificity, how to identify fear by the nonverbal communication that is
present—and absent—and how to isolate real goals. In this chapter you learn to build momentum through strategies that work with
action and reaction, similarities and differences, goal achievement
and problem avoidance mechanisms, and the as if technique. You
also learn nonverbal and physical techniques for dealing with
derailments and stalls; procedures for gaining perspective, managing pressure, and challenging relevancy; and ways of encouraging physical movement that fosters mental shifts.

In Step Seven, you bring closure to the parties and the process.
I start this chapter by showing you how to help parties make decisions. You discover how to ensure that parties have validation for

their decisions and how to raise their awareness of settlement realities. You learn how to use two levels of messages to create offers that people will listen to, weaving in nonverbal elements that compel people to give proposals serious consideration. This chapter walks you through techniques to guard against buyer's remorse once the agreement is signed and to deal with the dynamics of fear and apology. It shows you how to put the parties in control, balancing their power so they craft the final agreement jointly, and how to create strategies that allow the parties to leave the conflict behind.

Maximizing Your Results

I Hear What You Say, But What Are You Telling Me? gives you practical information you can use right away. These grassroots approaches have been created over many years of real-world experience in many forums. They have been tested and retested. The examples are composites, to ensure anonymity of the subjects, but the information they convey reflects years of experience.

Before you dig into reading and using this material, however, I must raise one flag of caution. I want to alert you to using this information appropriately. This book is intended as a guide only in reference to communication. I have written it to provide you with suggestions about using nonverbal communication strategies in mediation. The book is in no way intended to offer legal advice. I recommend that you always consult an attorney for legal information and opinions.

That said, I encourage you to enjoy experimenting with the material. Learning the techniques will be simple for you. Strategic execution takes longer. However, practice pays off. These nonverbal communication strategies have worked for me for more than fifteen years. I invite you to let them work for you too.

Recognizing That Techniques Are Just the Beginning

As you progress through this book, you will discover many techniques. All of them are there to help you create your own strategies in mediation. Successful execution, however, requires a marriage of technical knowledge and respect. This respect requires that you notice the nonverbal communication that people offer you and respond to it in a discrete and courteous way. That usually means acknowledging nonverbal communication by returning it in the form of nonverbal communication. This respect is key to achieving outcomes that are profound and elegant.

Relying on process alone can produce disastrous results. Mediators who do so have never heard the woeful tale of an old friend of mine. Many years ago he enrolled in a monthlong intensive training program. In that sequestered environment he was taught technical execution of nonverbal maneuvers. In no session, however, did he hear about respect or elegance. The day he returned home, his friends surprised him with a birthday party. Surrounded by chums and inspired by his new techniques, he decided to "share" his new wisdom with his buddies. As he talked to each friend he acted mechanically and without finesse. Without their permission, he told all of them the particular nonverbal patterns they were exhibiting, even though these patterns existed outside their awareness. Within minutes the room emptied. More than that, most of those friends never returned.

Being a Successful Strategist

The most effective way to develop your skill is to read this book in the order it is written. First, learn the definitions, so the explanations of the techniques will be clear. Next, build your technical skills in the order of the typical mediation sequence. That will make it easier for you to practice the techniques when you attend mediations. I also recommend that you rehearse the questions and scripts included in Part Two. You might even want to memorize them. Although the wording is colloquial, to fit the typical mediation environment, it is well thought out. It has been developed over a number of years to maximize the effectiveness of nonverbal strategies. Once you have covered all the material, you may want to reread the text to learn the techniques more thoroughly. Alternatively, you may choose to revisit selected sections for review.

However you choose to proceed, I suggest approaching this learning with a sense of adventure. Keep in mind the advice of communication expert Robert B. Dilts. In a 1992 Toronto workshop on creativity, *Tools for Dreamers,* he stated, "There is no such thing as a failure. It's only a solution to a different problem." I encourage you to become creative about solutions as you use this material. I believe you will find the parties in front of you already have all the resources they need. You simply have to recognize those resources and proceed respectfully. Your strategies will take care of the rest.

Avoiding Tailspins

Gregory Bateson was a brilliant anthropologist, researcher, and expert in communication patterns. He was also renowned for his expertise in epistemology—learning how to learn. At the Esalen Institute in 1978, Bateson encouraged those around him by saying that "before you start thinking about something you should first think about how you are going to go about thinking about it." I recommend his advice. Pause a moment. Sort out what you want from this book. As you read about the different approaches, wonder how you might come at using them. Think about how you can execute strategies while staying respectful to those around you. Have fun in the process. Practice. Practice. Practice.

Learn to anticipate the turns and twists. Be vigilant and prepare for them. I make this suggestion as a result of the time in my student pilot days when I had to learn to recover from "incipient spins." After one relentless hour of practice, I came back, exhausted, to the old flight shack. I was miffed because I thought my instructor had just wasted my time. As I filled in my log book, I spotted this sign on the bulletin board: "The mark of a superior pilot is never putting yourself in a position to have to use your superior skills." I finally understood.

The advice was true for spins. Today I also believe it is true for mediation. The path to greatest success in mediation is preparation for every possible contingency.

I Hear What You Say, But What Are You Telling Me?

Part One

Essential Definitions and Practical Applications

Chapter One

Essential Definitions—
Terms and Tools

As someone who deals constantly with conflict resolution you realize just how much preparation is necessary before you walk through any mediation door. A similar level of preparation is necessary before you use nonverbal communication strategies in mediation. This chapter introduces the ideas and applications of nonverbal communication and gives you a language for thinking about them and discussing them. Once you get comfortable with these ideas and terms, you will be ready to start learning about patterns and techniques. The first term in this language that needs to be defined is nonverbal communication itself. *Nonverbal communication* is a process in which people transmit and receive messages without using words. Research documents that from 65 percent to 93 percent of all our face-to-face communication is sent through nonverbal means. Even though nonverbal messages do not have words, they may contain sounds. A *nonverbal-vocal communication* is a message that has vocalizations but no words. Examples are hooting at a football game and of course all the ah's and er's and um's that we utter in ordinary conversation. A *nonverbal-nonvocal communication* contains neither words nor vocalizations. Examples are waving and shaking hands.

Some of the following terms may seem familiar; some may sound foreign. I suggest you read all the definitions with care and awareness. Expressions that you may have heard in other environments may carry a different meaning in the world of nonverbal communication. Other words and phrases that are standards in the field of nonverbal communication may be new to you. Some are terms that I have developed over the years because there was no other language available to explain to clients, students, or lawyers what was happening and what they could do about it.

The definitions are clustered in ten conceptual categories and explain ideas relating to our systems of understanding, the communication cues we exchange, our use of verbal language, our use of paralanguage, our levels of awareness, our sense about physical space, our beliefs about touch, our understanding of time, our use of objects, and our use of physical symbols. This approach allows you to learn related ideas together, and that will assist you in applying them appropriately later.

Systems

Many things affect the way we receive and store information from our senses. To begin with, it's essential for mediators to be aware that this receiving and storing process is automatic and systematic. More than one system is available, and different people may prefer different systems.

Representational Systems

A *representational system* is the process through which we understand information collected through our senses. It affects our subsequent behavior and communication. The process happens in stages. First, information is gathered by an individual through his five senses of sight, sound, taste, touch, and smell. Then this initial information is automatically organized and re-presented to the brain in the way the individual understands most easily. Finally, the person behaves or communicates according to the information he has received.

The brain may organize information through one of three systems. It may utilize a *visual representational system,* or *visual system,* in which it has a heightened awareness of sight-related information. It may use an *auditory representational system,* or *auditory system,* in which it has a strong responsiveness to sound-related information. It may use a *kinesthetic representational system,* or *kinesthetic system* or *kinesthesia,* in which it has an enhanced cognizance of touch, taste, smell, and feelings. For example, at a debate, the visual representational system would discern the appearance of the debaters, the auditory representational system would hear the sound quality, and the kinesthetic representational system would sense the hardness of a chair.

A *representational system file,* or *system file,* is a theoretical storage area in the mind. You might think of it as a mental file folder in which a person saves a piece of information acquired through one of the representational systems. For example, a person seeing a Christmas tree might store the memory of that tree in a visual system file. *Accessing* is the process by which the brain retrieves the information that has been stored in a system file. *Transderivational search,* or *cross-filing,* describes the process of accessing a series of related files. People receive a piece of information through one of their senses. The information is sent to the brain to create a system file. Once the file is created, the brain can search to see if there is another file with a piece of information related in any way to the information that just arrived. If there is no more information, the process stops. If there is a related file, the brain goes to it. This linking process can continue over and over. A remembered image of a Christmas tree might cross-file to an auditory system file that contains the sound of tinkling bells. That bell sound might then cross-file to trigger a kinesthetic system file holding the smell of fir needles and eggnog.

Neuro-Linguistic Programming, or *NLP,* is a process that examines a person's experiences and then looks at how that person perceives those experiences. Communication about those experiences takes place when the person retrieves information from representational system files and then expresses his thoughts. For example, if a traveler visits a beach, NLP might explore whether he talks about seeing waves, hearing fog horns, or feeling sand underfoot. Many nonverbal communication terms, like representational systems, have their origins in NLP.

Preferred Representational Systems

A person's *preferred representational system,* or *preferred system,* is the system that person uses most frequently to send and receive information. It is also called the *primary representational system,* or *primary system.* It may be a visual, auditory, or kinesthetic system. The person prefers it because she finds she can make the most distinctions about her respective world through it. For example, people who prefer a visual representational system might be given verbal (that is, auditory) driving instructions but then imagine a mental map (that is, imagine visual instructions) to understand better. People who prefer a kinesthetic system might be given those same verbal instructions and might then trace a map (that is, make kinesthetic instructions) to get their bearings. People are often aware of their preference and will ask to receive information through their primary system. For example, people with a kinesthetic primary system may want to touch a sample to evaluate a fabric, whereas people with a visual primary system may ask to see the swatch colors.

A *secondary representational system,* or *secondary system,* is an alternative to a person's primary communication process. People do not depend as heavily on this process as they do on their primary process. Moreover, usually they are not as aware of their reliance on this system. A *tertiary representational system,* or *tertiary system,* is a person's third communication process. Most people rarely use their third system consciously, although they do use it without knowing they do.

When information is coming into all three systems but the person is not alert to the information coming into one of them, that person is said to have a *blocked system.* People's behavior is often highly influenced by the information other-than-consciously received by blocked systems. For example, a person with a blocked kinesthetic system may react with fear to the tone in which certain words are uttered. Yet he may believe he is reacting to the words themselves because he is consciously attending to the words. He is not consciously aware of the tone that triggers the blocked kinesthetic system; nevertheless he reacts to it.

System jamming is a related term used to describe the interruption of communication flow. This disruption often happens when communicators fail to use the message receiver's primary or secondary systems.

Cues

A *cue* is a signal that one person sends to another person. It may be verbal or nonverbal. It may be detected through sight, sound, touch, taste, or smell. A cue provides information about the communicator. For example, if a person perspires, it may signal that she is hot or that she is stressed.

Let's look first at some general characteristics of cues (their direction, their number, and the significance of cue sequence) and then at specific cues a mediator will see in individuals (system cues, eye cues, physical cues, fear cues, and breathing cues).

Afferent and Efferent Cues

The terms *afferent* and *efferent* distinguish incoming and outgoing cues. A cue is afferent, or inbound, when it carries information inward to the receiver's central nervous system. An example is the feeling of a hot stove. A cue is efferent, or outbound, when it carries information outward from the sender's central nervous system. An example is sweat or tears.

Multiple Cues

Multiple cues are signals that happen consecutively or simultaneously. Their order or association may create a meaning different from the meanings carried by these same cues considered individually. A *pattern loop* is a type of multiple cue. People displaying a pattern loop move consistently back and forth among two or three representational systems. For example, a person who signals with a visual cue, then a kinesthetic cue, then a visual cue, then a kinesthetic cue, and so on, is using a visual-kinesthetic pattern loop. Once pattern loops are identified they can be used as *predictors*. Once a mediator identifies a subject's pattern loop, he can forecast from the current part of the pattern loop the part of the pattern the subject will enact next, and he can prepare for it.

Congruent and Incongruent Cues

Congruent cues are two or more signals that occur simultaneously and match. The related action is a *congruity*. For example, people who say they are hungry as they wolf down a meal are sending congruent cues. When two or more cues do not match, they are called *incongruent cues,* and the action is an *incongruity.* An example of incongruity is perspiring people saying they are cool during a heat wave. A *kinesic slip* is a specific kind of incongruity, a verbal message that conflicts with a nonverbal message. An example of a kinesic slip is a frowning teacher telling a student how happy she is about the student's grade. Gregory Bateson and a group of his associates created the term *double bind* to describe another specific type of incongruity. Double binds occur especially in interpersonal relationships. One person sends contradictory messages that cause confusion and leave another person with no appropriate way to respond. The double bind can be seen in the example of a work-at-home parent who tells children "the door is always open" (that is, sends the signal *come here*), glowers when the children start to enter (that is, *go away*), and then asks the children, as they are retreating from the room, why they do not speak (that is, *come here*), confusing the children by making their behavior seem wrong no matter what they do.

System Cues

A *system cue,* or *representational system cue,* is a signal that indicates to the receiver the representational system preferred by, or at least in current use by, the sender. A system cue can relate to the visual, auditory, or kinesthetic representational systems. These cues often take the form of eye, language, and paralanguage cues.

Eye Cues

An *eye cue* is a signal sent by a person's eye movements. It may offer information about the communicator's preferred representational system. It may also indicate whether the communicator is remembering something or imagining, or constructing, something. In this context, the words *imagining* and *constructing* are used as synonyms, and there is no positive or negative presumption attached to the eye position that suggests such imagining. It may indicate that a party is pulling together information from different system files so she can create a comprehensible response. Information being gathered can in fact be remembered or imagined. The party may be imagining how it all would fit together to create the final response. When a party's eyes go to the position that suggests imagining or constructing something, mediators must be especially prudent about their assumptions.

An eye cue can indicate emotion. It can reflect social position. Observers interpreting eye cues need to be alert to cultural differences in their significance. For example, when communicators in some cultures cast their eyes downward, it is appropriate for observers to interpret that cue as a sign of respect. In other cultures, the same eye cue is appropriately taken as exhibiting shame. *Oculesics* is the term used to describe the study of eye movements during communication.

More specifically, an *ocular accessing cue,* or *eye accessing cue,* is one of several neurological patterns of eye movements that involve moving the eyes to specific positions. People are usually unaware they are sending these signals. They make these eye movements when they are remembering or constructing information (that is, *accessing* it in some way). For example, when a person's eyes constantly look to the side, that person is likely remembering or imagining sound-related information.

In addition, people will typically look consistently to one side when *remembering* sight-related and sound-related information and will look consistently to the other side when *imagining,* or *constructing,* sight-related and sound-related information. Most commonly, they look to their left when remembering sights and sounds and look to their right when imagining sights and sounds. The left side tends to be the *nominally dominant* hemisphere of the brain. The nominally dominant hemisphere of the brain contains the language center and is not necessarily neurologically dominant.

A person sends a *cross-wiring cue,* or exhibits *cross-dominance,* when his eyes move in patterns that seem inconsistent. For example, he might exhibit a typical pattern for remembering something visual, looking up and to his *left,* but might look sideways and to his *right* when remembering auditory information. Cross-wiring cues often create confusion for observers who expect consistent patterns. In this case, they would ordinarily expect the person to look to his *right* side when imagining sounds and to his *left* when remembering sounds.

Physical Cues

People send *physical cues* through gestures, facial expressions, and other movements and through their physical appearance. An example of sending a physical cue is pointing a finger to a spot where someone is to sit; another example is clapping hands at a political rally. *Kinesics* is the study of body, head, and face movements as communication.

Fear Cues

Fear is an emotion. It affects people mentally and physically. People may experience *internal fear cues,* indicators of their fear that provide information to them about themselves. For example, a person who is afraid may notice such indicators as a dry mouth or upset stomach. People may also transmit *external fear cues* about their fear to other people. For example, people who are trembling or breathing shallowly may be demonstrating fear cues.

The *fight-or-flight response* is an automatic arousal mechanism that is activated involuntarily when people perceive a threat. It puts the body on alert and is produced by the interaction of the *sympathetic and parasympathetic nervous systems*. These are the two major divisions of the autonomic nervous system, which balances and regulates body processes. The fight-or-flight response stimulates the body to protect itself by moving toward the threat through fighting or by moving away from the danger through fleeing. This response can be communicated to other people in different ways. For example, the fight response might be seen in belligerence and the flight response in refusal to talk.

Breathing Cues

A *breathing cue* is a signal sent by a person's breath patterns. For example, different rates of breathing and whether breathing is deep or shallow can indicate a person's preferred representational system. Some breathing cues suggest the person is feeling fear.

Language

That verbal language is just one of ten communication categories in this discussion is telling all by itself. I focus here on ideas about how we determine the meanings of words and the role of verbal communication in identifying a person's preferred representational system.

Verbal Communication

Verbal communication is a process in which people send and receive messages containing words that are either spoken or written. These messages are discerned through sight and sound (and in the case of Braille, touch). A *verbal-vocal communication* is a message that contains words and sound. An example of this is a face-to-face discussion about settlement at the end of a mediation. A *verbal-nonvocal* communication is a message that contains words but no sound. An example of this is a letter or an e-mail.

When you are using and listening to verbal communication, it's important to remain aware that a word by itself does not convey a precise meaning. It needs to be attached to a context or it lacks a definite message. The *container fallacy* is the term used by William Haney to describe the misconception that words in isolation carry exact meanings. Words communicate specific meanings in relationship to the environment in which they are placed. For example, *taping* refers to capturing sound and pictures on videotape in a television studio but means sealing packages in a shipping room. *Text* is a linguistic term describing a unit that contains words; a one-word traffic sign is a text and so is a novel. Texts, too, need contexts to be fully understood. *Referent* is the linguistic term that describes a word in its capacity as a linguistic representation of an agreed-upon concept or object. For example, the term *the president* has no specific meaning unless people agree that it references George W. Bush, Abraham Lincoln, John Kennedy, and so forth.

In some instances, context supersedes the text. *Contexting* is a communication process first described by Edward T. Hall. When communicators use contexting, they imply a message rather than say it outright. The unspoken message is considered to have a deeper meaning than the message that is articulated. In *high-context communication* people use many words or phrases. They send implicit messages by talking all around a subject; they avoid being direct or abrupt with listeners. In *low-context communication* people use few words or phrases. They send explicit messages by being direct or frank with listeners. For example, when considering a job offer, high-context communicators talk about job benefits but do not actually say yes or no. Low-context communicators simply say yes or no.

System Words

When people use language that reveals how they are understanding information, they are using *system words*. System words are terms that relate to the three representational systems: visual, auditory, and kinesthetic. Examples of the system words that people commonly use are *see, hear,* and *feel.* In communication studies, a *predicate* is a statement or expression used by a person that indicates how that person is making sense of an experience. System words are predicates. They send signals to listeners about the specific systems people are using as their method of understanding information. "Sight for sore eyes" suggests a visual frame of reference, for example; "You don't say?" suggests an auditory frame; and "leaves a bad taste" suggests a kinesthetic frame.

Translation is the process by which messages presented in one language are changed into another. This change takes place so the original message can be understood in the second language. Speakers inadvertently force listeners to translate their messages when they send those messages in one representational system to listeners who prefer another system. *Shorthanding,* in contrast, is the process in which speakers consistently use words from listeners' preferred systems. By using a preferred system, speakers make it much more likely that their messages will be understood instantly by listeners. *Leading* is the process of using language that forces a listener to respond in terms of a system the listener would not spontaneously use. As a result the original speaker cannot accurately gauge the respondent's preferred system. Additionally, those who are led in this way enter a mental state in which they are less consciously critical and can be influenced significantly. *Contamination* occurs when communicators purposely or inadvertently influence listeners by nodding their heads in a pattern that indicates yes or by shaking their heads in a no pattern. This nonverbal communication accompanying the verbal communication can influence listeners' answers. Then again the original speakers often do not receive the respondents' true response. Instead they receive a reflection of their own signal. The result of such contamination is sometimes "buyer's remorse," as people later regret their response.

Nonsystem Words

When people use words that are not aligned with any representational system, they are using *nonsystem words*. These words are in effect neutral, which makes them a valuable communication tool. When speakers use nonsystem words, listeners usually respond spontaneously, using system words that indicate their preferred system. This response tells speakers how to send messages most effectively and facilitates communication flow. Moreover, listeners are not fatigued by being forced to translate messages into their own preferred systems to understand them. Examples of neutral expressions are "let me know" and "understand."

Butting

Butting refers to sending contradictory verbal messages. People are butting when they use words that erase or negate the message that just preceded them. Examples of butting words are "except," "however," and of course "but."

Language Structures

Some terms from linguistics are helpful to mediators for discussing and understanding verbal patterns. A *language matrix* is a pattern of the way words fit together. These patterns form *language models*. Language models vary from person to person.

Messages can have both a *surface structure* and a *deep structure*. *Surface structure* is the literal meaning or text of the message. Surface structure is what a person actually says. *Deep structure* lies beneath the surface of the literal message. It reflects behavioral and language patterns. Deep structure carries the more abstract part of the message. Through deep structure, communicators let listeners know how they see the world.

Paralanguage

Paralanguage refers to voice quality and vocalizations. Paralanguage may occur in the context of words or by itself. It sends its own message in either case. When coupled with words, the paralanguage message might be carried in a person's tone or pitch. Occurring by itself, paralanguage could be a grunt. Paralanguage may be congruent or incongruent with the words with which it is combined. When language and paralanguage are incongruent, it is the paralanguage, rather than the words, that delivers the credible message. For example, the message sent by "thanks for the help" said in a grateful tone of voice is clearly different from the message sent by the same phrase said in an ungrateful tone.

Voice Quality

Voice is the sound produced by the vibration of the vocal cords in the larynx. *Voice quality* is the character of that sound. There are a number of components that make up voice quality. *Pitch* refers to the high or low sound of the voice. Pitch changes as the frequency of vocal cord vibration varies. The higher the frequency, the higher the pitch of a person's voice. *Articulation* is the process in which vocal organs, such as the tongue, change position in relation to other parts of the mouth. These changes modify the air flow that produces speech sounds. The quality of the articulation affects the quality of spoken consonants and vowels. *Timbre* refers to the overtones or resonance in a sound. The timbre of a sound depends on the shape producing the sound, the frequency of overtones, and whether the sound is at the beginning, middle, or end of its production. The timbre of vowels depends on how open or constricted the resonating areas of the head and chest are. *Cadence* refers to the balance and rhythmic flow of vocal sounds. Sometimes cadence also refers to the sound of the voice falling at the end of a sentence. *Tempo* indicates the speed at which the voice produces sound.

Vocalization

Vocalization is the name given to the sound created when air passes through a person's respiratory system and up into the vocal folds and tract. At that point vocal sounds are formed and uttered. Examples of vocalizations are growling and snorting.

Vocal Segregates

Vocal segregates are vocalized hesitations, pauses, exclamations, and other fillers that are not standard words. Examples of vocal segregates are "ooo," "um," and "uh."

Silence

Silence is also a component of paralanguage. Like sound from a person, lack of sound from a person conveys a message. Sometimes these messages are very clear. For example, silence conveys an obvious message during a wedding ceremony when the minister requests that people "object now or forever hold your peace." However, silence can also be easily misinterpreted.

Levels of Awareness

Sensory information is the raw data people take in, consciously or not, to the nervous system. This information, as its name indicates, is collected by the senses—sight, sound, touch, taste, and smell, or more formally, the visual, auditory, tactile, gustatory, and olfactory senses. Perception starts when sensory receptors are stimulated. The stimulation triggers a chain of events that eventually translates information about the stimulus into a signal for the nervous system. That coded information is then forwarded to brain areas that make sense of the information. At that point, people can distinguish individual pieces or quantities of information and understand what the sensory information means. For example, if coffee is brewing, a person's olfactory sense might detect information that is translated into a coffee aroma. At the same time, the person's auditory sense might take in information that is translated into the sound of water percolating.

However, as I discussed in the Introduction, one communication reality is that we are able to consciously deal with a limited number of items of information at any one time. In discussing representational systems earlier in this chapter, moreover, I pointed out that people can experience a blocked system when they are not conscious of the information flowing into that system. A knowledge of levels of awareness, then, is critical to effective communication.

Conscious Awareness

Conscious awareness, or *consciousness,* describes a state of alertness. When people experience conscious awareness, they are cognizant of information they are receiving through their senses. People are usually conscious of approximately seven, plus or minus two, pieces of information simultaneously. Even when people's conscious awareness is fully occupied by those seven pieces of information, however, they are still receiving and making sense of other information. As I will discuss in a moment, this additional inbound information is absorbed, even though people are not aware of it. This information remains *outside conscious awareness* until people need to focus on a piece of it. When people make this shift in focus, a piece of information currently in conscious awareness is automatically dropped outside of conscious awareness in order to, in effect, make space for the new information. For example, people may enter a room and notice the cold temperature, room light, coat hooks, desk, chairs, flip chart, overhead projector, and screen until they hear a noise outside the room. At that point the cold temperature or the furniture that at first seemed so noteworthy may drop outside of their conscious awareness as the noise enters and takes the place of that other information.

An *altered state of consciousness,* or *altered state,* is a change in conscious awareness. When people experience this shift of consciousness, observers usually see it. Often people in altered states seem to be distracted or asleep with their eyes open. When people are in this state, they tend to be less consciously critical about the information they receive.

Other-Than-Conscious Awareness

The term *other-than-conscious awareness,* or *other-than-consciousness,* describes a state of alertness. It functions simultaneously with conscious awareness. It has sometimes been called the *unconscious.* In this state, people send and receive information all the time even though they are not cognizant that this is happening. The information resides in their other-than-consciousness. Other-than-conscious communication is purposeful rather than rational. It has the most profound influence on how people interpret information. For example, audiences may be consciously aware of rational messages in commercials that talk about thriftiness. If the spokesperson, however, is dressed in haute couture clothing and leaning against a foreign sports car, the contradictory message would be retained distinctly in other-than-conscious awareness, and this message rather than the overt message would tend to form the basis for consumer action.

Other-than-conscious communication, then, describes the sending and receiving of verbal and nonverbal messages of which people are not consciously aware. People find other-than-conscious information the most credible part of any communication. For example, if a disorganized and flustered-looking lawyer tells clients with a visual preference that he is well prepared, the other-than-conscious visual communication contradicts his conscious verbal message. The clients believe the other-than-conscious communication.

We might think of other-than-conscious communication as *no-fault communication,* in an acknowledgment that people transmit and receive messages automatically. This blame-free view recognizes that people communicate instinctively in the way they prefer because they believe other people understand messages the same way they do. They are not aware of other people's communication preferences. Nevertheless, this lack of awareness often causes misunderstanding and confusion. Consider for example how frustrated a person with a visual preference would feel if the manufacturer of an object she had to assemble enclosed only written instructions and no diagrams or pictures.

Acknowledgment is the process of recognizing and responding to communications that exist outside a person's conscious awareness. For example, a person identifies one element of another person's other-than-conscious communication, and then he reproduces that behavior. In doing this, he is responding on a level outside the person's conscious awareness. He might, for example, lift an eyebrow after noticing another person's raised eyebrow. Like saying "hello," this acknowledgment need be done only once.

Distraction is an act that draws people's attention away from what they are doing or from something on which they are focused. It is executed on a conscious level to change the direction of people's conscious awareness. People tend to stop thinking about what was in their conscious awareness at the time the distraction occurred. *Redirection* is an act that is also done on a conscious level and that also diverts people's conscious attention from something. However, it then goes on to point their attention toward a new thing or idea. That is, it causes people to lose awareness of their original focus and to become aware of the new thing.

Filters

When people automatically receive, screen, and sift information into core beliefs, core values, and attitudes they are engaged in *filtering*. The information is received on an other-than-conscious level, and the mechanisms that do the work, the *filters,* do so intuitively. The ways the filters organize this information are both influenced by and lead to people's specific understanding, opinions, and convictions.

A *meta-program* is one kind of internal filter that processes and sorts information. During this process, some incoming sensory information is selectively deleted. Such deletion is necessary to avoid overloading the senses. Some information is distorted or shifted. This is done so the sensory information fits people's perceptions of the world. It also allows people to be creative and plan. Some information is generalized. That way people can draw general conclusions based on a few experiences.

Norms are filters that cultures create. They are the perceived set of rules or behaviors of a culture. People regard these filters as standards for evaluating behavior. They are assumed to define the typical and the normal. *Ethnocentrism* is a filter that causes a person to presuppose that people from all cultures act and communicate in the same ways she does. *Beliefs* are filters, especially when they are core, or central, beliefs. A belief is a conviction or acceptance of the truth of something. People have many beliefs. They organize these beliefs into structures, or *belief systems.* These systems provide a set of assumptions and presuppositions that people use as compasses to navigate in their social, ethical, moral, and religious worlds. *Core values* are filters. They are the mechanisms that people use to gauge whether an act is right or wrong, useful or worthless, good or bad. Core values are set after people have an established belief system that tells them how to function in the world. *Attitude* is a frame of mind that reflects a feeling toward something or someone. This mental position occurs as a result of people's belief systems and core values. Figure 1.1 summarizes the levels of awareness.

Space

Proxemics is the study of how people use personal space. Proxemics tells us that people's perceptions about space vary and that people's use of space is a form of nonverbal communication.

Figure 1.1. Levels of Awareness.

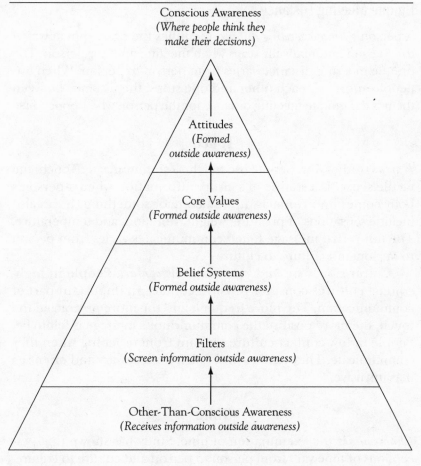

Conscious Awareness
(*Where people think they
make their decisions*)

Attitudes
(*Formed
outside awareness*)

Core Values
(*Formed outside awareness*)

Belief Systems
(*Formed outside awareness*)

Filters
(*Screen information outside awareness*)

Other-Than-Conscious Awareness
(*Receives information outside awareness*)

© 2000 Unicom Communication Consultants Inc. Reprinted with permission.

General Area Requirement

A person's *general area requirement* is the perception he has about his need for space. This requirement will vary depending on the situation. People need the least amount of space in an intimate environment. They feel the need for more area in a personal situation. They need even more in a social gathering. People require the greatest amount of space in a public environment. The *distance zone* is the space that people need between themselves and others to be comfortable.

Unique Meeting Distance

A person's *unique meeting distance* identifies the exact spot at which that person automatically stops when meeting another person. The unique meeting distance varies from person to person. When two people approach each other and one stops, the distance between them is the unique meeting distance for the person who stopped first.

Touch

Haptics studies how people use touch to communicate. Touch, the tactile sense, is a source of sensory information when a person's body comes into contact with someone or something. It can also include sensations of pressure, weight, vibration, and temperature. The nonverbal message touch communicates varies from person to person and culture to culture.

Cultures may be *high contact* or *low contact*. People in high-contact cultures consider physical contact an important part of communication. The more frequent and the more protracted the touch, the more positive the communicator's message is felt to be. People in low-contact cultures refrain from touching when they communicate. They tend to find touch unnecessary and often see it as intrusive.

Time

Chronemics is the examination of time. Study has shown that perceptions of time vary from person to person and culture to culture. How people deal with time sends nonverbal messages.

Monochronic and Polychronic Concepts of Time

A person's concept of time may be m*onochronic* or *polychronic*. People with a monochronic model of time tend to deal with one thing at a time. They regard time as linear. Tasks are separate and follow one after another. Some cultures tend to be monochronic. People with a polychronic model of time tend to deal with many things at the same time. They regard time as multidimensional and nondirectional. Some cultures tend to be polychronic.

Perceiving Events in Time

A *time line* is a chronological concept. It is used to illustrate the manner in which people store past memories and imagine future events. To create a time line, people imagine a line that represents the flow of time. They then imagine events placed along this imaginary line, associating the time of the events with the time represented by the line.

Some people perceive events in time from an *off-line* position. That is, they imagine themselves standing off the time line. When they then look at the time line, they see it running from left to right or from top to bottom in front of their eyes. Others perceive time from a *midline* position. That is, they look at events as if the events were running along the time line, and they imagine themselves standing in the middle of that line. As a result, some events seem to have happened behind them and some happen in front of them.

When people remember events in time, they are engaging in *time accessing*. For some people, this process is *random access*. These people can locate any memory immediately. For other people, remembering requires *sequential access*. These people must start in the present and go backward through each event, in consecutive order, to remember a specific event. Discovering one's own time line is a useful exercise that can help people understand how they store past memories and imagine future events.

Objectics

Objectics is the study of the ways people use material articles and artifacts to communicate information nonverbally. This information could be about a person's likes, beliefs, or occupation, for example. Instances of such articles and artifacts are conservative clothing and nose rings.

Symbolism

Symbolism is a passive form of nonverbal communication. It is the practice of using one object to represent something else. Some symbols are *code symbols*. People generally agree on their meaning, so they send the same information to everyone. For example, a flashing red traffic light at an intersection is understood by all drivers to mean that cars must stop. Some symbols, however, have different meanings to each observer. Their meanings depend on context and situation. For example, the color orange may symbolize one thing to a primary school child painting a picture and another thing to someone living in Ireland.

Chapter Two

Practical Applications— Representational Systems

The key to using nonverbal communication strategies most successfully is to identify a person's nonverbal communication pattern and then use the most productive application or technique. Now that you are equipped with the underlying ideas and a working vocabulary to express those ideas, you are ready to examine some of these patterns, applications, and techniques.

The patterns I discuss in this and the next chapter can be considered typical examples of patterns mediators see in their work. This chapter focuses on characteristics of representational systems because identifying the system a person prefers to use gives you much useful information and a foundation for applying many nonverbal communication strategies. Chapter Three centers on other characteristic patterns and on applications and techniques, because these are the bases on which mediators build the balance of their nonverbal strategies.

To fully appreciate the patterns, applications, and techniques described in Chapters Two and Three, I recommend that you keep in mind your own past mediations. Remember the parties with whom you worked who exhibited patterns similar to those I describe. Then think about situations in which you believed you had no alternatives. Consider what might have happened if you had been able to spot patterns and use some of the techniques offered in these two chapters.

This chapter first examines determining people's system preference from their eye, physical, language, and paralanguage cues

and patterns. Then it looks at making appropriate and ethical decisions about techniques and applications, given cue incongruity and
people's vulnerability.

Eye Cues and Patterns

People are sending and receiving messages all the time. You'll
observe that as they make sense of messages their eyes travel to distinct positions. These eye positions are directly related to whether
people are creating mental pictures, hearing sounds, or experiencing sensations. Even though people are unaware they are making these patterned eye movements, observers can see these cues
clearly.

Determining System Preference

One way to detect people's preferred representational systems is
by studying their eye cues. The following cues are typical in right-
handed people with left nominal dominance. The eyes of people
who are making mental pictures move upward or stare in an unfo-
cused manner. The eyes of people who are hearing internal sounds
move to one side or the other or move downward and to the person's left. The eyes of people who are experiencing the sensation
of touch, taste, smell, or emotion move downward and to the person's right side.

Eye cues are repeated consistently. This indicates that these
cues are not random but patterns. These patterns relate directly to
the visual, auditory, and kinesthetic representational systems.

Eye patterns also indicate whether people are remembering or
imagining (constructing) information. Although there are exceptions, when a right-handed person is facing an observer, typically
the observer sees the eyes travel upward and to the person's left
when the person is remembering an image. This cue is called
visual remembered. The observer sees the eyes move up and to the
person's right when the person is constructing images (*visual constructed* cue). The eyes shift to the person's left side when the person is remembering sound-related information (*auditory remembered*
cue). The eyes shift to the person's right side when the person is
constructing sound-related information (*auditory constructed* cue).

The eyes look down and to the person's left side when the person is remembering internal dialogues, conversations, and chatter (*internal dialogues* cue). Finally, the eyes go down and to the person's right side when the person is getting a feeling (*kinesthetic* cue). The positions are summarized in Figure 2.1.

Understanding Variations

I have found value in remembering two points about eye patterns. The first is that eyes never close, only lids do. Eye movements occur and you can watch them even when eyelids are shut. The second point is the generality of these patterns. Each person has the potential to be different.

The common eye patterns just described are demonstrated by right-handed people with left brain nominal dominance. My experience has shown that about three-quarters of the population use these patterns. Over the years, however, I have noticed a number of variations that have been meaningful for evaluating preferred systems. For example, half of the remaining 25 percent of the population are left-handed people who replicate right-handed patterns. Another small percentage are left-handed people who mirror right-handed patterns: that is, where a right-handed person would look right they look left, and vice versa. A final small minority, however, do not follow the general eye patterns at all. This group exhibits eye cues from a mixture of representational systems. For example, during one mediation I observed a party whose eyes indicated that she remembered images and sounds on the left side: this was a typical right-handed pattern. However, when she was remembering dialogues, her eyes went to her right side, and when she was remembering sensations, they went to her left side. This auditory-kinesthetic pattern switch reversed the typical right-handed pattern she exhibited otherwise. Such blends, or *cross-wirings,* may be the result of cross-dominance in the brain, or they may indicate that people have learned their patterns from atypical models.

Another eye pattern variation I have noticed occurs in a small group of people who possess an unusual psychological or sociological pathology. Members of this population often create their own mental worlds and live by their own rules or no rules at all.

Figure 2.1. Eye Cues and Patterns.

VISUAL ACCESSING CUES

| Remembering
Pictures
(Up Left) | Constructing
Pictures
(Up Right) | Making
Pictures
(Defocused) |

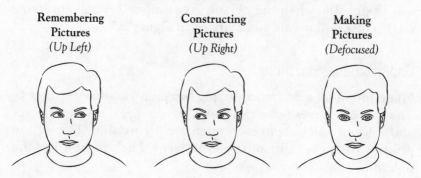

AUDITORY ACCESSING CUES

| Remembering
Sounds
(Side Left) | Constructing
Sounds
(Side Right) | Hearing Internal
Dialogues/Chatter
(Down Left) |

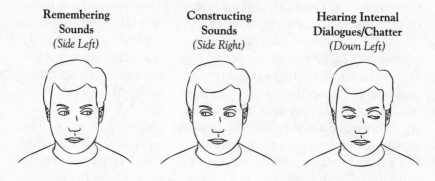

KINESTHETIC ACCESSING CUES

Accessing Touch,
Taste, Smell, Feelings
(Down Right)

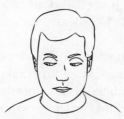

They have unreliable eye patterns because they have a capacity to "re-create" situations that never actually happened. I exclude their eye patterns when I assess their preferred representational systems.

Finally, I have come across eye pattern variations that relate to cultural norms. Some cultures require people to look in specific directions in the company of certain others. These mandates force people to use eye movements that differ from the automatic, or "typical," eye patterns. For example, cultural norms that require lowering the eyes may cause people to routinely use downward eye movements ordinarily classified as auditory remembered or kinesthetic cues. In these cases, I have found it useful to watch for different automatic eye movements occurring under people's eyelids. In cultures that instruct their members to look people in the eye, I have seen people with a visual preference defocus while they continue to look in the direction of the other person. They do this in order to visually construct their information in the space between themselves and the person talking to them.

Using Pattern Loops

Eye pattern loops, like eye cues, are produced outside a person's awareness. Once observers spot the loops, they can predict how people will operate next and how they will want information relayed to them. Observers identify the loops, as described in Chapter One, by tracking whether a person either uses one system or bounces back and forth between two systems. Once they note a person's sole system or his alternating order, they can communicate using his preferred system or exactly the alternating sequence of systems that he uses.

Pattern loops facilitate communication and provide predictability. I find this predictability gives me a real edge in presenting information and anticipating what type of communication to use next. Even though I am aware of the loops, the people using them are not. As a result, I can communicate on two levels with them. The first is the information I communicate in their conscious awareness. This consists of approximately seven pieces of information. However, these consciously apprehended items have much less impact than the second level of information I introduce to them, information that is outside their conscious awareness. People are vulnerable to this information because their conscious filters are not working to screen out other-than-conscious information.

Physical Cues and Patterns

During mediation the parties offer the mediator a wealth of information through physical cues. By examining these signals, mediators can notice how people are making sense of their worlds and how they want others to give them information. When mediators put all the cues together, they can see both patterns and inconsistencies. Once again, these patterns often indicate a person's preferred representational system.

Determining System Preference

When a person's head is tilted upward, it is a cue that she is using a visual representational system at that moment. Tilting the head left, holding it level, or holding it so that one ear is pointing toward the speaker, is an auditory system cue. Tilting the head down to the right is a kinesthetic system cue.

When a person leans his torso forward that is a visual system cue. Leaning the torso to the left is an auditory system cue. Crossing the arms and resting them against the torso is an auditory system cue. Leaning the torso to the right or swaying is a kinesthetic system cue.

When a person's fingers draw in the air, touch her brow, or rest around her eyes, that is a visual system cue. Resting the fingers in or around the mouth or ears and tapping, drumming, interlacing, or making repetitive motions with them are auditory system cues. Moving the hands with the palms turned upward, making parallel or balancing movements with the hands, and tracing or rubbing along the midline (that is, close to the heart) with the fingers are kinesthetic system cues.

When a person crosses his right leg over his left leg (sometimes referred to as *crossing into auditory*), it is an auditory system cue. Moving the legs up and down repetitively is also an auditory system cue. Crossing the left leg over the right (also known as *crossing into kinesthesia*) is a kinesthetic system cue. Similarly, crossing the right ankle over the left indicates an auditory preference, and crossing the left ankle over the right indicates a kinesthetic preference. Tapping one's toes repetitively is an auditory system cue.

Insofar as a person's skin tone indicates blood flow to the surface of the face and neck, it is another indicator of the person's preferred system. Skin tone with a pale flush is a visual system cue. Skin tone with a medium flush is an auditory system cue. Skin tone with a high flush is a kinesthetic system cue.

When a person demonstrates taut muscle tonicity, high shoulders, and a tense abdomen, she is sending visual system cues. Moderate muscle tonicity and rhythmic movements are auditory system cues. Slack muscle tonicity, sweeping motions, and a relaxed abdomen are kinesthetic system cues.

Finally, when a person exhibits breathing that is rapid, shallow, and comes from high in the chest, he is displaying a visual system cue. Breathing that is even, comes from midchest, and has the whole chest moving smoothly is an auditory system cue. Breathing that is slow and deep, that comes from the abdomen, and in which there is much sighing is a kinesthetic system cue.

Understanding Variations

People sometimes display physical cues that deviate from these typical patterns. These inconsistencies arise for various reasons. Physical limitations can restrict movement. People with neck and back injuries from car accidents, for example, may have difficulty with some movements. Psychological issues can change typical movement patterns too. Many years ago I experienced this myself. As the elementary school class to whom I was teaching French sat around me on the floor, one observant eight-year-old noticed a scar on my knee. The little girl, with great alarm, advised me that I had a "run" in my leg. Even today, with the scar long faded, I sometimes cross my legs to cover the "run."

Along with physical and psychological reasons for variations from typical physical movement patterns, cultural norms can have an effect. A gesture that resembles a system cue may actually be a unique ethnic signal. For example, a North American who other-than-consciously rests her fingers around her eye area is usually indicating a visual system preference. In some European cultures, however, a person may consciously tug at the corner of his eye with a finger to communicate his slyness. And if he nods at another person while he is making this gesture, he is communicating that she is the one who is cunning. On the North American continent, placing fingers under the chin can be an other-than-conscious auditory cue, but in some other cultures flicking them from there is done consciously to insult the observer.

Language Cues and Patterns

A person's language also reveals significant system information to the person listening for those cues.

Determining System Preference

People with a visual system preference tend to use sight-related expressions. For example, they might use the terms "sight for sore eyes," "horse of a different color," "naked eye," "short-sighted," "eye-to-eye," "tunnel vision," "perspective," "seeing is believing," and "whites of their eyes." People with an auditory system preference are more likely to use sound-based terms, saying things like "I hear you," "rings a bell," "call on," "utterly," "word for word," "voice an opinion," "a calling," "you don't say," "call off," and "tell me about it." People with a kinesthetic system preference lump sensation-based expressions into their language, like "come to grips," "in touch with," "bad taste," "stuffed shirt," "smells fishy," "gut feeling," "slipped my mind," "stiff upper lip," and "grabbed me."

When mediators use listeners' systems, they eliminate the listeners' need to translate the mediator's ideas into the listeners' preferred system. Mediators who insist on using their own preferred systems risk fatiguing the parties at the table.

Stepping Outside the System

Mediators can also find great value in using nonsystem words during mediation. These neutral expressions allow mediators to stand back and let listeners use any system they want. For example, when I am unclear about a person's preferred system or when there is more than one listener present, I use nonsystem words so all parties can send and receive information using their respective preferred systems. If I were to introduce my own preference first, I could contaminate their responses and lose my opportunity to learn their preferred systems. Additionally, I would be forcing them, other-than-consciously, to use my preference. Although they might be able to communicate in my preferred system, the mediation process would slow down due to the constant need for translation. Tension and weariness would result.

Paralanguage Cues and Patterns

Paralanguage cues also reveal preferred systems. Voice is a key indicator. For example, a jerky or quick tempo or speech characterized by rapid strings of words is a visual system cue. A moderate tempo with an even cadence and rhythmic delivery of words is an auditory system cue. A slow tempo with long pauses is a kinesthetic system cue. Voice timbre indicates system preference too. Timbre that is high pitched and at times nasal is a visual cue. Timbre that is monotone or melodic is an auditory cue. Timbre that is husky and low pitched is a kinesthetic cue.

Deciding on a System

Determining the most productive representational system to use in communicating with another person is more than a matter of adding up the observed cues and patterns. The mediator must interpret incongruous cues and be respectful of the other person's vulnerability to other-than-conscious communication.

Dealing with Cue Misalignment

When you examine system patterns, you will often notice misaligned, or incongruous, cues. A person's eye, physical, language, and paralanguage signals may not all point to the same representational system.

Most cues about preferred systems are sent other-than-consciously. They originate in the system files in which information is stored. Although the brain works rapidly, it is not organized in a way that stores all related files in the same place. As a result the brain seeks and retrieves information from files associated with all the representational systems. For example, remembering a trip to the grocery store might call up a visual system file containing a picture of the storefront, an auditory file holding the checkout person's dialogue, and a kinesthetic file retaining the feeling of soft fruit.

When I pick the information to work with overtly, I look at the patterns that people use consistently in the communication of which they are consciously aware. Those are the systems I use with parties when I am conveying information within their conscious awareness. Take the example of parties who continually ask for visual information and appreciate sight-related materials and language. I identify the visual system as their preferred system because that is the system they are using consciously. In addition to using visual language with them, I will make sure they have visual aids like colored markers, a neat environment, and space to imagine pictures in front of them.

Acknowledging Vulnerability

When I look at the cues that do not originate from people's preferred systems, I note that the parties are seeking and retrieving information from other systems. They are likely to be doing this on a level outside their conscious awareness. These other-than-conscious cues let me know the systems in which people are less consciously critical. These are the systems in which messages will receive less filtering. Information introduced through these systems can have the greatest impact on people.

As an ethical mediator, I am prudent in my communication at all times, but I am most judicious and circumspect about communicating through these less filtered systems because I am sending messages into a vulnerable system, a kind of unguarded backdoor. This backdoor becomes even more obvious when I track pattern loops. Pattern loops reveal primary and secondary preferred systems. These are much more in people's awareness than their tertiary system is. Once I recognize the pattern loops, I know from the start of mediation each party's point of vulnerability. The system least used by a party is his Achilles' heel.

Cues originating in other-than-consciousness often show mediators what system is driving a certain type of communication and allow them to respond appropriately. People may, for example, use words (that is, auditory cues) to ask directions to a rest room in case they need it "some time." Their rocking back and forth may be an other-than-conscious kinesthetic cue that sends another message.

Deciding What to Believe

I pay attention to both the conscious cues and the other-than-conscious cues. If I have to make a choice of which to believe, I always trust the other-than-conscious cues. I learned this in my days as a jury consultant. During *voir dire*, prospective jurors are asked whether they have seen or heard details about a case. In addition to observing other cues, I watch to see the side to which their eyes move. If prospects reply they have not seen or heard about a case and their eyes do not move to a visual or auditory remembered position, I am inclined to believe they can deliberate using the evidence offered at trial. If their eyes do move to a visual or auditory remembered position, I am concerned that they might be prejudiced by information gained prior to trial. In one case a defense counsel chose a juror against my recommendation. Later I learned it was that very juror who led the rest of the jury to a guilty verdict. All the signs had been broadcast in the selection process. Someone just had to notice.

Chapter Three

Practical Applications— General Patterns and Techniques

Identifying the preferred representational systems of all the parties to a mediation is one step in preparing for a successful mediation. In addition, mediators can undertake three things to make the mediation process more successful for all involved. First, they can learn to understand a number of additional important messages sent by means of the patterns and cues discussed in the previous two chapters. Second, they can carefully and systematically track and profile each party's communication patterns in order to improve their ability to work with individuals. Finally, they can master specific techniques for using nonverbal and preferred system communications to create rapport, gather information, and clear hurdles and thereby help people reach satisfactory agreements.

Understanding Messages in Patterns of Communication

Through their physical, language, paralanguage, space, touch, and time patterns, people send many messages. Recognizing these messages and responding appropriately to them can be the key to a successful mediation. Here are a number of general patterns that deserve close attention.

Physical Patterns

One way to make sense of individuals' many physical communications is to look for relationships among them. In addition, it is vital to be alert for the physical cues that tell you when the parties to a mediation are experiencing fear.

Cue Chains

Each person has unique patterns of physical communications, some deliberate, some less so. For example, many years ago a famous entertainer with her own television show tugged one ear-lobe; said, "Good night"; and the show ended. After the second or third show, the audience began to notice the entertainer repeating this pattern. And in every show after that the same pattern took place. The audience did not know the entertainer's reason for the pattern. Its relevance for audience members was that observing these two cues gave them the ability to predict that the show was about to end.

In mediation also there is a consistency in people's patterns. Knowing these patterns can help you predict communications and can assist you in creating nonverbal strategies. As in the example, each party demonstrates chains, or patterns, of cues. These chains advertise information, such as whether a person will say yes or no. For example, the president of a multinational corporation used to tap his right toe three times just before he said yes. When I mentioned to him that he did this during union negotiations, he was astounded. Until then he had not been able to understand how union negotiators seemed to know when he was ready to concede. He now saw that the negotiators, outside their conscious awareness, were noticing his toe-tapping pattern. Inside their conscious awareness, they had only a *sense* that he was about to agree. (I advised the executive to stay away from interactions in which his legs were exposed. He would have to avoid, for example, sitting on couches that faced each other and sitting in front of the glass-top tables in his office.) Cue chains can have any number of links. To ensure accuracy in predictions, I collect at least two or three cues.

There is nothing inherently good or bad in having a chain of cues, or a pattern. However, the existence of these other-than-conscious patterns does make people's conscious responses predictable, and that may make people vulnerable during mediation. They believe they are conveying only certain types of information, but their nonverbal, physical patterns may be either reinforcing or contradicting their words. After mediating parties have been in contact for a while, they quickly develop a sense for the meanings of the physical patterns of the other party. This sense relates to communication happening outside their conscious awareness. So they may not know why they feel another person is about to act or respond in a certain way, but they follow their hunches and are usually correct.

Sometimes cue chains are unique to a culture rather than to an individual. Knowing what each party's cultural patterns are and what the patterns mean in that culture can be relevant to a mediation. Because most cultures are ethnocentric, when cultural patterns are an issue I suggest to mediating parties that they interpret these patterns within the context of the message senders rather than the message receivers: that is, that they avoid assuming that their interpretation of a particular pattern is the only interpretation.

Fear

Fear is an emotion that produces a set of physical patterns. When parties feel afraid, their bodies automatically shift into a *danger* mode. Different levels of fear exist, appropriate for different situations. These fear levels run from simply noticing something and getting an awkward feeling through concern, apprehension, trepidation, alarm, and terror and finally to existential fear.

I have often noticed, however, that the parties to mediations usually respond to frightening situations as if their existence were being threatened. Their patterns show that they are afraid and that they cannot distinguish the severity of the danger. They exhibit automatic behavior tied to the fight-or-flight response, an archaic response originally designed for survival. The signal that triggers this response varies from person to person. It could be a physical cue or a tone of voice. Whatever its form, this signal stimulates the oldest part of the brain, the part that prepares the body to battle enemies or escape from them. Mediators face a challenge when parties get this signal and react as if the situation were a life-or-death event.

Physical patterns appear when this fear mechanism kicks into operation. Initially, the person's heart rate, blood pressure, vaso-constriction, bronchodilation, blood sugar, and metabolism increase. Immune system activity decreases. Hormones are re-leased, and the skeletal muscles are strengthened. These changes result in more obvious physical patterns, which manifest themselves at the mediation table. Often breathing comes from high in the chest and in short inhalations and exhalations. This breathing change may be followed by the face paling and the hands shaking. In other cases there are breathing changes with facial and full-body flushing, followed by the fists closing. However, patterns are as var-ied and numerous as people are.

I have frequently benefited from knowing the cue chain that starts a party's unique fear pattern. The most relevant flag is a shift in breathing. Breathing is the most useful barometer of change because it is such a subtle cue. Nevertheless, because breathing change is also detected other-than-consciously by the other parties, even this minimal change can affect the nonverbal dynamics of the group. As a result, I make a covert effort to break up a fear breath-ing pattern by changing my own breathing pattern to a deeper, more protracted rhythm so that the parties can follow. By altering parties' breathing, I can change their fear responses and assist them to get the mediation back on track.

Language Patterns

When I deal with language patterns during mediation, I consider them in the context of the no-fault communication paradigm. In this communication model, words and language patterns are seen to float freely. They may be productive or unproductive. Their value is a function of the environment in which they occur. Most language patterns are a result of people's natural prefer-ence for one representational system or the influence of an envi-ronment. Environmental influences may include patterns modeled at home or in the larger culture. The following sections look more closely at cultural language patterns and at a few spe-cific patterns that can create particular challenges for the parties to a mediation.

Cultural Influences

Cultural language patterns arise among people when they have a common religion, ethnicity, or geography, to name just a few factors. These patterns are easily discerned and easy to reproduce. The mediator's task is to track them and use them under appropriate circumstances. For example, although mediators may hear a party talk about "the luck of the Irish," it may not be an appropriate expression for a mediator to use if he or she is not Irish. Rather than creating rapport, this use of another's language pattern could destroy it. I am always mindful about which language patterns I reproduce at the table.

Some regionally based language patterns are as unique as regional accents. For example, "y'all" ("you all" or "you") is used in the American south, "How d'y'" ("How do you do?") greets Americans in the west, and "G'day" ("Good day") welcomes Australians. There is no right or wrong about such usages. They are just expressions of ideas. In mediation, I have found that using parties' regional language patterns often relaxes the parties. Other-than-consciously they feel more at home in an environment that reflects their habitual expressions. Again, I exercise vigilance to make sure I am developing a link with parties and not sounding patronizing.

Once I have picked up the parties' culturally based language patterns, I focus on whether they employ high-context or low-context communication. Then I match that preference. High-context cultures seem to be more adept at reading nonverbal communication, and their ethnocentrism encourages them to believe that other cultures are competent at it too. Low-context cultures rely heavily on verbal messages to convey explicit information. If parties are talking around a subject, I notice their high-context communication and avoid going directly to the heart of the matter. Instead, I talk circuitously about issues also. Alternately, if parties express themselves directly and frankly, I interpret this as low-context communication. I speak directly and get to the point quickly to avoid looking as if I am dodging an issue. People from high-context cultures—the Japanese, Arab, and Greek cultures, for example—might interpret the directness I use with people from low-context cultures as tactless and offensive. They might well regard it as unresponsive to the implicit messages they are sending. Conversely, people from low-context cultures—the German, Scandinavian, and American cultures, for example—might find the indirect approach I use with people from high-context cultures vague and inefficient.

Individual Patterns That Cause Difficulties

The phrase "you know" is a language pattern that many people use repetitively outside their conscious awareness. Many speakers use this language pattern constantly, like the uh's and um's in paralanguage. I believe that people use this phrase to balance the rhythm of their speech, fill silence, and hold their linguistic "space." It offers no real information and does not really ask for the affirmative answer, "Yes, I know." Many listeners hear it once or twice and then automatically delete it from the incoming message dropping it out of conscious awareness. Other listeners, however, continue to hear it and find it annoying. The result is tension that develops outside their awareness. Therefore, when my clients use this pattern, I suggest they drop it completely.

Patterns of contradictory messages are another challenge. Earlier I described the pattern of *butting*. I suggest to clients that they recognize the antagonistic effect the words "but" and "however" can have on listening parties. Linguistically, "but" equals "and not." Repeated use of this technique means that each time the speaker offers a positive comment, he quickly withdraws it. A lawyer, for example, might say, "I really like your offer but . . ." Before the next word is out, most listeners will experience an automatic negative response. Many of them will actually miss the words that follow. They know this language pattern. They are already in an altered state and not listening anymore. As a result, I strongly recommend that parties replace "but" and "however" with "and," unless they really want to negate what they just said.

Another contradictory and challenging pattern occurs when a person's language contradicts her physical patterns. People experience these kinesic slips all the time in mediation. For example, one party stares out a window while uttering how deeply interested she is in the other party's issue. Verbal messages that are contradicted by physical messages erode the communicator's credibility. Because verbal language forms such a small part of people's communication, the nonverbal message is the one that is believed.

Paralanguage Patterns

Paralanguage provides a whole set of tools for conflict resolution. To maximize its value, I start by checking for a number of paralanguage signals that might affect the mediation or send incorrect messages.

I listen for accents because they can tell a mediator about a person's culture and his educational levels. A cultural accent may indicate that the mediation sessions will require a translator, and it also suggests the need to be attentive for cultural patterns in areas such as eye cues and gestures. Accents reflecting educational levels suggest the mediator might need to explain the same thing in different ways during the mediation process.

Voice modulation (its tone and pitch) can indicate educational and social levels. It gives the mediator an idea of how parties might present themselves. It also indicates how parties might be perceived by each other. Modulation can be an indication of a perceived or a real educational or social imbalance at the table.

Speech impediments sometimes have a subtle impact on communication. This sound modification can cause mediation to proceed at a slower speed, produce feelings of discomfort for either or both parties, and create fatigue.

Vocal segregates, like um's and uh's tagged to the end of phrases, indicate speakers want to pause, fill a silence, or simply hesitate. When these sounds occur, I act as if the speakers are making an effort to hold that space for themselves. Unless this pattern continues in a way that excludes other speakers, I allow speakers to continue to use this pattern with which they are comfortable.

Volume sends messages that vary from culture to culture. I have noticed that a loud volume, which is quite normal for North Americans, is sometimes seen as vulgar or belligerent by people of other cultures. Conversely, I have also seen North Americans treat a lower volume used by people of other cultures as a covert activity.

People's rate of speech also varies from culture to culture. Sometimes people from cultures where speaking slowly is appropriate are incorrectly perceived as being less intelligent or lazier than people from cultures where speaking quickly is valued.

In addition to these signals, there are three more paralanguage patterns to which mediators can pay special attention: tone, cadence, and silence.

Tone

Tone is an even more subtle paralanguage influence than the communication patterns just described. It affects mediation strongly because its interpretation is totally subjective. It is not the tone itself but the *meaning* of the tone to listeners that has the impact. For example, the word *fire* has a range of very general meanings until the brain goes through separate system files to give the word a context and with that context a more specific meaning. Then the meaning of the word may be made even more specific when the listener attaches a tone to the word.

In mediation, message interpretation is typically not as dependent on the words as it is on the tone attached to the words. For example, in an estate mediation, I asked counsel to stop reading a will out loud. I did not want the listeners, the beneficiaries, to attach counsel's tone to the words. I knew it would be valuable for beneficiaries to read the words for themselves. That way, they could "hear" their father's voice in their minds as they read. That would help them understand the will's instructions as the wishes of their father rather than as an impersonal legal edict. This in turn could encourage them to move to the feelings that were driving their positions. As a result, they could explain their reasons for conflict to the other family members at the table.

When I hear less-than-productive tones exchanged by parties, I stop the conversation as soon as possible. Rather than asking people to change their tone, I ask if they can say what they just said in another way. Habitual sets of words, or ways of saying things, often are stored together with specific tones, sometimes offensive ones. Changing the words often brings out new, more productive tones and starts more positive trends in the mediation.

Cadence

During caucus a lawyer once asked me why the other party's counsel was not taking her well-articulated arguments seriously.

I suggested she might be sending an unintentional message because her voice rose at the ends of all her sentences.

Like many people, this lawyer had not been aware of the paralinguistic message her cadence was sending. Usually statements end with a fall in pitch. Questions end with the voice rising. Parties whose sentences always rise at the end sound tentative, seem to crave mitigation of what they just said, and convey a sense of unsureness. Combining statements with the cadence of questions is confusing and gives listeners the impression that speakers do not really mean what they said. In turn, speakers get frustrated. They believe they have made statements, yet people respond as though they had asked questions or asked for permission.

The intervention I use to assist in these situations is to restate the speaker's sentence myself with the appropriate cadence. That way, the last sound listeners hear is the dropping cadence, and they know they have heard a statement rather than a question.

Silence

Silence is another paralinguistic component that affects mediation. Some cultures honor silence; others regard it as uncomfortable. Look at Lao-Tzu's proverb cited in *Tao Te Ching*, "Those who know do not speak; those who speak do not know." It exemplifies one culture's positive perception of silence. Conversely, silence is viewed negatively by some North Americans, who often perceive it as uncomfortable and at times embarrassing. Accordingly, parties who fill the quiet with chatter risk being perceived with disdain by cultures who value silence, and vice versa.

When people from cultures with different views about silence attend the same mediation, I make a concerted effort to balance talking time with quiet time. Otherwise both sides are uncomfortable, and communication is interrupted.

Space Patterns

Parties coming to mediation have varied space requirements. Some cultures focus their attention on objects. Others focus on the space in between objects. In general, most North Americans need to keep a certain distance between themselves and other people.

General Area Requirements

The specific amount of space required depends on the occasion. Most North Americans operate in four major distance zones: public, social, personal, and intimate. The *public zone* requires the most distance. People in this zone leave twelve or more feet of space between themselves and others. In this zone, people talk most loudly and formally. People in the *social zone* leave distances from four to twelve feet between themselves and others. This is the zone in which parties first become comfortable talking about business and having social conversations. People in the *personal zone* leave eighteen inches to four feet between themselves and others. In this zone, parties feel at ease holding personal conversations. Finally, people in the *intimate zone* leave eighteen inches or less between themselves and others. Here parties are always aware of and sometimes hypersensitive to nearby people.

Implications of Culture and Systems

Other factors that affect spatial dynamics are culture and preferred systems. The set of distance zones favored by some cultures varies from the North American model. For instance, I have frequently found that parties from northern European cultures require more space than do parties with a Mediterranean background. Moreover, my background in foreign languages has shown me over and over that people often assume the postures and distances of the culture whose language they are using at the moment. For example, after a colleague of mine first heard me speak French, he told me how stunned he was as he watched my whole demeanor and posture go through an instant metamorphosis as I switched from speaking English to speaking French.

Finally, people's preferred representational system affects their space needs. Parties with a visual preference need space in front of them to construct their mental pictures. People with an auditory preference have no special space requirement except to be in a position to hear clearly. Parties with a kinesthetic preference are the most highly sensitive to distances, because they have a heightened awareness of touch and smell. They are the ones most likely either to benefit from or be distressed by the space allocation at a mediation, depending on how comfortable or uncomfortable it is for them.

Touching Patterns

I have found that touching patterns can be indicators of the degree of familiarity between people. They can also be a cue that suggests a person's preferred representational system.

How Touch Indicates Familiarity

Touch can display individuals' levels of closeness or intimacy. Because touch necessitates physical connection, it delivers a powerful message.

Touching patterns range from functional to social, friendly, loving, and sexual. Often the intent or circumstance of a touch is the factor that determines the communicated message. For example, if a person encircles a dear one's waist with his arms, it may be interpreted as loving or sexual. The same touch may be interpreted as functional, however, when done by a passenger riding on the back of a motorcycle. I encourage clients to make sure that the intent of both parties is exactly the same before establishing a level of touch. If there is doubt about intent, I ask clients to use the functional touching pattern and wait for the other party to approach with a closer level.

Environment, culture, and timing also dictate the meaning of a touch. For example, a kiss on the cheek may be deemed by most North Americans to be a loving or friendly touch, but in Quebec or Europe a kiss on both cheeks can be quite acceptable as a relaxed greeting among business colleagues. Twenty years ago North American men greeting each other would only have shaken hands, but today a bear hug is an acceptable greeting exchanged by, among others, football players and politicians.

I have come to believe that the most common touching pattern is the most misinterpreted one—the handshake. I believe the most effective way to shake hands is to match the handshake of the other party. This seems to be a simple concept, but people still miscommunicate with their handshake message. Parties who want to send friendly greetings through their handshake may not realize the message is in the receiver's mind. If the receiver believes the grip is too tight or lasts too long, the handshake may seem inappropriate. For example, in the 1970s many women were encouraged to squeeze men's hands with a vicelike grip. They were assured, by well-meaning coaches, that this would assert their equality. Unfortunately those instructions arose out of misinterpretation of the pressure of men's handshakes when shaking hands with women. Coaches assumed that the pressure was intentionally excessive when it was simply the automatic pressure men were accustomed to returning to other men. As a result, many women seemed foolish as they appeared to make an effort to break bones with their handshakes.

I also caution parties that some cultures see a lingering handshake as too familiar. Some cultures interpret the hand-on-top-of-hand handshake as a personal, positive bond. And different people have different thoughts about moist handshakes. Many people perceive perspiration as a normal occurrence on the palms or other body areas. Other people tend to think of sweating palms as unpleasant and perhaps a signal of nervousness or an indicator of guilt. If clients do have moist palms, I suggest they roll antiperspirant on them before mediation and then squeeze a tissue just before they enter and shake hands, so they do not inadvertently send these signals.

Implications of Systems and Culture

Parties with a kinesthetic system preference understand the world through touch, taste, smell, and feelings. The mediator's challenge is to deal with this preference at the table. Parties with this preference have a different sense of space than parties do who prefer visual or auditory systems of communication. People with this preference often welcome closeness or actual physical contact. I find the most neutral way to accommodate their preference is to speak to them in kinesthetic terms and to work with models and miniatures (such as toy cars) during the mediation process. I also make a point of connecting with these parties by using professional touch, like shaking hands or making contact with their papers.

Mediators can also watch the parties at a mediation to see whether they come from high-contact or low-contact cultures. When two cultures are represented at the table, the mediator can then treat the parties from each culture in the manner they perceive as appropriate. High-contact parties can receive more touch (that is, longer handshakes, pats on the back) than do low-contact parties (who receive the same messages through words).

High-contact cultures also require less space between individuals than low-contact cultures do. To keep an equilibrium between the two cultures, at first I use the distances favored by the low-contact culture. If I did not, the parties from low-contact cultures would literally keep moving away from the table. No progress would ever be made. Parties from high-contact cultures will always gravitate toward other parties, so they tend to be more malleable in this respect, especially at the start of mediation. Moreover, using low-contact distances at first allows for positive change to be accompanied by the parties' moving closer together physically and actually shaking hands on agreement.

Time Patterns

An understanding of the different views of time held by monochronic and polychronic cultures and of the different ways that individuals perceive events in time can guide the mediator in managing the mediation schedule to the parties' satisfaction.

As I described in Chapter One, monochronic and polychronic cultures perceive time very differently. These different perspectives spill into mediation and affect how it runs. Relationships are secondary to prearranged schedules in monochronic cultures but are more important than schedules in polychronic cultures. Activity schedules and meeting times are rigid in monochronic cultures but are flexible and fluid in polychronic cultures. Tasks are performed serially in monochronic cultures but are performed simultaneously in polychronic cultures. Work time is set off from personal time in monochronic cultures but merged into personal time in polychronic cultures. Breaks and personal time come before personal relationships in monochronic cultures but run second to personal relationships in polychronic cultures.

In addition, individuals perceive time differently. As they imagine events on a time line they may perceive themselves as standing off-line or at midline. People with the off-line position tend to be dissociated from their memories. Time flows linearly and seems quite long to them. They believe in the adage that "time is money."

They value it that way. Like monochronic parties, they are prompt and expect everyone else to be on time too. They view time as if events were occurring in a line right before their eyes but have a real challenge recalling a specific time because they remember events mainly as parts of more complex experiences. People with the midline position see their pasts behind them and their futures right before their eyes. In response to a question about an event, they can go right to the specific experience and associate with it. These parties live in the present. They are not always mindful of time and can be a real challenge because they may resist ending a mediation session. They are often late.

The key to managing both these types of individuals and to managing people from monochronic and polychronic cultures is to balance their needs. I stay alert to time to ensure that schedules are met. That way I honor the needs of parties with off-line positions and those from monochronic cultures. I also tend to reserve a little time before breaks and just before the scheduled end of sessions to accommodate the needs of people with midline positions and those from polychronic cultures who may wish to spend additional time discussing some subject.

Object and Clothing Patterns

At a mediation, clothing sends nonverbal messages from person to person whether the garments are tailored suits, tattered jeans, or saris.

I have noticed unwritten dress codes. There is a formal level that seems to require suits and similar clothing, an informal level that calls for casual attire, and a totally open level in which it seems acceptable for parties wear anything from Gucci to garden shoes. Americans generally expect all parties to be dressed in a similar way and at a similar level. Canadians, too, anticipate that all parties will be dressed similarly although they are not entirely surprised when parties appear in ethnic or cultural garb.

When both parties wear the anticipated type of clothing, neither party pays much attention to dress. For example, if two tongue-studded, nose-ringed parties came to the table, they would be observing the same dress code. It is when parties appear in extremely different types or levels of clothing that they consciously notice the difference. At the same time, their other-than-conscious filters decide what message the other party is sending.

I have seen counsel bring unspoken lawyer dress codes into the mediation room. This type of formal dress can comfort those clients who look to their lawyers as sources of power and leadership. The potential downside is that this type of uniform dress sometimes fosters the appearance of camaraderie among the lawyers for the different parties. It also sends an exclusionary message to their clients who are not dressed that way. Communicating nonverbally, these lawyers risk creating an other-than-conscious belief among their respective clients that they are aligned with each other rather than with those clients.

Expensive clothing may communicate a message. In North America, money is often equated with power, therefore the quality or cost of clothing can send a message of power. Take the example of two parties wearing suits. If one party sports a designer suit and the other wears a cheap off-the-rack garment, the gulf between the parties may increase. The power balance often shifts toward the expensively clad party.

Symbolism Patterns

Symbols communicate messages between parties too. Parties may wear religious objects and other symbols that hold one meaning for them but are likely to be interpreted differently by people sitting across the table. One party may derive comfort from the article whereas another may see it as a symbol of something distressing. Some examples of unproductive communication seem clear, others not so apparent. It would seem obvious that people should refrain from wearing a swastika in the presence of a Holocaust survivor. It might not be as clear that accessorizing an outfit with a second-hand military medal might offend a war veteran.

Identifying Individuals' Cues and Patterns

At the very first contact mediators have with mediating parties, they can begin a systematic process of learning the most effective ways to communicate with each party and what the party needs to communicate successfully in return. This process involves tracking cues and patterns and compiling a profile of each party. The profile addresses a person's system preferences, action triggers, and working frameworks.

Tracking

Tracking is a technique I use constantly in mediation. It is a process in which I carefully observe and listen to parties. I note their actions, words, and any other cues they offer. Then I compile and sort the information so I can spot their patterns and incongruities. These patterns and incongruities become the basis for profiles of the individuals and for many nonverbal strategies.

The Foundation: General Trends and Baselines

Tracking can be compared to watching a movie in which the subject is moving all the time and the information is changing. Picking up all the important details requires a high level of awareness. A similarly attentive process can provide mediators with much information about parties. In general, the process works like this. First, I look at trends. Then I organize the initial tracked information for each party into specific patterns that show the party's communication inclinations. I call this refining process *setting a baseline,* or *baselining.* If tracking is a movie, then a baseline is a snapshot that reflects a person's profile at the moment the results were recorded.

Establishing this baseline is critical. Once it is documented, the mediator can know whether parties are demonstrating their typical patterns or are deviating from them. For example, a party's baseline pattern when he is supplying (verifiably) accurate information might be raising his left eyebrow, pulling his mouth taut and down to the left, and saying the word yes. If he deviates from this baseline pattern during mediation, the mediator would probe further. She needs to determine whether the party is giving her a second affirmative pattern or uttering the word yes consciously while making a negative response other-than-consciously. When the conscious and other-than-conscious responses contradict each other, I always believe the other-than-conscious communication, reask the question, and dig deeper.

The SIR Formula

To aid their tracking process, mediators can use the SIR formula (*S*enses, *I*nterpretation, and *R*esponse). Following this formula allows them to gain accurate information, decipher it, and respond to people in a productive manner.

To use the SIR formula, first collect information by using only your senses. To make sure you track correctly, preface each piece of information you collect with, "I can see   ," "I can hear   ," "I can touch   ," "I can taste   ," or "I can smell   ." If you cannot insert the piece of information into the blank space in one of these sentences, do not use that information. A piece of information you can use is called a *marker*. Next, interpret the markers. Compare them to the party's established patterns, and note whether you have found a new pattern. Finally, you can respond appropriately to the party, because you have based your interpretation on data. In communicating, many people skip the first or second steps entirely. As a result, they bound into a response that is often an arbitrary reaction. When people eliminate the first step, they cannot collect information to interpret. When they skip the second step, they end up mind reading.

When incongruities arise, mediators should respond prudently. Countless times I have resisted the urge to challenge parties. Instinctively, I want to tell them that I question their answers because they are using patterns different from those they use when they state facts. Instead, I make myself a note that there may be another pattern existing outside the party's awareness. Then I either leave the issue and return to it another way or simply record the inconsistency and see what I uncover later.

Profiling

Profiling is a method of charting communication. It graphs verbal and nonverbal patterns that the parties exhibit. Although parties may demonstrate some of the same patterns, each party will have a unique combination of patterns.

I created Figure 3.1, the *Profile Element Grid*™, or *PEG*™, to document each person's pattern combination. The PEG makes tracking easy. The *profile* is the completed picture of a party's unique patterns. The *elements* are the sections within the PEG. The *grid* is the matrix that is formed by each person's unique set of patterns. Using the PEG, a mediator can quickly record parties' baselines.

Once a PEG is completed for everyone—including counsel— the mediator has a set of *profile markers* (that is, pieces of profile information) and can craft communication to accommodate each person's patterns. PEGs act as quick reference guides. You can keep them beside your notes so you always have the information handy and ready to scan in a distilled format. These summaries are particularly useful when many things are happening concurrently during mediation. It's best to PEG parties at the beginning of mediation, but you can do it later if necessary. The downside to waiting can be missed opportunities to create positive communication or neutralize counterproductive messages.

Identifying Preferred Systems

Preferred systems form part of each party's profile. Verbal patterns (choice of predicates) clearly articulate whether the visual, auditory, or kinesthetic system is the preferred system and which systems are the second and third choices. Physical cues appear and form patterns that conform to or contradict the verbal patterns. Together, verbal and nonverbal patterns tell me which systems parties are using inside their conscious awareness and which systems they are using other-than-consciously. When the verbal and physical system patterns reflect the same system, parties are using a preferred system within their awareness. When the language and physical patterns do not match, parties are aware of the system articulated in their language but unaware of the influence of the system expressed through their physical patterns.

Identifying the Language Matrix

The language matrix is an intrinsic part of each party's profile. It is an overview of all the language patterns and tells me *what* communicators are thinking and *how* they are thinking about it. It is formed automatically as the profile takes shape. Each party has a unique matrix dependent on how he or she perceives the world.

The matrix is like a kaleidoscope. There are only a certain number of elements in it, but each time the kaleidoscope is turned, the pieces form various combinations and create different

Figure 3.1. PEG™.

Name: _____ Date: _____ Notes:

SYSTEM

_____ Visual   _____ Auditory   _____ Kinesthetic

ACTION TRIGGERS

Language Touchstones

_____

_____

Initiation

_____ Active   _____ Reactive   _____ Both

Mental Movement

_____ Toward   _____ Away   _____ Both

Validation

_____ Inside   _____ Outside   _____ Both

Rationale

_____ Opportunity   _____ Necessity

Decision Factors

Activity: _____ See   _____ Hear   _____ Do   _____ Read

Time Frame: _____ Reflex   _____ # of Examples   _____ Time   _____ Constant Proof

WORKING FRAMEWORKS

Thinking
_____ Micro   _____ Macro

Focus
_____ Self   _____ Others

Affiliation
_____ Loner   _____ Group   _____ Collaborator

Preference
_____ People   _____ Objects   _____ Systems

Operating Code
Self: _____ Definite   _____ Variable   _____ No   Others: _____ Definite   _____ Variable   _____ No

Pressure Reaction
_____ Inside   _____ Outside   _____ Inside-Outside

Perception
_____ Similar   _____ Similar with Exceptions   _____ Difference   _____ Difference with Exceptions

Targets
_____ Perfect   _____ Optimized

Placement
_____ Starter   _____ Maintainer   _____ Completer

designs (just as people's profiles are made up of the same elements but the elements are configured into a variety of pattern combinations). People use their word patterns, like their other patterns, automatically, consistently, and outside their awareness. As they use their word patterns, the surface and deep structures reveal both the meaning of the words and how their worlds operate.

The words that make up the surface structure of a verbal message are much like the images on a television screen; the words are what is apparent. Communicators are aware they are sending this part of the message. Listeners are aware they are hearing this part of the message. People's words, however, are created after they have systematically deleted, distorted, and generalized information so that it is configured to fit their world. So surface structure is only one part of the communication.

Deep structure is the second part of the message. Just as what is contained within a television is what makes the apparatus work, deep structure demonstrates the way people work. The deep structure message is enclosed in the patterns people use when they talk about their experiences. Communicators are unaware of the deep structures they are exhibiting. Listeners are unaware of them too.

For example, in the sentence, "Let's meet early so we don't miss the bus," the surface meaning of the words indicates what the person is consciously thinking. On closer examination, the phrase "so we *don't miss*" indicates a deep language structure typical of an avoidance pattern. I work with these patterns and requirements during mediation.

Filters and context, concepts discussed in Chapter One, are two factors that affect how matrix elements combine. Filters affect people's beliefs, values, and attitudes. This happens at a level outside their awareness. As a result, they are not consciously aware that they have formed these perceptions even though they are expressing them through their language matrices. The context or environment in which the language is elicited also affects matrix patterns. Some of the patterns may hold across contexts; others will be unique to a particular environment. For example, a person's language matrix may exhibit an avoidance pattern in a mediation environment but a goal-seeking pattern in a family setting. I complete a different PEG for each environment in which I deal with parties so I can use the appropriate pattern for each context.

Action Triggers. The next section of the PEG begins to accumulate information for the deep structure revealed by the language matrix by identifying an individual's action triggers. An *action trigger* is the mechanism that prompts a party to make a move during mediation.

Language touchstones. A *touchstone* is a standard, or yardstick, against which people measure things. *Language touchstones* are the exact words or phrases in which parties announce their standards and most highly held values. These touchstones tell mediators specific words they must use to please or satisfy parties during mediation.

Active and reactive initiation. In communication terminology, an *initiation* is a trigger for an activity. An *active initiation* is a stimulus mechanism that prompts parties to undertake activities and make things happen. A *reactive initiation* is a stimulus mechanism that prompts parties to wait for something to happen before they act.

Toward and away mental movement. *Mental movement* describes a thinking process. The process triggers action. Parties who use *toward mental movement* process ideas in terms of moving toward goals. Parties who use *away mental movement* think in terms of avoiding problems.

Inside and outside validation. *Validation* is a process in which a decision is made regarding something's value. Parties use this process to corroborate their decisions. Parties who make decisions for themselves and depend on their own judgment for a decision are engaged in *inside validation.* People who rely on other people or other factors to evaluate situations in order to come to their conclusions are engaged in *outside validation.*

Opportunity and necessity rationales. A *rationale* is the reason a person does something. It is an action trigger that is particularly dependent on context and timing in parties' lives. Parties who are stimulated to act by an *opportunity rationale* do things when they are interested or when they perceive opportunities or options. Parties who are triggered by a *necessity rationale* believe they have limited options or no choice. Some may think they are obligated to do something.

Activity and time frame decision factors. *Deciding* is a process that occurs when parties reach a conclusion or make up their minds. *Decision factors* are elements that help convince people. *Activity* and *time frame* are the two major factors. People typically have an activity (involving seeing, hearing, doing, or reading something) that must precede a decision they make. They also take a customary length of time to decide something (they may agree reflexively, that is, immediately; they may need to obtain a certain number of examples; they may need a specific period of time; or they may need constant proof, that is, each time they deal with the issue they may have to be convinced all over again). Activity and time frame decision factors exist outside conscious awareness. Every party has a distinctive pattern. Parties who are forced to make decisions without having both factors satisfied inevitably experience buyer's remorse. This means that they feel bad about the experience or that the resolution falls apart—or both.

Working Frameworks. The final section of the PEG identifies parties' working frameworks. A *working framework* is a party's perception of the world around him, the people in that world, and how he relates to both.

Micro-thinking and macro-thinking. *Thinking* is simply the process in which people use reasoning. During this process they break down and communicate information. They automatically separate pieces of information into large chunks or small chunks. *Micro-thinkers* are those who like to deal with minute details. They break information into small chunks. *Macro-thinkers* are those who like to see the *big picture* and deal with large chunks of general information.

   Self-focus and others-focus. *Focus* describes where people's attention is centered. Parties who demonstrate *self-focus* are self-referenced and inward looking. Parties who have an *others-focus* are aware of others and concentrate on the people around them.

   Loner, group, and collaborator affiliations. People's communication patterns show the way they affiliate with, or connect with, each other in their working relationships. I have noticed three distinct types of *affiliation: loner, group,* and *collaborator. Loner affiliation* describes the communication pattern for parties who prefer to work alone. A computer programmer might have a loner affiliation. *Group affiliation* describes the communication pattern for people who like to work in a joint effort or as part of a team. Members of a relay swim team are very likely to exhibit group affiliation. *Collaborator affiliation* describes the communication pattern for people who prefer to work independently but who accept that there must be people around them so they can do their jobs. Presenters and teachers may exhibit a collaborator affiliation.

People, objects, and systems preferences. People may prefer to work with people, objects, or systems. Parties with a *people preference* seek to work with other people. Recruiters, teachers, and entertainers are likely to have a people preference. Parties with an *objects preference* seek to work with things. Mechanics and carpenters might well have an objects preference. Parties with a *systems preference* seek to work with a number of related parts (or people) to create a final, interwoven unit. Business systems technology experts and workflow specialists might have a systems preference.

Definite, variable, and no operating codes. *Operating codes* are codes of conduct. They show how people perceive rules. When people have a specific set of rules for themselves or others, they have what I call a *definite code.* When people believe that rules can vary, they have a *variable code.* When people do not live by any rules, they have *no code.* People may have one code for themselves and another code for others.

Inside and outside pressure reactions. *Pressure* describes what a party is feeling when stressed. A *pressure reaction* is the pattern parties communicate to observers when the parties are under stress. People who communicate an *inside pressure reaction* are reliving situations as if they were happening at the moment. People who communicate an *outside pressure reaction* are dissociated from the situation and are describing it. People who communicate an *inside-outside pressure reaction* are going back into an experience to associate with it and relive it temporarily. Then they dissociate by coming out of the experience to tell about it.

Similarity and difference perception. *Perception* is the process in which parties picture ideas in their minds. In this process, information is noticed and sorted automatically and outside of conscious awareness. When people consciously call upon this information, those who perceive *similarity* notice things in the information that are alike. Those who perceive *differences* notice things that are dissimilar. In addition, people may perceive mostly similar things and then notice some exceptions or mostly different things and then notice some exceptions.

Perfect and optimized targets. A *target* is a goal people strive to reach. People who set *perfect targets,* or *perfectionists,* are relentless about reaching goals. They are unforgiving of themselves if they do not reach them. They are equally unbending with others who do not attain their objectives. People who set *optimized targets,* or *optimizers,* do their best to get results. If they fail, however, they pardon themselves and move ahead. If others fail, they allow them to go forward too.

Starter, maintainer, and completer placements. A *work line* identifies the flow of a job or project from start to finish. It describes it as if it were a line that had a beginning and end. *Work line placement* describes the location on the work line that a person intuitively likes to occupy. People who choose *starter placement* (or *starters*) want to brainstorm and begin a project. People who favor *maintainer placement* (or *maintainers*) like to shepherd a project once it is underway. People who prefer *completer placement* (or *completers*) get their satisfaction in wrapping up and closing down a project.

Applying Nonverbal Techniques During Mediation

There are a number of specific nonverbal and special verbal techniques that mediators can use to enhance communication. This section introduces techniques for creating rapport, gathering information, and clearing hurdles that may stand in people's way during a mediation. In Part Two, many of these techniques are described more fully as they occur in mediation contexts.

Creating Rapport

Creating rapport (accord, or harmony) between the mediator and the parties to a mediation and among the parties themselves can be an important part of helping parties to deal with issues realistically and also to achieve an outcome that satisfies them. Techniques such as anchoring, mirroring, and chasing away pink elephants help mediators establish rapport and then clarify issues.

Anchoring

An *anchor* is a stimulus associated with a particular response. Anchors can occur naturally. For example, people may hear waves (*stimulus*) and think about past vacations (*response*). The sound of the waves is the anchor for remembering the sights, sounds, and feelings of the holidays. Anchors can also be set and stimulated deliberately. For example, a person can set an anchor by putting her index finger to her mouth and saying, "shush." After that, when she touches her lips with that finger, people fall silent. *Anchoring,* or *setting an anchor,* is the term used when a communicator intentionally and purposefully exposes a party to a particular stimulus so the communicator can trigger a specific response at a chosen time. For most productive effect the communicator sets the anchor outside the party's awareness. I often do this by testing various tones during mediation. When I notice a tone that has a useful effect on a party, I reserve that tone for specific times. Then I use that tone with that party when I need to invite the party into a more productive frame of mind.

Employing the Match-Pace-Guide Technique

Match-pace-guide is a three-part process for productive communication. Mediators can use this process to gain the confidence of the parties and lead them into successful results. The first step is to identify a party's preferred representational system and use it in response. This is called *matching* (that is, matching systems). The second step is to replicate the party's system, breathing, and eye cues and her physical and language patterns. This is *pacing.* The third step is to lead the party into worthwhile ideas by introducing new patterns. This is *guiding.*

This process prevents conscious resistance to a new pattern by acknowledging the party on an other-than-conscious level. It allows the mediator to introduce suggestions on a level outside the party's conscious awareness.

Using Metaphors and Analogies

A *metaphor* is a figure of speech in which there is imaginative identification of one thing with another apparently different thing. Alfred Noyes's famous poem *The Highwayman* yields an abundance of metaphors. For example, the wind is a "torrent of darkness," the moon is "a ghostly galleon," and the road is "a ribbon of moonlight." An *analogy* is a linguistic device used to suggest similarities and correspondences between things that may not be immediately obvious to most people. For example, calling an airplane "a high-priced bus with terrible food" is an analogy.

Metaphors and analogies are gentle ways to create and maintain rapport. Mediators can use them to explain new information, introducing a topic to a party through something she already knows or to which she can relate. These communication tools are also especially useful to mediators for mitigating an unpleasant situation while continuing to acknowledge its presence.

Mirroring

Mirroring is the process of replicating other people's communication signals and then sending the signals back to the original communicators. Mirroring can be done consciously or other-than-consciously. Mediators can use it to create rapport with a party.

Chasing Away Pink Elephants

Chasing away pink elephants is the name I have given to a technique that clarifies issues and maintains rapport. This technique guides communicators to tell people what they want and to avoid stating what they don't want. It is based on the fact that the brain functions primarily in a positive state. That means people must know what something is before they understand what it is not. For example, look at the command, "Don't think of a pink elephant." The listener's first activity is to imagine an elephant. Then she must imagine an elephant that is pink. By the time she has finished dealing with the command (that is, "not pink elephant"), she has, in an extremely rapid process, searched over and over for that pink elephant she was not supposed to think about. Using a communication structure that includes "not" triggers an automatic response that yields exactly the opposite of what the communicator seeks.

People frequently err when they believe they can get results by telling others not to do something. The outcome is usually the opposite of the goal. Parents see this often after saying to children, "Do not trip with your drink," or, "Do not dirty your clothes."

A mediator can chase away pink elephants by minimizing his use of negatives (like "not" and "don't") and by rephrasing the negative communications of the parties during conflict resolution sessions. A mediator can also make sure he tells parties what he wants rather than what he does not want.

Playing Back

Playback is a communication technique that encourages speakers to send clear messages to listeners. It compels listeners to attend carefully to other parties. It helps clarify issues. In this technique, each party at the mediation takes turns speaking and listening. The first speaker makes an opening statement. After the opening statement, the listening party repeats, or *plays back,* what she heard. If the listener's report is inaccurate, the speaker is invited to point out any errors. The listener then restates the information as she heard it the second time. The speaker may continue to suggest corrections until he is satisfied the listener is repeating the exact meaning of the information. Once this occurs the parties switch roles.

Using the Polarity Response

A *polarity response* is the inherent, automatic reaction of some people to separate from something and go in the opposite direction from it. This response can be a conscious or other-than-conscious action. Some people experience this reaction frequently. Other people go through it only occasionally. Mediators see the polarity response when they ask a party to do something, and the party chooses to do exactly the opposite. This response can be counterproductive unless mediators recognize it. Then they can use it to create valuable results. I choose to take advantage of the response. I use it to encourage parties to do things that benefit the mediation. For example, I might say to a party who exhibits the polarity response, "I think it would be a bad idea for you to feel really great about this mediation experience."

Reframing

Reframing is used to change a person's perception of a situation or event. Mediators take a party's original idea about an experience and modify the setting or context around it. This change creates a different mental environment or frame of reference for the original experience. Once the party's perception is altered, the meaning of the experience also changes. As a result, the party has a new representation of the experience and new feelings attached to it.

The reframing technique is used constantly in organ donation programs, for example. Medical or other staff seeking donations often talk to family members about making the "meaningless" accidental death of their loved one (*original idea*) into something meaningful by giving life to someone else (*reframing*). In employment mediation I often suggest that the conflict (*original idea*) that brought parties to the table might be viewed as the catalyst (*reframing*) for creative policy change within the organization.

Gathering Information

Mediators need to gather accurate information from parties in order to help them reach a satisfying agreement. Here is one tactic mediators must attend to when they notice parties using it, two methods mediators can use for accessing information that is not immediately forthcoming, and two clues that there is yet more information to gather.

Bracketing

Bracketing is a negotiation tactic. Its name comes from the practice of bracketing when firing artillery. Bracketing starts with firing the first two shells so one explodes above and one below the target. Personnel then fire continuously, dividing the bracketing distance until a shell hits the target. In mediation, a party may want a specific financial settlement figure, and he may use bracketing to try to get it. He names a figure far above his actual financial goal. He assumes that if the other party offers a low figure, eventually both parties will end up agreeing to a midpoint. That midpoint is what he considered a reasonable sum in the first place. However, this technique does not always work as parties hope it will. Mediators need to recognize when bracketing is occurring because they may need to intervene.

Employing the Columbo Technique

Columbo is a technique I named after a television series detective who sounded and looked awkward but was in fact clever. This technique assists mediators in collecting and verifying information. Mediators using the Columbo technique refrain from appearing slick or polished. They sometimes question parties in a seemingly inane or obsequious style. They appear quite pedestrian. They avoid making pointed inquiries. This style reduces parties' feelings of threat and confrontation. As a result, parties may offer invaluable information to the questioner.

Onionskinning

Peeling the onion, or *onionskinning,* is another technique mediators can use to collect information. Mediators applying it are dogged in their questions, in a process similar to removing the layers of an onion. The persistent series of questions can focus on any subject. Often this technique is used to disclose the core mediation issue. Mediators ask many questions about the issue that seems to be the basis of the conflict. They keep asking questions—*onionskinning*—to verify whether that issue is really the one at the heart of the dispute. They want to know whether that issue is what makes up the onion "all the way down." During this peeling process, hidden issues are sometimes uncovered.

Recognizing a Wedding Dress

A *wedding dress* is a clue about incomplete information. It derives its name from a mediation that almost dissolved because among the amounts of money one party claimed was an unsubstantiated sum. That sum turned out to be exactly the price of a wedding dress one party had promised to a niece. The party was hoping to get the cost of that dress out of the mediation even though the dress had nothing to do with the mediation issue. Mediators need to look for and flag any unusual portion of a party's claim. Then they can investigate whether or not the sum is related to the accounting in hand. Once they have actually identified an unrelated amount, a wedding dress, they can work with that knowledge.

Minimizing Door Knob Issues

A *door knob* issue is an important point that one party brings up *after* the mediator and other parties believe all subjects have been canvassed and resolved. It gets its name from the fact that parties are usually walking out the door as this matter is articulated. The key to preventing door knob issues is to ensure that all matters have been resolved before parties start to walk out the door. Watching for nonverbal cues that say no at the same time the party is verbally saying yes is essential to spotting areas where there is more information to be gathered about issues.

Clearing Hurdles

When obstacles to the mediation process appear, communication techniques like the following can often help parties change habitual patterns of response and overcome the barriers raised by their old responses.

As If

As if is one technique mediators can put into action when parties believe they are faced with insurmountable barriers that are preventing them from moving forward. The mediator invites parties to imagine they are working on other mediation issues as if the original obstacles had been resolved and were in the past. The mediator asks parties to imagine what that new situation looks like, sounds like, feels like, tastes like, and smells like. This activity stimulates parties to change their mental states and operate as if the original matter has been resolved. The mediator then helps the parties to work through other pending issues. Once these other matters are dealt with, parties can return to the troublesome questions, which may no longer look as daunting or may no longer be relevant at all.

Backing

Backing is a technique I developed for parties who literally cannot see anything except a problem right before their eyes. The problem is like an object blocking their vision. In this technique, the mediator requests that parties use their imaginations. They are asked to visualize taking hold of the "problem" in front of them as if it were an object. Then they are instructed to move the hand holding the "object" behind their heads. They are told to deposit it out of sight. They are asked to bring their hand back empty. At that point, parties can look at other mediation issues again.

Crumpled Paper

Crumpled paper is a technique that mediators use to help parties get rid of vexatious issues that have nothing to do with the mediation but are impeding its process. The mediator uses this technique in caucus or with all parties in the same room. First, the mediator asks the parties to determine their troublesome issues. Then the mediator instructs the parties to write the issues on a piece of paper.

(Each party sees only her own piece of paper.) When the parties have finished writing, the mediator asks them to crumple their respective pieces of paper and throw them away.

Hanging Balloons

Hanging balloons is a technique to use when parties raise issues relevant to the mediation but not applicable to discussion underway at the moment. The mediator first acknowledges the topic by thanking the party who raised the issue. Then the mediator asks if it would be acceptable to that party to "hang the issue up." As she says this, the mediator makes the gesture of suspending an imaginary balloon in the air. She requests permission to leave the issue there until a later time. She "pulls down" the balloon at an appropriate time to deal with the issue.

Kelly Decision Wheel

The *Kelly Decision Wheel*™© is an instrument designed to assist parties to make optimum decisions. The concept was developed by Kathleen J. Kelly in 1989. It can be used for different types of decisions. These can include making choices and prioritizing options.

Magic Button

The *magic button* is a technique I created to use with parties who hit an impasse because they have a limiting belief. This belief is that there is no possible solution. In this technique, the mediator asks parties to visualize a magic button. The button is on the table in front of them. The mediator then suggests to parties that they can push the button. As they press on it, parties imagine they can have *anything* they want to resolve the conflict. The mediator advises parties that their choice is limitless. This allows them to experience that a solution is possible.

Marking Out

Marking out is a technique mediators use to isolate physical locations in the mediation room. They associate each physical spot with either a positive or negative idea. They then stand in the positive spots to reinforce progress that is being made. They point at the negative locations to separate and dissociate counterproductive activity from the mediation. This technique relies heavily on other-than-consciousness. It automatically associates positive or negative thoughts with the information the mediator associates with each spot.

Option Circle

The *option circle* is a technique that produces new communication choices. It interrupts old, automatic responses to a stimulus and allows people to choose new communications in response to that stimulus. Both mediators and parties can use this technique, which relies on a physical process. Parties receive the old stimulus but refrain from using their instinctive response. Instead, they inhale and exhale deeply to interrupt their automatic response and give themselves as much oxygen as they can. With eyelids open or closed and starting in the visual remembered position, they move their eyes in a clockwise or counterclockwise direction. The eyes move as if they were running along the edges of a square, as shown in Figure 3.2. The direction does not matter as long as the parties move their eyes through all the eye positions. The eyes return to the visual remembered position. Then the parties inhale and exhale again and choose a response, either their old one or a new one.

I have found this exercise generates new choices and new creativity. It allows people to do a transderivational search through system files they would not ordinarily access during mediation. This process invites people to connect other-than-consciously with productive information that would ordinarily be missed at that moment. Figure 3.3 outlines the entire process.

Switched Hand

The *switched hand* technique is another way to produce creative solutions when mediation is stalled. The mediator asks the parties to place their pens in the hand they do not typically use. The mediator then suggests that the parties imagine solutions. Finally, the mediator tells the parties to record their results, using the pen in their switched hand.

Relevancy Challenge

The *relevancy challenge* is one more technique mediators can set in motion to clear away obstacles. The parameters of the challenge are established during the mediator's opening remarks, when

Figure 3.2. Running the Square.

Touch All the Eye Accessing Positions

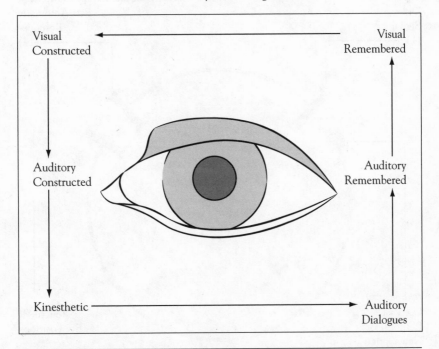

Visual
Constructed

Visual
Remembered

Auditory
Constructed

Auditory
Remembered

Kinesthetic

Auditory
Dialogues

© 2000 Unicom Communication Consultants Inc. Reprinted with permission.
Note: The figure shows the typical eye movement of a right-handed person with
left brain nominal dominance who is facing you and running the square
clockwise from his or her point of view.

ground rules are explained. At that time, the mediator makes a
pact with parties. In this agreement the parties resolve to focus discussion on specific issues, to remain relevant. The agreement
discourages parties from digressing from contracted points.

Consider this example of a party who strays to a topic like un-
paid support payments during a family mediation concerning
scheduled visits. The mediator can start by saying, "When we set
up ground rules that limited this discussion specifically to scheduled visits, we agreed other issues would be excluded." Then the
mediator can preempt further discussion about support by adding,
"Chris, since this matter isn't related specifically to scheduled visits, it's not on the table today." Alternatively, if the mediator wants

Figure 3.3. Option Circle.

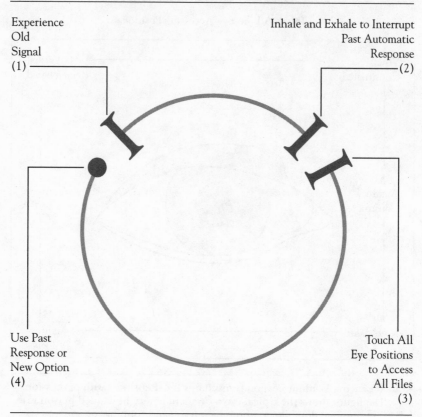

Experience
Old
Signal
(1)

Inhale and Exhale to Interrupt
Past Automatic
Response
(2)

Use Past
Response or
New Option
(4)

Touch All
Eye Positions
to Access
All Files
(3)

© 1993 Unicom Communication Consultants Inc. Reprinted with permission.

to flesh out the comment and still control whether the issue stays on the table, she can choose to follow up on the original statement by saying, "Chris, if you can't tell me how this issue specifically relates to scheduled visits, it cannot be on the table and we will resume our discussion where we left off." At that point, the onus is on the interrupting party to link his issue to scheduled visits. If he cannot, that issue is automatically excluded and the mediation continues.

Wondering

Wondering is a technique mediators can use when they want to encourage creativity in parties. When mediation starts to move slowly, the mediator asks the parties to "wonder" and to "get curious" about a situation. These words consciously stimulate parties to become creative. At the same time, the mediator moves her eyes up and to her right to guide parties into a visual imagination accessing pattern. This other-than-conscious communication prompts parties to wonder too. When using this technique, mediators must avoid terms like "think about" and "dissect." These expressions invite parties back into an analytical state. Mediators should also keep their eyes away from their left side. That too will lead parties other-than-consciously back into analyzing.

Part Two

Seven Steps to Getting Results

| Be Prepared

Many years ago, it was common to see bumper stickers reading "PLAN AHEAd." The final "d" was almost squeezed off the paper's edge. Although the sticker's novelty has long passed, the idea remains meaningful. In Part One, I outlined the terminology, patterns, techniques, and applications of nonverbal communication in mediation. By introducing the material this way, I invited you to become familiar with the existence of nonverbal communication in the mediation environment. With this new awareness, you are now ready to take the first of seven steps to get results using this information.

Planning Ahead

Even before the first client contact, you can take advantage of knowing about nonverbal communication. As I show you in discussing Step One of using nonverbal communication in mediation, you can prepare to use nonverbal strategies by setting up the mechanics and logistics of your working environment appropriately and by examining incoming information for clues about clients.

Preparing Forms

In Part One, I discussed the importance of tracking nonverbal information right from first contact. Results from tracking lay the foundation for each person's profile and form the basis for most nonverbal strategies. The most effective way to document this vital information is by PEGing™. I keep a fresh stack of Profile Element

Grids by my telephone. That way, I have a new one for each initial telephone conversation I have with a party to a mediation. I know the PEG form thoroughly (Figure 3.1). I simply check boxes as the other party talks. The only writing I do on the PEG is filling in language touchstones. I use these touchstone expressions during that conversation or later during the mediation. My only other notes are jotted additional details on the side of the PEG sheet, if I need them. With the PEG in front of me, I can listen for both the content and structure of the conversation. By the end of the call, I am ready to begin to create a communication strategy relating to the person with whom I spoke.

You may find it more comfortable to create a form of your own on which to record information systematically. If you do, ensure that it contains all the essential elements needed to profile the person with whom you are talking on the telephone or in person and to gather information useful for mediation. The first phase of developing a form for yourself is to review an old case file. Read the notes you took during the initial telephone call or meeting. Identify the vital information that came out during mediation. Ask yourself if you could have gathered any of that mediation information during the initial call. Recall the original telephone call again. Determine whether you picked up any information regarding the person's communication patterns or simply case detail.

Now, as a second phase, review one or two dozen old files using the same process you used in the first phase. Look for consistencies. Create your own form around them. List topic names for the general kinds of nonverbal information you have been overlooking and would now find useful, such as preferred system, mental movement, and so forth. Add any other sections that matter to you. For example, you may want to ask callers about potentially disruptive parties who should be excluded from the mediation. You may want to list people who should be present to validate the decisions of parties who require such external support. Translators may be a need you have on a regular basis. Test your form for a month with each call you make or receive. Adjust it where necessary. Keep the topics that are useful for you. Drop the ones that are not. Make your final template, and run off or print copies. Always keep a batch of your forms by your telephone.

Gaining Proficiency in Systems Language

The next component of planning ahead is becoming comfortable using language from the different representational systems. Start by drawing up three columns to list words and expressions from the visual, auditory, and kinesthetic systems. Make a fourth column for nonsystem, or neutral, words. Fill in each representational system column with at least twenty-five expressions that reflect that system. Find at least five expressions for nonsystem words. (Chapter Two offers some examples, and Appendix B contains a sample list.)

I predict you will find it easy to complete some columns and will struggle with others. At this point stop and reflect. You can surmise that the columns you complete easily reflect systems you favor most of the time. Conversely, the challenge you experience in finding words in other systems may be the same difficulty others go through to understand your information. You may be inadvertently forcing them to translate all your messages if they prefer another system.

Now continue your exercise by going to other sources to complete your lists. Watch television interviews; listen to radio; read print articles and newspaper items. Pay attention to the language of friends, family, colleagues, and clients. Let all these people be resources for your lists.

Finally, begin to use the listed words and expressions in your conversations with family, friends, colleagues, clients, telephone solicitors—everyone. If you hear visual system terms, respond with visual predicates. If someone chatters using auditory system words, match them with auditory expressions, and so forth. Pay special attention to the systems with which you have greatest difficulty. When you become comfortable using all systems, your approach is balanced, and you are ready to communicate effectively on an other-than-conscious level.

Tracking and Profiling

Get used to developing an awareness of all verbal and nonverbal information being hurled at you. Begin to practice tracking and profiling. Use all your senses. Sponge up all the verbal and nonverbal communication people are offering to you constantly. As you listen to television interviews, build profiles of the interviewees. (The unrehearsed interviews on public television are the best for this practice activity.) Pay attention to the communication of restaurant diners, clients, partners, family members, and subway riders. Every person is broadcasting information continually. You just have to tune in to receive it. Track that information. Get comfortable with being alert to valuable material. It is out there, just waiting for you. Develop ease with the process. Once you do, attending to conscious and other-than-conscious messages during mediation will be second nature to you.

Having Useful Equipment on Hand

Two years ago, a skillful mediator I know was awarded a contract by a high-profile lawyer whose office was in another city. The case related to a design copyright. The mediator had been waiting years to snag a lawyer of this caliber and was ecstatic about the opportunity. The two managed swimmingly until information had to be exchanged. The mediator did not own a fax machine or a scanner. He worked with a computer program that was five years old. He kept insisting he did not need a fax or a scanner and that his word processing software was just fine. The result was much lost time, frustration, messenger costs, higher billings, and most significantly, the mediator's inability to provide the lawyer with the visual information the lawyer wanted in a way he needed it. To this day the mediator insists that he did "just fine" without the equipment. The lawyer has sworn never again to deal with or to recommend that mediator.

Choosing Equipment to Meet Clients' Needs

You must have a fax machine that sends and receives information clearly. This is vital for working with parties who must see, read, or touch something before it is real to them. If you use a stand-alone fax, you can send written information or pictures without scanning. You can also send material in its original size. Parties may appreciate this.

Stand-alone faxes do have paper and memory limits. They also can send and receive only in black and white. Along with a stand-alone fax machine, you may also want to have a computer fax card that allows your computer to send and receive faxes. This is an economic consideration if you often receive multipage faxes and need only peruse some pages and not print them. It also places no limit on the number of pages it can receive. If you want clients to feel comfortable about faxing at their convenience, however, you must always leave the computer running. If exact reproduction size is important to you or your highly visual clients, computer faxing may not be for you. Letter-size originals with fax headers appear in a slightly compressed format on the computer screen and when printed in order to fit the text plus the header inside standard margins, and legal-size originals are even more squeezed and distorted. If you opt for a computer fax card only, you will also need a scanner so you can capture and forward visual information not available directly from your computer files. Additionally, optical character recognition (OCR) software can gather and deposit information from the scanner directly into your computer files when you need it. If you get a scanner, you may not need a photocopier.

Consider installing two telephone lines so you can dedicate one line to faxing and e-mail. Clients can fax without calling you first. The e-mail system will give clients easy and inexpensive access to your office twenty-four hours a day, from anywhere. Easy access for clients sends a message about your professionalism. Arrange for a telephone answering system or service that is congruent with the image you want to convey to clients. This is the time to avoid tinny, twenty-five-dollar answering machines. If you record your own message, make sure it sounds welcoming, energetic, and like you. Rehearse and record the message until it conveys exactly what you want current and prospective clients to believe about you.

The next type of equipment I recommend for a mediation professional is a visual caller identification display. When you see the caller's identification before you lift the receiver, you gain an enormous advantage. In the split second between seeing the caller's name and picking up the telephone, you can inhale and exhale, run the eye square, and shift your attention to focus on the calling party. Then you can take good care of the caller.

If you subscribe to call waiting and your telephone company offers visual call waiting identification, you may want to invest in this too. Without this display you receive a waiting call beep but have no way of knowing who the second caller is. The beeping may be a distraction you convey paralinguistically to your current caller. With the visual call waiting display you can quickly choose to let your voice-mail pick up the second call or you can stop the in-progress call. You can also be prepared mentally for the party on the second line.

Many years ago a multinational computer manufacturer hired me to teach several interpersonal communication programs. During one class, curious participants asked if preferred systems had any affect on computer equipment. I told them that corporations like theirs were affected profoundly. Their company, for example, built computers that responded to language-based and letter-based commands. This was fine for people who have an auditory preference and who like to read as they subvocalize the words. It was problematic, however, for those who like to use picture or movement commands. Enter another company whose founders thought differently. The latter company provided users with a visual framework (icons) and a kinesthetic vehicle (a mobile mouse to point and click) to execute commands. Predictably, most established clients and word-based corporations stayed with the multinational company. Their systems were already entrenched. Visually oriented and kinesthetically leaning companies, however, as well as individual consumers with these preferences, flocked to the products of the new manufacturer.

Today we have a mixture of both styles, although die-hard vocalizers still prefer letter keyboarding. I suggest you select the system best suited for your preferences. If your industry requires an alternate type of software, I recommend you become proficient in it too. Then you and the parties with whom you deal will be able to send and receive information easily. If you do not accommodate people in this way, you erect a nonverbal barrier before your first face-to-face meeting.

Positioning Equipment

Consider how to position your equipment. Look for comfort and avoid muscle strain. Place your general equipment and files conveniently close to you so they are handy if you need them while on the telephone. You will stay relaxed and communicate this in your tone. If you usually compute figures during telephone conversations, have a calculator close by. Make sure its noise is muted. If you get faxes frequently, situate that equipment away from your desk so incoming ringing is not intrusive. If you share equipment like a photocopier with others, locate that machine away from your desk. That way you avoid disrupting telephone communications. You also refrain from giving callers the impression that background voices might be people who could breach confidentiality.

When placing your telephone set, put it on your left side if you are right-handed and on your right side if you are left-handed. That way, you can write notes easily as you talk. When it is on your nominally dominant side, you may also find conversation easier, because you will be "tipped" toward (that is, accessing) the hemisphere that holds words for you.

Be careful where you place the computer keyboard in relationship to the telephone mouthpiece. If you document conversations by typing on your computer keyboard, your note taking could flatter or annoy people hearing the keystrokes. Either way, if keying is loud, listeners will be aware of the noise. One option is to use a headset that has a unidirectional mouthpiece (one that picks up sound from one direction) rather than an omnidirectional one (one that picks up sound from all directions). Place the mouthpiece close to your lips and push the keyboard as far away from you as is comfortable.

In setting up your computer monitor, I suggest you consider the advice I gave one company. They asked how to locate equipment and furniture so communication was most effective. One piece of advice I gave them was to forget about predrilling desk holes for monitors. Screen placement does not have a one-location-fits-all solution. Monitor locations are as individual as preferred systems. When you locate your screen, I suggest you first identify your preferred system. Then place your monitor where your eyes naturally rest. By doing this, you avoid forcing your eyes to move away from the monitor, travel to your primary system to access information, and then return to the monitor so you can enter the information into the computer. For example, if you have a visual preference, put the screen in a high location. If you have an auditory preference, locate the screen so you are looking directly at it. If you have a kinesthetic preference, set the screen down and right.

Be careful if you decide to place your screen down and to the left. That location brings eyes down to the position that typically accesses old dialogues and conversations. If you decide to locate your screen there, you may find that you are hearing unproductive internal messages. Move your screen immediately to another spot if this happens.

I have discovered one other tip about monitor placement. Any time I want to change my thought process, I change my eye information accessing position. I do this by moving my screen (which hangs from a monitor arm) or by adjusting the height and location of my chair in relationship to the screen. My eyes are invited into a new accessing position, and I begin to think differently.

Gathering Facts

As you gather facts in preparation for the mediation, you will benefit not only from considering as many sources of information as you can but also from examining likely biases and filters.

Reviewing Briefs, Reports, Pictures, and Videotapes

In preparing for mediation, it's wise to consider all the valuable information and resources you have in hand. If you are reviewing briefs and reports, sift through the legalese, and glean the writer's preferred system. Many times, the language reflects the other-than-conscious representational system bias of a judge or tribunal board member. If you read enough of the person's respective decisions, you can often pinpoint the preferred system. For example, in one case I was retained "to read" a judge in court. Prior to attending the trial, I obtained a copy of a previous decision handed down by the judge. By the time I had read the second page I could advise my lawyer client that the judge's language showed a 95 percent visual predisposition. That meant the lawyer went into court equipped with pictures, colored charts, and a strong vocabulary of visual predicates.

If you have access to pictures and a videotape, they can provide you with two types of information. First, simply note that the visual information has been included in the information package. Begin to wonder if inclusion by itself might be one indicator of the sender's preferred system. Probe further.

Next, examine the content of the pictures and videotape. It may also allow you to gather factual information about the parties and how they like to operate. Get curious about pictures showing the parties in their natural environments. For example, if the surroundings are generally neat and have lots of pictures, you may be looking at a person who prefers visual information. If the environment has material strewn everywhere, looks almost chaotic, but appears to have mementos around, you may have uncovered someone with a kinesthetic preference. If you see material that is strictly alphabetized, itemized, and highly organized, you may have found someone with an auditory preference.

Pictures and videotapes can reveal cultural information, from which you can create strategies. Look at clothing and jewelry to ascertain ethnicity and economic levels. See whether religious artifacts are present. Videotape, of course, provides the dimension of language and sound. Listen to the parties' articulation on the videotape for accent, educational level, evidence of geographical region, and paralanguage. All of these details offer invaluable information from which you can create nonverbal strategies.

Considering Source Bias and Filters

In preparing for mediation, I have noticed a real benefit to stepping back from information I have received. Doing this, I can consider the source. By taking an even longer perspective, I remind myself about the filtering and translation process through which all information goes.

First, our senses receive cues. We cannot understand the information directly, however. In fact, what we ultimately "understand" is actually third-hand information. This means we receive cues first collected consciously or other-than-consciously, then put through filters, and finally brought into awareness. Once you recognize this process is happening to you, then take one more step back. Consider how many more filters have been used to sift the information you receive from another party. The sender has filtered it, consciously and other-than-consciously, even before sending it to you.

The process of stepping back twice can provide you with a new outlook about the abundance of bias built into any piece of information you gather. With the first step, you remember the process of receiving your own screened information. With the second, you appreciate you are getting filtered information from others.

Accordingly, I suggest you separate the message content (or facts) from the message delivery package (that is, the person or the type of material conveying the message). For example, a well-written brief from a lawyer does not ensure the lawyer's client will be well educated or articulate. If you hear counsel with an accent or see ethnic garb, that does not mean the mediating party sounds or looks the same way. As a result, when you consider any information from which you are gathering facts, keep in mind that the people submitting information may not always be the parties for whom you are preparing. You must be ready for those who submit information and for others too.

Making as Many Preliminary Calls as Possible

The final way to prepare yourself is to replicate your fact-gathering process as many times as possible. The more contacts you make, the more information you can track. The more information you can track, the more profiles you can begin. Each piece of information provides you with more dimensions and a greater appreciation for each party. Moreover, hearing accounts of the same issues from different parties allows you to triangulate on agreed points and to isolate disagreements before you walk through the mediation door.

The more knowledge you have before mediation, the better prepared you are to get creative in devising and using nonverbal strategies.

Maximizing the Initial Telephone Contact

At the time when I was starting to train lawyers to use nonverbal strategies, an attorney with a strong visual preference moaned to me about her extreme disadvantage on the telephone. She said she needed face-to-face contact with other parties to collect all the information she required. I bet her a lunch that she could pick up almost 50 percent more information if she used two small nonverbal strategies. She was game. I told her to forget about housecleaning her desk while she talked on the telephone. I also instructed her to close her eyes and *really* listen. A week later she laughingly called me to ask me to pick a restaurant.

Because many mediators do much preparatory and other information-gathering work by telephone, anything they can do to increase the amount of knowledge they gain from each call will benefit everyone involved in the mediation. Step Two in using nonverbal communication in mediation, then, is to maximize what you can learn from the initial telephone contact, and all subsequent contacts, with the mediating parties and their representatives. Four areas need particular consideration: listening for physical cues and patterns, managing the conversation, attending to the nuances of paralanguage, and asking effective questions.

Physical Factors in Telephone Communication

The way people behave physically when they are talking on the telephone affects the amount and kind of information they can absorb. Mediators can do several simple things to get more from telephone conversations.

Maximizing the Information You Collect

The lawyer I described at the beginning of this chapter had two traits that worked against picking up the maximum amount of information. The first was that she used her time on the phone for her desk-cleaning routine. She would never have done this if a client had been in front of her, but she didn't have a problem with doing it when the client she was talking with couldn't see her. Because she, like most people, could consciously focus only on a limited number of bits of information (seven plus or minus two pieces), she was missing pieces of information offered over the telephone that she would otherwise have heard. She was losing the opportunity to garner as many vital, nonvisual details as she possibly could. They would drop into other-than-consciousness if they were the eighth or ninth bits of information offered concurrently with the housecleaning images she had in front of her.

The second habit that diminished her results was her unexamined assumption that visual information was the only information worth knowing. According to expert information (such as that presented by Dave Dobson in a 1985 workshop), visual information does occupy about 47 percent of a person's attention. If the visual information is unrelated to the most important event going on, however, in this case a telephone call, other vital clues are lost. Once the lawyer became willing to gather information in other ways, she could close her eyes in order to become more aware of nonvisual information and other-than-conscious cues. Some of these cues were ambient background noises. They told her, for example, whether or not it was a productive time to be on the telephone. She might hear altered breathing, background voices, and people who sounded ill. On occasion she found herself saying, "It sounds as if you might be busy right now. Is there a more convenient time to speak?" Parties were amazed that she seemed to have developed an instinct for being sensitive to their needs. She was courteous about people's demands and set up times in which both parties could hold focused conversations.

As this lawyer learned to do, you can close your eyes to better hear background cues. Sometimes you will hear conversations. At times the content of these discussions will be informative. At other times background voices may indicate it is a poor time for respondents to be candid or to provide you with useful off-the-record information. You will pick up other information too. If you hear fax machines, doorbells, and other pieces of equipment, you will realize that they are competing with the seven or so bits of information that are all you and the party can each deal with on a conscious level. You can then choose to put yourself and the other party in an environment or time frame in which you are both able to focus. That way you can pick up maximum information.

Another strategy for picking up as much information as possible involves the way you use your telephone apparatus. In Step One, I talked about placing the telephone on your desk. By leaning toward the natural side that allows you to access the nominally dominant and analytical part of your brain, this action allows you to be more alert to facts and find words for dialogue. If you want to get more creative during a conversation, switch the telephone handset temporarily to your other ear and lean to that side. By doing that, you assist the other part of your brain to access the creative process. Your words may temporarily be replaced by ideas and feelings. Relax. The words will return shortly after you inhale and exhale and lean again to the first side.

Maximizing Your Effectiveness

I suggest, as discussed in Step One, that you use your own tracking form or a Profile Element Grid when initially talking to a party with whom you will be dealing at mediation. A form keeps you centered on information you need for a working profile, and checking off items takes less of your attention than writing or computer keying does. Once you have tracked even a few pieces of information, you can use them as a springboard to vault over obstacles and retrieve more information. That way you can optimize your effectiveness during the latter part of the conversation.

To become even more productive on the telephone, consider using the option circle (Figure 3.3) to increase your flexibility and make yourself more creative. Inhale and exhale two or three times, and run the square (Figure 3.2) with your eyes. When I do this, inevitably I move out of my stalled state and come upon one or two alternatives resulting from the transderivational search that I started by running the square.

Another way to maximize telephone effectiveness is to alter breathing patterns. If you are breathing in a pattern different from the other party's pattern, decide whether you want to match the party's breathing or to have the party match you. Either way, you develop rapport with the party through breathing. When you change your breathing, do it subtly so the other party detects the change only other-than-consciously and responds to it. For example, if you want to invite a person into a visual mode, use visual language and breath rapidly from the top of your chest. If you want to encourage the person to adopt an auditory frame of mind, breath evenly and from midchest. If you want the person to follow you into a kinesthetic, relaxed mode, breathe evenly and deeply from your diaphragm.

Even though you can use breathing to set up a subtle, nonverbal rapport on an other-than-conscious level, you may find that parties still need consciously to perceive a common interest. Although the initial telephone contact is ostensibly made to discuss and settle logistical details about the mediation, you can use this occasion to forge links that can be strengthened during mediation. This is an ideal time to ask about cultural, religious, or other special requirements that may affect mediation. By inquiring about particular needs, you may detect kinds of conditions or even biases that would not ordinarily surface until mediation itself. With this advance warning, you can plan accordingly. During this conversation, you can sift through information that may have a meaningful impact during mediation as you establish and strengthen your connection with parties. You can also arrange to send the kind of follow-up material that the parties prefer to receive. Along with mediation documentation, you might choose to forward written instructions to some parties and maps to others. This kind of attention to detail builds a strong connection with parties before you meet them personally.

Conversation Management

During the initial telephone contact, you will need to guide the conversation on both conscious and other-than-conscious levels to create rapport, reduce barriers to open communication, and focus the discussion effectively. You can also identify and begin to deal with individuals' unproductive ways of speaking.

Finding a Common Interest

Have you ever wondered why people talk about the weather? Do you think they feel meteorologically challenged, or do you sense something more basic in these questions? Weather, I have discovered, is a universally benign topic. It allows people with a low level of familiarity to connect. It acts as a bridgehead into people's worlds. By asking another person about the weather, an individual is literally and figuratively checking the climate for interaction. People want to know how safe it is to venture forward. They are really asking for the information that the word containers (like tone) carry. Questions about weather are a gentle way to ask for permission to enter another person's world.

Initial contact is an opportune time to wash away barriers with such small talk. Small talk is like little puddles of conversation outside the storm being mediated. These little pools may touch on children, cars, sports, or any other noncontentious topic likely to be of interest to both parties. During this chatting time, I carefully listen for words that suggest specific interests of the party at the other end of the telephone. Then I pursue the reason these words are special to the party. I want to learn whether there is a connection that I can acknowledge. I do this by picking up a thread of the conversation and moving forward with that thread.

Here is an illustration from a conversation I had with a lawyer about a possible mediation location. The lawyer said, "I've been to that place. You know, it has a lot of stairs. Every time I go there, it reminds me of one vacation and the time I spent climbing to the top of the Statue of Liberty." I heard *vacation* and *climbing* threads. So I picked up the climbing thread, saying, "I know the feeling. Every time I work there, I think about the dust that's collecting on my stair-climbing equipment." The conversation then went on to areas like past vacations and exercise. It was a benign conversation that elicited interests we had in common. The thoughts were not directly linked to the mediation. Nonetheless, rapport was built on these pieces of a positive foundation. The more such pieces you accumulate, the more solid your base is going into mediation.

Matching High-Context and Low-Context Speakers

Once you have established some common interests on a conscious level, I suggest you also match the speaker's context pattern if you want to increase your rapport on the other-than-conscious level. Listen for parties who use lots of words to articulate their message. If they are high-context communicators, steer the conversation by giving them implicit messages. For example, you can talk about the value of a location, its accessibility, its convenience, and its professional staff, but avoid saying directly, "Let's book this spot for the mediation." If you hear parties being very direct with you and you identify them as low-context communicators, manage the conversation with low-context messages. Continuing the example of finding a mediation location, you might say, "It's good value for the money. Let's book it."

Along with matching the speaker's number of words, I suggest you match the length of the speaker's words. This method is one of the most subtle conversation managers you can use on an other-than-conscious level. I used to work with a therapist who was a genius at using this technique with children and teenagers. Whereas other clinicians struggled to develop linkages with youngsters, he just matched the youngsters syllable for syllable. The responses you would hear him using in his sessions were "huh," "nope," and "yup." The youngsters were totally unaware of the technique. Rapport was instant because the structural bond was established wholly outside their conscious awareness and without reference to therapeutic content. When you match the length of a speaker's words, you can achieve the same conversation management.

Matching Language

After matching context pattern and word length, you might reproduce the speaker's language patterns to manage conversation. Start with systems. If you do not know initially what system speakers prefer, use neutral expressions, such as "do you *understand*" or "do you *know*." Speakers will respond in their preferred system. I suggest you then match the system the speaker uses. That is the easiest way to send and receive messages and create rapport in the initial contact. It telegraphs your message so listeners get your point immediately. It also avoids jamming their systems because it eliminates their need to translate your preferred system into their preferred system. If they answer with visual predicates, then use expressions like "I *see* what you mean," "When I *look* through different *lenses,*" or "I have the same *perspective.*" If they answer with auditory predicates, use expressions like "I *hear* you," "You can *say* that again, and "I *chimed in.*" If they answer with kinesthetic predicates, use expressions like "We're *on the same page,*" "I'll *take it* from here," or "I *have a hunch* they might *boot it* out of there." When you do this, you make information easy to understand because you are sending the facts of your message within the structure the other party understands most easily. You manage conversation flow by using the other person's systems.

I also suggest that you use buzz words the way other parties do. By communicating using their buzz words, you create a bond outside their awareness. For example, if speakers refer to mediation attendees as "parties," use that term instead of "people." If content-related jargon surfaces during the initial conversation, use those words too when the context is appropriate. Buzz words allow you to manage the conversation covertly because you are matching the party's model of the world through language. You can further this impact by dropping some of the party's language touchstones into your discussion. For example, if a mediating party says she wants to "replace the vehicle" and receive "acknowledgment for inconvenience," you parachute those two exact expressions into your conversation at some point. The more touchstones you accumulate and deposit into the exchange, the more control you have in managing the discussion.

Deescalating Speakers' Language

The times I suggest you avoid matching speakers' language are rare, but they do happen. These are the times when parties use language that is inflammatory, types of words that ignite arguments and create unproductive environments. To manage conversations, you can steer speakers away from certain expressions and toward others. Repeat their ideas, but remove the commands from them. Replace commands with rhetorical questions and suggestions. You might want to do away with the expressions "you should," "you must," and "you ought to" unless you have no choice. These expressions often trigger a polarity response. They also beg the question, "According to whom?" Instead, rephrase and replace those terms with constructions like these: "Do I understand you to mean that it might be productive if . . . ?" or, "Are you suggesting that it might be useful if . . . ?" These sentences suggest a possibility (something "might be" so); their content is tentative. They also introduce the possibility of a positive idea (in the words "productive" and "useful"). This type of language construction removes any hint of command and replaces it with recommendation.

Some parties like to create catastrophes in their verbal descriptions. They seem to derive some sense of satisfaction from making something sound much worse than it is. This pattern often raises tensions and emotions among the parties. To deescalate speakers' language, I rephrase superlatives and replace inflammatory words. For example, if a speaker says, "It was the most horrible event of my life," I avoid contradicting him. Rather, I restate his idea and at the same time bring his language down a notch. I might say, "It seems that you are talking about a very disturbing occurrence." This notching downward often calms speakers. If they choose to reescalate, I again deflate their language, until they come to accept that I understand their idea and emotions even though I use less inflammatory terminology.

Paralanguage Nuances

As you plan for the mediation, it is also important to pay attention to paralanguage nuances during the initial contacts. You may learn about people's backgrounds, their health, and in particular, whether or not they are feeling fearful.

Gathering Parties' Background Information

Just as language clues tell you to make certain preparations, paralanguage signals you to prepare for mediation in other ways. Accents can indicate that mediating parties come from different worlds and have different models of expectation for behavior and language. Foreign accents can also alert you that you may need to arrange translation at the table. Different educational levels may filter through parties' language. When you hear these different levels, you may decide to plan a simplified set of proceedings and explanations, or you may see a benefit to preparing sophisticated materials.

As you listen for vocalizations during the first telephone conversations, you may get a reading of parties' health. Hoarseness and shortness of breath may indicate chronic conditions and parties who will need frequent breaks. Raspy, wheezing sounds and the throat clearing of long-term smokers may mean you will need to accommodate nicotine breaks. Sneezing and nasality from a cold or the flu could indicate that mediation should be delayed until all parties have the focus and stamina to sustain the process. Also listen for indicators of good health. Normal breath flow sounds and clear articulation should be present. If these or any other good health indicators are absent, question parties about their health. Determine whether their health will be a factor during mediation.

Separating Fear from Other Indicators

When people speak rapidly, that pace may indicate either representational system preference or fear. You will need to explore the possibilities more deeply. When parties use visual predicates (like "seeing is believing," "couldn't take my eyes off," and "a picture is worth a thousand words") while they are speaking rapidly, they could be showing you their visual preference. When the same parties talk quickly and breathe shallowly from the top of the chest, this breathing pattern too may be normal for them. To differentiate their fear cues from their representational system cues, you will have to look for other signs, like stammering or tonal shift, which may be unusual for these parties. When parties with either an auditory or a kinesthetic preference breathe shallowly from the top of the chest yet use predicates from their respective preferred systems, they may be showing you they are afraid. In both cases I suggest you match the parties' preferred language systems. Then alter your breathing to a slower, deeper rate, so parties can change their breathing to match. Those who are afraid can shift out of their fear response. Others can become more relaxed.

A cadence in which the voice rises at the end of statements can be a sign of fear or simply habit. People sometimes use this paralinguistic tactic to mitigate the content (that is, the information) of the statement they have just delivered. They are afraid of the consequences of saying something outright. At other times this vocal rise is just habit, and people are unaware they are sending a mixed signal. When you notice this rising cadence, investigate its origin if possible. If it is fear, you may want to articulate the fear for the party while you explore the reason for it. For example, you might say, "I understand that mediation is sometimes a little unsettling to people who haven't yet experienced it." If the rising cadence is merely habit, you may want to gently alert the party that she sounds tentative. You can do this by asking after each sentence, "Are you sure?" At some point her other-than-conscious awareness will trigger a conscious reaction, and she will ask you why you are asking her about her statements. Once she has opened the subject, you are permitted to suggest that she sounds as though she is asking questions rather than making statements.

In some initial conversations with parties you may hit a wall of silence. When you do, determine whether the quietness is a sign of fear, a cultural communication pattern, or an issue. If it is a sign of fear, the lack of words may be the flight part of the fight-or-flight response. In this case, adjust your breathing to a deep, even rhythm. That way, the party can alter his breathing and shift out of his fear response and back into a more rational frame of mind.

People from some cultures drop into silence as a method of communicating. If you believe the lack of discussion is a cultural issue, I recommend you respect it, ask few questions, and create rapport through lack of conversation.

If a fluid conversation suddenly stops, you may conclude that the silence is an issue indicator. You may opt to go on to another issue and return later to the matter that caused the silence. Another way you may handle it is to introduce the subject of the silence with deescalated, no-fault language. Here is the approach I often use: "I notice I was able to gather a great deal of valuable information about many things so far; however, I'm not being very successful here. I don't know why. I wonder if you could help me. Is there something I should be asking about? Perhaps there is some way I should be asking you about this matter that I don't know. Can you help me here?"

When I ask questions in this way, I am helping the other person by shouldering the load of the responsibility for the silence. As a result I receive less resistance than I would if I were to finger point. I also encourage the parties to guide me, because I have directed their attention away from the troublesome issue and toward helping me. Asking for assistance in an area other than the issue itself coaxes them out of the silence.

Questioning

Many years ago I heard a story about parents caught short by their inquisitive child. The tot asked, "Where did I come from?" Unprepared for a sexually explicit question, the parents did not know how to answer. Finally, the perplexed child became annoyed. He said, "Billy's parents told him he came from Chicago. Why can't you tell me where I came from?" Questions are a useful method that you can use to increase effectiveness during your initial telephone call. You will get the most useful answers to your questions, however, when you follow a few pointers.

Preparing the Groundwork for Responsiveness

First, I recommend you lay some groundwork before the initial query. Prepare yourself by establishing the questions you want to ask, the most productive ways to position them, and the best time to broach them.

Make it easy for parties to respond by building some latitude into questions. For example, you cannot predict whether questions about personal points of sensitivity such as age or confidentiality might ignite an explosion. Accordingly, build in cushions that add humor to the situation or release the questioned party from feeling pinned. For example, if you are talking in general terms about settlement, you might ask if the party is thinking in the range of a hundred dollars, a hundred thousand dollars, or a hundred million dollars. If you are asking about age, you might want to soften the question by saying, "Some states require people to be at least eighteen years old to collect lottery winnings. May I take it I could roll the truck containing the money up to your door when you win?" Parties will usually see questions like these as humorously probative rather than direct and offensive.

Give parties the perspective they need to form new insights and respond to you within the context of the question. As the anecdote about the curious child illustrates, the value of questioning is getting the correct answer to your question, not the correct answer to another question. In each initial call, create an environment in which the party senses you are asking for information and clarification rather than collecting facts that will later be used to score points.

Asking Productive Questions

Here are five types of questions that can be useful tools in your initial telephone contact.

Questions that break the ice act like fire kindling. These questions are tied to benign subjects. They are meant only to ignite communication between parties. They loosen conversation, bring down walls of silence, and start a two-way flow of ideas. These questions can relate to the mediation but are primarily meant to connect two human beings. They might be about the weather or colleagues you have in common. You might ask if the other party has mediated before in the potential meeting spot you are considering. For example, you might say, "Can you believe the snow that's falling right now?" or, "I understand that you specialize in insurance matters. Have you ever worked with [a particular colleague]?" The topics are irrelevant. The communication flow is paramount.

Questions that ask for assistance request that parties help you. Sometimes you actually need the answers to these questions. Sometimes you are using this type of question to achieve other communication goals. I find asking for assistance directs parties' thoughts away from the substantive issues and focuses them on becoming part of the solution process. With a question like, "Can you help me understand the sequence of events that led to [a certain situation]?" or, "Do you think you could walk me through [a particular event]?"

you and the other party work together to develop understanding. This type of question diffuses the tension of a direct question-and-answer pattern. Acknowledging that other parties know something that you do not often flatters those parties too.

Questions that are open-ended invite parties to respond in some detail. (They are the opposite of *closed-ended questions* that require only a yes or no response and then shut down the communication process.) I ask open-ended questions like these, "Could you describe the circumstances of [a specific topic]?" or, "Could you tell me about what happened when [someone did something]?" Open-ended questions start conversations and fuel discussion. They will give you facts with which you can work to create ongoing discussion. This type of question lets respondents go in the directions they want, so they feel free to explain in as much or as little detail as is comfortable for them. The structure of the response often indicates whether respondents are high-context or low-context communicators. Answers often help to fill in language matrices by indicating elements like parties' mental movement, focus, and perception.

Questions that reframe provide you with a vehicle to deliver information to parties. By using this kind of question, you can often make the initial telephone contact more effective. For example, if parties indicate they have a negative view about a subject, you can reorient their thoughts on that subject. Look, for example, at the situation in which parties view mediation as only one step (*original idea*) in an arduous, litigation process. You might use a reframing question like this: "Can you see how this mediation might actually be the final step [*reframing*] that eliminates more discovery and long delays until trial?" In addition to reframing, this question illustrates two other beneficial elements. First, the word "how" (as in "can you see how . . .") invites explanation that continues the conversation between you and the other party. Second, the word "might" offers an expression of possibility that is softer and less confrontational for the questioned party. Well-executed reframing questions often end as rhetorical questions that allow positive conversations to flow from them.

Questions that ask for curiosity or *for analysis* also form part of your questioning tool kit. They allow you to select whether you want to tap into people's creativity or their analytical processes. When you ask people to "get curious" and to "wonder," you invite them to become innovative. When you ask people to "think" about something, they become analytical. When preparing your questions, decide which result you want. For example, if you want parties to become inventive, you might ask, "Can you *wonder* about [the topic needing a creative approach]?" Alternately, if parties are not as focused on issues as they could be, you might ask questions that direct them to "examine" and "think about" an event or issue.

Posing Risky Questions

During a trial a lawyer avoids putting a witness on the stand unless the lawyer knows in advance what the witness is going to say. The risk of the unknown is too great. When you design your questions, I suggest you consider adopting a similar attitude toward risk. Here are three common types of risky questions.

Questions that are too direct may seem confrontational to respondents. People often take overly direct questions as personal affronts. Moreover, direct questions tend to turn off the flow of conversation because they are often regarded as commands or statements. For example, if you ask a party's attorney, "Can you tell me why you took this case?" the "can you" segment of the question may drop away as the attorney hears the question. People tend to feel trapped or embarrassed when faced with this structure because they believe they have no verbal wiggle room. If you must uncover certain information and are willing to take the risk of posing a question about it, mitigate the question's structure. When framing your question, I recommend you use the following example as a model: "I wonder [*suggests curiosity*] if you could [*requests a possible action*] tell me how you came to [*softer than the direct word "why"*] take this case?"

Questions that influence responses risk tainting results. Parties' perceptions and then their responses can be altered by changing the words the question uses. For example, a mediator who wants to change a perception about an event can choose words that are either blander or more acute. The mediator might ask, "Can you tell me how the other party grabbed [*escalating language*] your arm?" Alternatively, the mediator might ask, "Can you tell me how the other party took hold of [*deescalating language*] your arm?" The first version of the question can incite parties to a more emotional reaction or perpetuate already heightened emotions. The other version of the question calms the emotional environment. I suggest that as a mediator you word your questions carefully, considering their likely influence on the mediation.

Responses can also be altered by emphasis. By stressing some words and not others, you affect how parties respond to your questions. I suggest you do this exercise. Imagine you are asking a party the following questions and emphasizing the italicized words. First, ask, "Can you tell me about *this?* Can you tell me about *that?*" Now, repeat both questions without emphasizing any words. Did you notice the difference you created? Mediators must neutralize their tone when they ask questions, otherwise their emphasis may inadvertently skew responses. Parties may play back responses in the structure the mediator has given them. Then mediators may hear responses that echo what the mediator believes is important rather than what the respondents believe is important.

Questions that are too complex lead to confusion and unreliable answers. That in turn can stop productive communication. Let me give you an example that often arises in criminal trials. Prospective jurors may be asked two questions. The first is, "Have you heard or read anything about details of this case?" This question is relatively simple. It asks for a yes or a no answer regarding hearing or reading. The complexity arises in the follow-up question. It asks, "Even if you have heard or read about this case, do you believe you could still render a decision based strictly on the evidence entered at trial?" If you analyze the elements of the second question, you can see that it contains a number of questions that can be answered yes or no. Here is the breakdown: "If you have read or heard about this case [*yes or no*], do you believe [*yes or no*] you could still render [*verb phrase asking about a possibility*] a decision [*yes or no*] based strictly on the evidence entered at trial [*yes or no*]?" There are many ideas here that require an answer, and the prospective juror's ultimate yes or no could be attached to any one of those ideas. Questions like this often arise during mediators' telephone conversations. For example, counsel may ask if mediators believe they can really be neutral after learning about information offered in briefs. When you find yourself retrieving information by asking questions with many components, I recommend you break each question down into simple units. The responses will be more reliable.

Managing the Environment

Environments send messages. The environment in which the mediation occurs can strongly influence the success of the mediation. This environment includes the physical surroundings that affect people's bodily comfort levels. It also involves some less tangible elements: the parties' relative levels of power, their feelings of safety, and arrangements that convey respect. I recommend that mediators pay close attention to all these details. You may find it helpful to create a reusable checklist of environmental factors so you can systematically evaluate each factor described here and any other environmental factors you encounter in your work in light of what you want to achieve in each mediation.

Examining the Power Balance

There is an admonition that warns, "If you think you will fail, you will be right." Viewing this expression through the lenses of mediation, you can appreciate that actual power and perceived power appear the same to parties. Both are treated as real. As a result, I suggest you discern, appreciate, and deal with power in order to achieve a sense of balance between the parties in the mediation environment.

Look at the factors contributing to the impression of power. Social status is one. You can hear it trickle subtly through the conversations of parties who drop names or who talk about connections to well-known personalities. You can see it telegraphed by expensive clothes. At times you will observe parties wearing costly clothes specifically to intimidate the other side. You may notice garments that delineate social standing or caste in other ways. When you see these indicators, you can help level the scales by creating a power balance through conversation.

You may not observe an actual blue collar at mediation; however, you may sometimes experience an almost tangible gap in employment status. When nonmanagement and executive parties come to the table, the relative difference in positions or professions often creates a sense of power imbalance. This chasm is particularly obvious during some employment mediations. If you think there may be a need for power balancing because of employment status and you believe you can begin to balance it, in a small way, with dress, check with the parties before mediation. Ascertain the kind of clothing they plan to wear. If a great disparity could affect mediation, nudge parties gently by discussing the value of similar clothing as a message that suggests rapport and common ground. Remember, sometimes small factors make big differences in mediation. Additionally, you will want to make sure that both parties are represented by competent counsel so there is a perceived power balance in this area too.

Parties' educational levels are another contributing factor to perceptions of power. The potential imbalance is clear in situations in which one party is accompanied by counsel and the other is not. The unrepresented party may see the party with educated counsel as having an advantage. As a mediator you must be prudent at these times about both balancing parties' knowledge and remaining neutral. You want to avoid communicating the impression that you are advocating for the unrepresented party.

The perception of power when no counsel is present is more subtle. The parties' educational levels may send different messages about power. Some parties see those with higher education or degrees as having an upper hand. Their confidence may dwindle. Previously acquired knowledge of the mediation process can affect parties' self-assurance too. Accordingly, whether parties are represented by counsel or not, I suggest you review the mediation process with all of them yourself. That way, you ensure they all feel knowledgeable and empowered.

Language facility affects perception and levels of power. Parties who express themselves easily feel comfortable discussing their thoughts and playing at verbal repartee with others. People who lack the confidence or ability to express themselves verbally may feel outmatched in the mediation process. For example, lawyers often forget that they are in a mediation environment, not an adversarial pretrial environment. When they have large, incisive vocabularies, they may go to work to eviscerate parties who use more basic vocabularies. When you are the mediator in such a situation, I recommend that you restate the lawyer's ideas and at the same time deescalate the language. You may also want to caucus briefly with the lawyer to advise her of the less-than-productive effect this type of language wreaks on mediation.

Parties whose native language is not English are subject to feelings of vulnerability in mediations conducted in English. This sense arises out of their frustration at their inability to understand others and express themselves as well in a second language as they do in their native tongue. Assist these parties before mediation by covering the terms they will hear used in the mediation. See that they know what steps the process follows. If they have counsel, ask him to preview with them all material they might hear during mediation. Have a translator available or on site if you know or suspect that one might be needed.

The final factor in determining levels of perceived and real power is the money that is available for legal proceedings. You may find parties with unlimited funds feel more powerful than those with financial limits. The former can more easily afford to go to trial. You may see moneyed parties attempting to coerce other parties as a result of this. If so, I suggest you unearth for the coercing parties the benefits of mediation that go beyond money. Caucus with affluent parties, and ask, "What's important to you in mediation?" and, "What will having that [important thing] do for you?" Collect each person's respective touchstones. Then drop these touchstones into your conversation with the affluent parties. You may be able to propel them to seek resolution in mediation.

Providing for Safety

Safety, like power, is an issue in which both perception and reality play strong roles. For example, the number of people at the table may affect feelings of safety. If there are many more people sitting on one side than on the other, parties with fewer representatives may feel overwhelmed or pressured. If you anticipate an imbalance of this kind, canvass both sides before the mediation session. Suggest to them that the presence of an equal number of people sends a message that supports the spirit of mediation and is conducive to achieving positive results. Suggest that if one party feels pushed into settlement, the final agreement may not be durable or may create powerful feelings of buyer's remorse.

The presence or absence of particular people during mediation can affect both how safe an environment is and how safe it seems. That is the reason some jurisdictions do not send cases involving domestic violence to mediation. These cases are excluded to preclude any opportunity for further violence and to reduce an abused or threatened person's fear of harm. I have attended multiparty mediations in which people have been asked to wait in caucus rooms because some parties would not enter the mediation room unless the people who had allegedly threatened them were physically absent from that room. All parties agreed to this physical separation. Although these arrangements were not ideal, they did produce the effect of a safe environment for all the people who gathered in the mediation room. These arrangements also allowed the mediating parties to work toward some type of solution rather than none at all.

Make sure also that obtrusive people are absent. This too communicates a message of safety. Arrange for this before mediation. Ask mediating parties about people who should be barred. The following models suggest how to ensure the absence of obtrusive or threatening people in several scenarios.

Model 1. During the mediation planning stage, ask both Party A and Party B if anyone should not be present at the mediation. If, for example, Party A responds verbally or nonverbally, flesh out the details. If the perception has no basis in fact but the feelings are real, deal with the perception and feelings appropriately before mediation. They could relate to general fear of the mediation. If the perception seems fact based, discuss the request with Party B. In either case, before finalizing the details for the mediation, get agreement from both Party A and Party B on who is to be present.

Model 2. When parties who are potentially troublesome for Party A appear unexpectedly to support Party B at mediation, keep these new arrivals in a physically separate location and away from the mediation. (It is safest that Party A and the problematic people literally not see each other.) Then caucus with Party B. Explain how it will be counterproductive to the mediation process if the bothersome people stay. You might say, "Since Party A is alone, I believe the process would be more balanced and work best for both parties if you were alone too."

Model 3. When multiple parties appear for both sides at the time of the mediation, ask that Party A and Party B each pick from their respective supporters one person to remain at the mediation. Then ask each party to thank the unselected people for coming and to inform them they are not needed at this time.

In addition to dealing with problematic people who may accompany the parties, you can encourage a feeling of safety by taking into account any party's need for translators and validators. Either or both might be required for parties to feel safe in expressing themselves and executing final agreements.

Parties may also draw on their own resources by bringing talismans for feelings of safety. The symbolism of a talisman is usually meaningful only to them. Still, I suggest you check with all parties before mediation to learn whether they plan to bring materials or objects that could be perceived as a threat to the safety of others. Moreover, you must be sure that no weapons will be present. This applies to ceremonial items that others might perceive as weapons as well. This is not a farfetched concern. Not long ago some people were banned from entering a public place because they wore ceremonial daggers. Although wearing these items was part of a religious rite, the public building had a zero-tolerance ban on any kind of weapon. To the people practicing their religion, the knife was part of a meaningful observance. To others, it suggested a threat to their safety.

Finally, look at the message of safety conveyed by the geographical location of the mediation. Canvass the parties about this location. Ask them about their feelings of safety. If the location is one that might be seen as generally unsafe or dangerous after dark, make other arrangements. Doing so will improve the effectiveness of the mediation. Parties can sleep the night before mediation and arrive rested because they are not worried about a dangerous location. They can concentrate during the mediation because they are not concerned that the mediation might run after sundown.

Establishing Comfort

When you consider the different factors affecting communication during mediation, the parties' comfort should be high on the list. Along with power and safety, comfort moderates the river of communication. Low comfort levels impede the stream. High comfort levels sweep mediation forward. Comfort has both physical and emotional components. By understanding the nonverbal messages communicated by the comfort of the environment, you can strategically moderate communication.

Deciding on the Meeting Location

Be mindful of the messages the mediation environment broadcasts and the frame of mind it invites. If you can influence the selection of the mediation environment, you can affect the messages. Parties might be somewhat uncomfortable in an unfamiliar environment. I suggest you do whatever you can to communicate welcome and control. Small acts can make large differences. Before mediation, send parties maps and directions so they know exactly where to go. Include the general inquiry telephone number of the facility too. Arrange for a site that allows parties the choice of public or private transportation. Invite parties to visit the location before the mediation to become more comfortable about driving the route and meeting at the facility. Tell parties in advance if parking is limited. Propose to counsel that they supply prepaid parking passes for parties. If you know about high prices for parking or food in the area, prepare parties for that fact too. Even if they do not like some of the details you convey, the knowledge gives them a sense of control. That sense establishes a productive mind-set for mediation.

Comfort levels are developed in visible and invisible ways. Twenty-five years ago I made a trip to see a lawyer. His office was located on the second floor. Even though I had visited him there many times, this trip was an eye-opener. This time, I was alone, on crutches, and could not pull the second-floor door toward me to open it without risking a fall backward down the flight of stairs. I was powerless until another building visitor came up the stairs to help. Today, legislation guarantees certain types of accessibility. Beyond regulations, however, is the message of intention that barriers or lack of barriers can convey. This message can be powerfully positive when accessibility goes beyond legal mandates. When necessary, I suggest you talk to parties about the strategic advantage gained by physical accommodation resulting from willing acts rather than legal compliance. This perception of accommodation is vital if parties are looking toward a feeling of resolution and not just legal settlement. Similarly, I recommend you find a location that goes beyond conformance to minimum legal standards. Locate one that is comfortable for all the people who are coming to the table.

Comfort levels are affected by issues of territoriality. Parties often consider that mediation held at one party's office site hands the hosting party a "home court advantage." Although the environment may be cost free and the ambience hospitable, small signals can create great feelings of discomfort among the visiting parties. Host parties are used to the office layout, decor, odors, and noises. Most significant, host parties are greeted by people they know and who know them. Visiting parties are strangers who literally do not know the way to the bathroom. I strongly suggest you consider not just the monetary savings but the larger costs attached to the visitors' feelings of discomfort when you have the option of mediating on one party's turf. Unless you determine an overwhelming reason to use one party's home ground, engage a space neutral to both parties.

Preparing the Main Room

If you want to know how to prepare the main and the caucus facilities most effectively, ask yourself, "What do I want to achieve?" and, "What must I do to get there?" You will already have canvassed the parties or their representatives for special accommodation needs. You know that parties operate with different preferred systems. You can anticipate other general needs as well. I suggest you consider all these factors so you can create the most effective nonverbal strategies for productive communication.

Begin with the location of the rooms. Ensure there are washrooms, water pitchers (or a water fountain), coffee, tea, soda pop, and juices near mediation and caucus rooms. Arrange to have coffee brewed and waiting. Serving coffee has useful social implications and sets up a strong kinesthetic, visual, and auditory welcome message for many parties. First, you welcome people with a familiar smell (of coffee). Next, you invite nearness and conversation through an environment in which one party pours coffee while standing beside the other. Give parties access to food from a cafeteria or delivery service. Bring candy or fruit and place it on the table. This strategy is appealing visually and kinesthetically, and these sugar-rich foods can also give parties a quick energy boost.

Select room color carefully. Room color affects parties in different ways. The famous Lüscher Color Test (discussed by Ian Scott in his book of the same name) indicates some effects. Reds seem to elicit uneasiness and sometimes aggression. Yellows can bring out feelings of diligence or envy. Blues and green evoke feelings of tranquility and safety. I suggest you also keep in mind Edward Podolsky's observations in *The Doctor Prescribes Colors*. Podolsky discusses how people sometimes feel cold in blue rooms and warm in yellow rooms even though the temperature may be the same in both rooms.

Parties with a visual preference appreciate artwork on walls. They need neat, clean, and attractive environments. When areas appear messy or disorganized, these people are strongly affected. They feel uncomfortable and lack the ability to concentrate. People with an auditory preference really care about hearing clearly. They have no real preference about how rooms look. They need environments that are free from ringing telephones, noisy conversations, buzzing faxes, and outside traffic noises. Their attention to sound is so acute that most noises disturb them and direct their attention away from mediation. They need a quiet environment to operate most productively. People with a kinesthetic preference do not care about a room's appearance or acoustics. They want chairs that mold to their bodies and table heights that make it easy for them to write. They like the feel of soft carpet under their feet and general coziness. On the practical side, all parties will feel more relaxed and in control after you tell them the location of pay phones, elevators, fire exits, and smoking areas.

I suggest you look for a mediation room that is large enough to accommodate everyone's need for space and that allows parties to move and stretch. Sufficient space is especially relevant for parties with a high visual component because they need an area in front of them for visualizing in order to make sense of communication. People with a kinesthetic preference need to move around. Even people with an auditory preference often have to change their physical position to shift their mental bearings. The ideal mediation room is one that has small nooks and a suggestion of separate areas. In it, parties can cluster to talk privately among themselves without leaving the room. Unfortunately, ideal rooms are not generally available. If you do get the choice of a room with this unusual configuration, take it. Parties can then meet together and separately without breaking the rapport created in the room.

I recommend you mediate in rooms with windows because the windows provide natural light and the rooms feel open and spacious. The windows must have blinds or curtains, however, to prevent interfering glare or distractions. Make sure all lighting fixtures work. Flickering lights distract people with a visual preference. Buzzing lights annoy people with an auditory preference. If you can meet in a room with adjustable lighting, you can alter the perceptions and mood of all parties in the room. I use strong lighting to wake up parties. I use softer tones to invite them into altered states of awareness in which they can consider matters literally in another light.

Finally, do your best to arrange for mediation and caucus rooms that have individual temperature controls. Rooms that are too hot invite doziness. Rooms that are too cold prevent parties from focusing on issues. Additionally, you may want to set a comfortable room temperature in the morning and then lower the temperature after lunch, when parties tend to get drowsy because an increased blood flow is temporarily routed to the digestive tract.

Preparing the Caucus Rooms

Caucus rooms provide a safe environment in which parties can find privacy. In these rooms, parties hold conversations among themselves and with mediators. Although caucus rooms may not be occupied as long as the mediation room, they must still accommodate parties' needs.

Before making room assignments, form an idea of which room would be best for each party. At the same time, be aware that parties must perceive equality in the assignments. For example, if there are two caucus rooms and a mediation room, parties automatically want to know why they are assigned to one room and not the other. They wonder if you have a special reason for making these room designations. If the choice is arbitrary, tell them. If you have reasons, let them know those too. Reasons could address the number of people in attendance or accessibility. You might give parties the choice of which rooms they use. This strategy provides them with a sense of control over this element in the larger, less manageable thing called mediation. Once parties go into their respective caucus rooms, you may invite them to stake their claim to that room for the day. That way, they feel they have a base of their own and are not just adrift in the mediation facility.

All caucus rooms must be equipped with materials that facilitate communication. See that they contain paper and colored markers for parties who make sense through sight, calculators for parties who need to figure, and comfortable chairs for parties with a kinesthetic preference. Have tissues in the rooms too, because emotions often surface unexpectedly here. On-site tissues relieve parties of embarrassment and tension. They communicate a clear nonverbal message that crying is an acceptable and normal event that happens during this stressful time.

If you have only one caucus room and a mediation room, pay close attention to alternating parties between these rooms. That way, no party will come to believe there is an advantage to the out-of-sight location. If such a belief does get started, it could create tension and make the caucus process divisive rather than constructive.

Finally, stay alert for the unwanted development of ad hoc, informal caucus areas. These are spots in which mediators and counsel may cluster to talk about the progress of the case without the parties being present. This is done surprisingly often and is not very private. Although this discussion is usually off the record, mediating parties are often startled when they stumble onto these conversations. People are talking about them without their knowledge or presence. The surprise is destructive to the process. More than this, it undermines the neutrality of the mediator and counsel in the eyes of the mediating parties. It can undo any good faith that parties invested in the mediator as a neutral. If you find yourself tempted to participate in these caucuses, stop. Avoid creating or being part of these ad hoc activities.

Arranging Tables and Chairs

I suggest that you arrive at the mediation room well before the parties do. You may want to rearrange the furniture. Table and chair positions, sizes, and shapes can influence your nonverbal strategies. You want to exercise awareness and caution when configuring this furniture.

Until rapport is developed with the parties, a face-to-face position might instigate a confrontational message. You will find that the ideal mediation table is round. It seats all parties in a circle. There is no head, or end, of the table. Accordingly, it sends a strong nonverbal message of mediator neutrality and party equality. Conversely, when the mediator sits at the end of a rectangular table, it may send an implied message that the mediator is judging rather than facilitating. So, if the on-site table is long and rectangular, you may decide to sit at one end with participant chairs close to you and positioned at a 45-degree angle facing you. I suggest you insist all parties sit along the sides of the table and not at the other end of the table. If some parties were to occupy that end position, it would convey a visual, nonverbal message of power. That would create a perception of mediation imbalance.

If you do not wish to sit at the head of a long, rectangular table, you can create a more informal setting by sitting on one side in the middle and asking the parties to sit across from you. This positioning invites the parties to talk to you first, avoids confrontation, and actually places the parties in a traditional, collaborative, side-by-side position. When the table is small and rectangular and only two single parties are mediating, parties can sit on either side of the same corner or sit on opposite corners of the table and face you. You begin conversation with them facing you. Either seating plan eliminates a confrontational position. Eventually the angle of the parties in relation to each other can change easily and result in a collaborative, side-by-side position as they listen to you. Then it can change back to the original configuration or to a face-to-face conversational position once they are in discussion with each other.

Chairs are the second major furniture consideration. First, look at their positions. If you are co-mediating, I suggest you and your co-mediator sit side by side. That sends a message of equality and collaboration to the mediating parties. This arrangement also makes it easy for co-mediators to exchange messages unobtrusively. When you are co-mediating, you may be asked to allow observers into the room. (This often happens in mediator training and community-based mediation.) Permit only one observer so mediating parties will not feel outnumbered. Seat the observer slightly behind the active mediators so mediating parties pay attention to each other or to the mediators and not to the observer.

Next look at the mobility, appearance, and height of the chairs. Chairs that move and swivel are ideal for mediation. Once mediation is underway, people can move their chairs unobtrusively, sometimes other-than-consciously. When parties are ready to talk to each other, their bodies automatically shift. If parties are sitting in moveable chairs, the angle of the chair turns toward the other party too. That movement is a key cue that parties are shifting mental positions. You can then be ready to deal with that change. If chairs do not swivel, at some point you may have to intervene. When you observe bodies shift, you can suggest that parties might feel more comfortable turning their chairs slightly so they can talk with each other more easily.

I recommend you position the chairs before parties arrive at the mediation. Make sure that all parties have identical chairs. This creates a perception of equality. If any chairs do not match, then get each person a different chair. When some chairs look alike and others look different and this cannot be changed, put some of the identical chairs on both sides of the table to avoid the impression of team against team. This positioning also sends a nonverbal signal of commonality to the parties (even if the common ground is just a chair). Unless all chairs are identical, be especially careful that the mediator's chair looks different from any party's chair. That way you avoid any other-than-conscious message of alignment between the mediator and the party sitting in the same kind of chair the mediator has.

See if you can get chairs that are adjustable. They can be set to equalize parties' different heights. This is often important to perception. Diminutive parties may have their size equalized by using a chair that is as wide as the other party's chair and that raises up enough that the parties can look each other in the eye. (This is the same illusion created constantly on television news broadcasts to equalize news anchors with different physiques.) Adjustable chairs allow parties to find their individual levels of comfort. Stationary chairs in which people are positioned very low in relation to the table can induce feelings of vulnerability. The party's physical relationship to the table may be the same as it was when the party was a small child and a table was too high. This feeling occurs outside conscious awareness and often drives unpredictable, unadult behavior. Chairs that are higher than other chairs sometimes create perceptions of higher rank (a fact made use of in some military environments). These perceptions cross-file into feelings of powerlessness for those not sitting in the higher chairs. Again, the emotion happens other-than-consciously, but the resulting communication is strong and usually counterproductive to the mediation.

Know the sides of the table on which you want to place your parties. Parties who turn to the left will access their auditory side much of the time. That means they will be relying heavily on logical, analytical thought. Parties who turn to the right side a great deal will often find themselves deep in feelings and emotions. You can use this positioning as an effective strategy if you want less emotion from one party and more from another. If you established before mediation that certain sides are nonproductive for specific parties, locate these people carefully in relationship to each other, their counsel, and you. If you are not in a position to change their locations, you can use other subtle physical, eye, paralanguage, and language cues as alternative ways to assist them to be productive.

Using Charts, Props, and Other Items

I suggest you arrange for a writing board that is erasable (a whiteboard or blackboard). One especially effective whiteboard medium captures an image of what is marked on the board and can print copies of the material. This tool invites parties to participate in the planning process and immediately gives them visual, auditory, and kinesthetic feedback on their progress. Alternatively, you can use an overhead projector, clear transparencies, and colored markers.

It is useful to have a flip chart as well. I suggest you write and draw on flip charts using various colored markers to differentiate information. Have a pencil available to scribble inconspicuous notes in the corners for later reference. If you use permanent ink markers, which can penetrate to the second page and look messy, use every other flip chart page. If you use dry markers, you may be able to use every page.

Flip charts can become the physical record of the beginnings and evolution of the process and of brainstorming sessions. Some parties may regard a flip chart as the tracking mechanism for the mediation. Others may see it as the record on which parties can rely. Parties feel safe in referring to it because they do not have to ask the mediator or other parties for the information. The notations are on the flip chart already. Also, you can sometimes turn sheets back to remind parties how far they have come in the process. Be aware, however, that looking back has the potential to backfire because it can act as an unproductive reminder of a troublesome, earlier part of the mediation.

If you can make arrangements to have two flip charts, do it. You can place one on the left and one on the right side of the table. Each chart then accesses a different representational system and can get different responses from the parties. With two flip charts you may also be able at times to allow the two parties to use the charts for their own planning and for presenting that planning back to the group. Having two flip charts also gives you another alternative. You can anchor, or attach, one chart to unproductive mediation notations (and the negative associations attached to them), put that chart aside, and then move the second flip chart to the center of the room and use it to record positive results.

Give thought to other props and articles you may want in the room. Bring a (silent) clock to increase the comfort level of parties for whom time is relevant. Place it in a visible but unobtrusive position. That way you acknowledge members of monochronic cultures and give members of polychronic cultures a marker in case they do not wear watches. Bring large crayons to use in the switched hand exercise, in which parties write with their nondominant hand in order to get creative. Bring miniature models of cars and trucks when you are mediating vehicular accidents. The miniature size diminishes fear, puts things in a new perspective for parties, and allows people with a kinesthetic preference to communicate effectively about the accident. In your final check, also make sure you avoid props or objects that might be offensive to parties.

See that the environment has devices on site that might be needed to make final resolution possible. Consider the possible need for a computer. Have a fax at your disposal if you think you might need one. When necessary equipment is not available, agreements may fall through before they can be committed to paper. I recall one mediation in which agreement was reached at 2:00 A.M. Because of timing issues, counsel and parties wanted to write up the final settlement immediately. The law firm on whose premises the mediation had been held had a networked computer system, but the last person who knew how to log onto it had left at 9:00 P.M. The system was there but locked off. No one at the mediation had a laptop computer, let alone a printer to produce documents. It was hours later when the very fatigued parties executed one very complicated, longhand version of the settlement. They left hoping they had made no errors.

Considering Other Ambience Issues

Explore other issues of ambience that affect mediation. Consider sounds that might be present. Are jackhammers working on the pavement below the window? Is this a quiet area of an office floor or a room next to ringing faxes, telephones, or elevators? Is it only a thin wall away from a loud-voiced speaker? A noisy environment can be disturbing and embarrassing. I remember holding a pre-mediation caucus in a boardroom that shared a wall with another office. The voice of the lawyer next door boomed through the wall. The lawyer also used his speaker phone all the time. My meeting with the client was disrupted constantly by nonstop shouting and private conversations. The client with whom I was meeting was disturbed both by the noise and the fear that his conversations might be as audible to others as the lawyer's were to him.

Before mediation starts, decide on your policy about communication devices and cellular telephones in the mediation room. I recommend that no-cost telephones be available to parties outside the room. If there is a telephone in the room, have incoming calls redirected. Make outgoing calls available to parties who want to pick up messages during breaks and to parties who need to check with external validating sources before they can move ahead. I recommend that cellular telephones and pagers be turned off. Even the vibration signal must be eliminated, or parties receiving calls will still be disturbed. That personal disruption will be communicated nonverbally to other parties in the room.

The final ambience check I suggest is for air quality. See that environment is smoke free and that there is separate accommodation for smokers if necessary. Pay attention to the environment around the proposed meeting place. Steer away from locations situated near overpowering smells like coffee bean roasters, industrial sulfuric smells, and abattoirs. Also make sure that the area is clean and dust free. Be alert for this particularly in newly renovated buildings, in which construction and plaster dust can be a health issue for some parties. When you are considering premises, ask about all these factors.

Planning for Food

Food requirements vary with the type and length of mediation. Most mediation locations make coffee or tea available before the process begins. This is a nonverbal signal of hospitality. As mentioned before, inviting mediating parties to be near each other while getting refreshments often acts as an icebreaker and encourages small talk. Even if the parties do not converse, at least they are literally in the same room with each other. Make available decaffeinated beverages or juices too. Parties may be tense already, so caffeine is counterproductive for them. You may want to arrange for muffins or bagels, to give people who skip breakfast an energy boost at the start of the mediation.

Some mediators like to have refreshments on the table during the mediation. That is strictly a personal choice. It may lend a hospitable air to the environment. If you know that the mediation will last through the lunch hour, I suggest you have food delivered. Canvass parties first about any medical, social, or religious dietary restrictions. Unless I have a specific reason for wanting parties to be physically separate, I usually suggest they stay on site while lunching. If parties leave, they tend to lose their linkage to any positive action that has taken place. I also recommend making a real effort to have parties eat in the same room, even if caucus rooms are available. Eating is a social (as opposed to adversarial) activity. It can be a benign way to have parties relax together without conflicting. Moreover, the delivery of the food or the choice of what to eat once the food is on the table can be a situation that encourages parties to communicate. A decision about food may be their first agreement, one that starts the path to resolution.

Introducing Music

I have discovered that music is an untapped gold mine in mediation. You can make it an inconspicuous element that raises the beat of activity or lowers it significantly. You can choose the times you want to use each musical piece to accomplish a different purpose.

Different kinds of music elicit a variety of responses. You must be thoughtful about what you want to achieve and mindful of the parties attending. If you have gathered any information regarding ethnic preferences, investigate bringing some of that type of music. If parties come from different backgrounds, select neutral music. Know the sounds you want to hear in the room. Know the effect you want to produce. Be as prepared for this component of mediation as for any other element. Be skillful in your choice. On the one hand your selection could be jarring and could interrupt the process. On the other hand it could create a refreshing pause or lead to an upbeat momentum. Preparation means knowing what music you will potentially use. It means bringing a variety of music selected in advance of the mediation.

Finally, test your sound equipment before mediation. Bring extension cords. Make sure there is an outlet or an alternate energy source such as batteries. The music will take care of the rest.

Conveying Respect

Everything you do to make the environment comfortable and safe conveys respect for the parties to the mediation. Perhaps what people will find particularly respectful, however, is attention to their particular needs for space and an awareness of time as they perceive it.

Meeting General and Cultural Space Requirements

In Part One I asked you to consider people's varying needs for space. Now, let's look more closely at the general and cultural space requirements that parties need fulfilled in order to feel comfortable and respected in the mediation environment.

Start with the strategy that the more space you have, the better. You can usually make the environment of a large room seem more intimate; however, you cannot increase the physical size of a claustrophobic room. A larger room allows for flexibility in chair placement and in the way parties sit in relationship to each other. Larger rooms allow for private discussions. Parties and counsel who need to talk privately are not forced to leave the room and break the rapport.

If you know parties will need to hold business discussions and socialize to break the ice, secure a room that accommodates the social distance they need, about four to twelve feet between individuals. Four feet is the minimum. Less than that—from eighteen to forty-eight inches—forces them into a space meant only for personal interactions. Finally, take into consideration that each party will need to maintain a comfortable distance from the mediator and from the other party yet still have available an intimate zone of six to eighteen inches to whisper highly confidential information to colleagues or counsel.

Make provision for special cultural or religious variations from general North American spacing. In addition to the points I mentioned earlier, some cultures require more space around women to ensure they are not touched. Indeed, some cultures require that women sit in a row behind men at mediation. Canvass all these factors before mediation. If you do not, be prepared to accommodate all these different circumstances when parties arrive.

Considering Attitudes Toward Time

To convey respect through your handling of time, I suggest you appreciate and work with the way parties perceive time. The potential fallout from the differing patterns of people from cultures that are monochronic or polychronic is particularly challenging. One party's lateness can ignite the other party's temper, hamstringing the mediation before it begins. I suggest you have a caucus room ready for parties who arrive on time, so they are not in a position to watch the parties arriving late. Give on-time or early parties tasks to do in premediation caucuses. That way, even if polychronic parties are late, monochronic parties do not take offense. They perceive the tasking as the way activities were slated to run.

Be sure parties understand that breaks and meals are scheduled at tentative times only, because once an exact timetable has been put forward monochronic parties will fight to stay on it, even if major progress is being made at that moment. If you stick to fixed times and interrupt a productive session, polychronic parties will find that disrespectful. If you set no times at all, monochronic parties will find that disrespectful.

Finally, assign mediation tasks to parties in ways that respect their views of time. Make sure you give people from a monochronic culture one thing to do at a time and assign multiple tasks to people who come from a polychronic culture.

Checking for Symbolism

When you read briefs and talk to parties prior to mediation, you may expose information that alerts you to possible problems resulting from symbols that are important to one or both of the parties. When you uncover this information, talk to the parties about it before mediation. You can defuse many situations this way. For example, if you know mediation parties come from gangs, you can count on their wanting to wear their gang colors. You must act before mediation. Advise all parties that they must show up at the mediation location without gang identification or they cannot be part of the process.

Get curious about information you receive before mediation. Ask questions. For example, if you are conducting an estate mediation, you might want to inquire about mementos or jewelry that people plan to wear on mediation day. Are there items that could be a red flag to other parties? If you hear about articles that may be problematic, advise parties to leave them at home that day.

Stay alert for other symbolism that may be less conspicuous but just as influential. For example, if mediation is slated to be held in a religious environment, some parties may feel awkward. If it is their own house of worship, they may not like experiencing this type of process in it. If it is not their own house of worship, they may feel uneasy and at a disadvantage. Canvass parties in advance to make sure environments associated with religions or other specific groups are acceptable. If a party objects, find an alternate location.

Assessing the Parties

You are about to have your first face-to-face contact with the mediating parties and their counsel, as they arrive on the premises. As the parties gather for the first session, you enter Step Four of using nonverbal communication in the mediation process, assessing the parties for their communication patterns and preferred systems. Using Profile Element Grid information garnered from the initial telephone contact, you move into a new stage where you track the parties more closely. You double-check the initial PEG information and add more information to make the profile more complete and valuable for working with the parties.

Your first challenge in this assessment is to take a formal reading of yourself. This chapter discusses the rationale for that self-assessment and then looks at techniques for tracking general information and detailed information about mediation parties. Finally it walks you through the categories on the PEG, so you can accurately identify parties' action triggers and working frameworks.

Knowing Yourself

My high school English teacher liked to tickle the minds of self-important senior classes. One day she stated that the end of wisdom was the knowledge of self. For many years I thought she was correct. Today, however, I disagree. I see self-knowledge not as the end but as the beginning of wisdom. This belief has particular resonance when I consider assessing other parties. I suggest you give this idea some thought too.

If you do not know how you operate, how can you distinguish where your patterns stop and other parties' patterns begin? How do you know whether you are leading a conversation or contaminating it? I suggest you create your own profile to discover the answers.

Considering Your Own Profile

Begin your profiling by asking yourself the questions for the Profile Element Grid that are suggested in this chapter or the questions for your own form. For even better results, ask a colleague to run through PEG questions with you. Asking another person to record your patterns lessens the potential that you might contaminate results with premature personal evaluation. Once you have all the data in hand, you can evaluate them. After reviewing the documented responses, learn about your own preferences and biases. Come to know how you might be tipping a conversation in one direction or another. For example, do you orient conversations toward similarity or difference? Do you tend to talk in terms of solutions or of problem avoidance? What is your preferred system? Do you insist that others use it? You owe it to yourself and to the mediation parties to complete all the profile categories before you assess other people. (The communication inventory in Appendix A can help you identify some possible preferences.) If you fail to do a self-assessment, you cannot know how you may be influencing the responses of others.

Recognizing Your Filters

You cannot be aware of information that resides outside your conscious awareness. You can, however, raise your cognizance of your belief systems, core values, and attitudes. Now that you have completed the PEG for yourself, take the next step by becoming alert to the ways you may filter information through your own ethnocentric world. Look back over some mediations or other interactions. Ask whether your filters gave you a sense that other people's views were "wrong" or that other cultures were strange. Question whether you have been viewing life in a certain way for so long that your expectations usually do happen. Answer honestly. If you are like many mediators, you will find that you have created self-fulfilling prophesies. Now, recall the axiom "If you think you will fail, you will be right." I suggest that if you think about everything in a certain way, everything will appear that way. Your final question is this: how has this type of perception been limiting your success at the mediation table?

Shifting into Neutral

The most effective way to gather information is to operate in a neutral fashion. When you influence answers, you give people your information. You do not get theirs. Accordingly, if you intend to track information about parties accurately, if you wish to create baselines and profiles, you need to shift into neutral. This means you must stay aware of your preferences and biases. You must be able to ask for information without appearing to favor any answer. You can do this in different ways. For example, use nonsystem words. Use all representational systems. Rotate through cues in all systems so people can gravitate to their preferences. Ask questions in an impartial way (for example, ask, "How is it that . . . ?" or, "Could you let me know how . . .?"). Stop your head from moving. Avoid nodding it yes or shaking it no, for example. That way, you avoid contaminating parties' answers; instead of just giving you back verbally your nonverbal yes or no, they can respond with their own answers. Remember that you can track information accurately only when you recognize your own biases first and stay in neutral.

Tracking the Big Picture

Because this is your first personal contact with the parties, absorb all the pieces of information you can. These pieces form intriguing jigsaw puzzles. Assembled into patterns, they prepare you to select and execute strategies later. To add to any information you may have collected over the telephone, act as if you were a camera taking a long, wide shot. Visually track preferred systems, space requirements, dress, and other profile factors as though you were observing from a great distance away. Then zoom in for details later.

Start by looking at people's gross physical movements. You may be able to detect system preferences. Are there any parties whose hands are drawing in the air? Are they leaving space between themselves and others that might be space for visualizing? Do they seem animated? Are they talking rapidly from high in the chest? Those people could have a visual preference. Can you spot parties with deep skin tone flushing? Do their hands appear to be balancing weights? Are their bodies swaying back and forth? Are they breathing deeply? Those parties are signaling a possible kinesthetic preference. Can you see some parties who continuously drum their fingers? Are they jangling keys or tapping toes rhythmically? Do they continue this noisy beat until they start to talk? Earmark those parties as possibly having a preference for an auditory representational system.

Notice how much space parties need between them and others. You need to know about this space so you can determine their relationships and requirements during mediation. Are parties interacting at distances that are public (twelve plus feet), social (four to twelve feet), personal (one and one-half to four feet), or intimate (less than one and one-half feet)? Listen to the general volume of conversations. You can often gauge space preference from it. Business and social conversations typically take place at greater distances than personal and intimate discussions do. These observations can give you a feel for how parties are relating to each other. When people are speaking loudly and it does not seem to be distance related, see whether anyone is using a hearing aid. Watch a loud speaker's eyes too. See whether that person focuses on another speaker's lips. That person's hearing might be challenged. Silence tells another story. Watch to see whether any parties are not speaking at all. Notice whether they begin to speak and are cut off by others or whether they stand mute without (literally) making a move to talk. How you profile these quiet people will lead you to a strategy of eliciting conversation and information from them at the table. Those who do not speak at all usually need more nonverbal cues before they will start speaking than do speakers who interrupt others.

Look at touching patterns. This is an ideal time to see how parties interact physically. You can judge the amount of contact that is comfortable for them. Look at every person. See which people seem to avoid touching; they might be from a low-contact culture. Differentiate them from people who appear to touch a great deal. The latter could be members of a high-contact culture. Make a note of these patterns because you will plan different nonverbal strategies around the various perceptions of touch. Look also for clues to kinesthetic preference. If you discern people with this preference, expect them to need some kind of touch during mediation. Touch is their method of communication so you have to plan around that piece of knowledge too.

In tracking the big picture, I suggest you look at clothing, accessories, and symbols. Do you see dress imbalances that might lead to a sense of power imbalance? If so, be prepared to equalize the parties at the table later. You might do this by identifying something positive about the underpowered party's grooming, dress, or accessories and making a point to acknowledge it. Observe whether a party's attire suggests a cultural or religious factor that might affect mediation. If you conclude that parties are sending a message by wearing such clothes, ask them about their intent in wearing them, so you can appreciate their reasons and be prepared to deal with this information if it surfaces during mediation. (You might want to do this before the mediation begins.) Notice whether any parties are wearing symbols that could implicitly or explicitly affect communication during the mediation. If you spot something you believe might offend another party in some way, have a quiet word with the party wearing the symbol. Before mediation begins you might discuss lowering the profile of the symbol during the conflict resolution session. Finally, check for any distinct odors. From a distance you may not detect any. As you approach people you may. Are these odors perfume, cologne, cigarette, or body odors? Some people find commercial scents very attractive. Others find them overpowering. Body odor may result from poor grooming. It may also be a result of fear. If you notice odors but the parties display no reaction to the scents, just note the presence of the odors. If you detect reactions by other parties, arrange party seating, air flow (for example, open windows and doors), and other logistics either to separate the parties or dissipate the scent.

Tracking Detailed Information

To compile detailed information about parties' cues and patterns, you might wish to use trackers. Trackers are neutral parties at mediation. They recognize and follow the communication patterns of parties and lawyers during mediation, relaying that tracked information to the mediator. The point at which a mediator decides to gather detailed information is the ideal time for that mediator to pair with a tracker.

Mediators, like everyone else, have a limited amount of conscious awareness. Most times, that awareness is directed toward observing parties, listening to them, or writing down mediation facts. If you arrange to have a tracker, you can listen to parties' *text*. Concurrently, your tracker can focus on parties' *patterns*. Then he or she can make discreet written suggestions to you about nonverbal strategies. During the mediation process the tracker can also detail your own patterns for you. That way you can be most effective.

I have acted as a tracker for other mediators. The results have been invaluable for the mediation process. I suggest you test the effectiveness of this dual approach with other mediators. Consider doing it in your next mediation. Ask a colleague to co-mediate with you, but rather than just alternating turns at the same tasks, use this approach in which one person is the mediator and the other the tracker. It will double your ability to profile parties and thus give you greater flexibility in employing nonverbal strategies.

However, even when you are a sole mediator and must do your own tracking, you can still be effective. Just pay attention to patterns as well as facts. The following sections analyze in more detail key patterns discussed in Part One: eye patterns, physical patterns, language and paralanguage patterns, and the particular physical pattern known as a cue chain.

Eye Patterns

Until now you have been gathering the big picture details from a distance as parties were milling about, getting coffee, and talking. When the parties move to the table to start mediation, you are closer to them and can fill in more details of people's profiles. First, look around the table. You should be facing the parties so you can see their eyes clearly and track their eye patterns to distinguish how they are accessing their remembered and their constructed information. Start by establishing their nominally dominant side. You can do this through multiple observations over a period of time, or you can use a shortcut. For quick assessment, ask each party to remember seeing something ordinary or nonde-script. Her eyes will travel upward and to the left side or to the right side. The side to which her eyes move is her nominally dom-inant side. She will repeat this eye pattern every time you ask her for simple, visually remembered information. For example, ask the party, "Do you remember how your first bedroom looked?" Her eyes usually move up and left or up and right. That right or left side is her nominally dominant side. Whichever side she looks up to is the side on which she remembers visual information. When her eyes move up to her nominally dominant side, that is her *visual remembered* eye accessing position. If a person does not move her eyes up to one side or the other automatically, ask another question. You might ask, "Do you remember where your bed was?" or, "Do you remember what color the room was?" or, "Can you see where your bed was in relation to the window?"

Use any question that invites a person to remember visual facts. You should be able to gain the information you need from the nonverbal response. If you get continued resistance to a question, change the subject immediately. It may be the subject that is prob-lematic, not the exercise itself. I experienced this once when ask-ing questions that referred only to "the first bedroom." The eyes of one party continually traveled to the kinesthetic position. Ulti-mately I stumbled onto the fact that this person had been molested in the first bedroom. Clearly this was not the information I needed nor the experience I wanted the party to remember. You too may come upon cases in which the content of the answer obscures the pattern you seek. If you find resistance to this seemingly innocent question—or to any other—move on. Test an unconnected area. For example, ask, "Can you remember the color of the first bicy-cle you rode?" Keep in mind that you are looking for the eye pattern associated with a visual memory, not with the content of the answer.

From establishing the dominant side, you continue to deter-mine baseline eye patterns. Ask parties about information they re-member hearing. Then ask them about feelings they experienced. Typical right-handed people indicate remembered visual and auditory information by moving their eyes to the left side. They demonstrate imagined visual and auditory information by moving their eyes to the right side. These parties also experience or recall kinesthesia on the right side. Their eyes go down and to the right side. Make a note if any party's patterns are reversed or mixed.

You need to know these eye patterns during mediation. For example, during mediation a party may say he "remembers" seeing something. At the same time he may demonstrate what you have identified as his visual constructed eye accessing position. You may conclude that this is not his typical eye pattern for remembering an image. His verbal and nonverbal messages are incongruous. At that point, delve more deeply. Investigation may show that your words triggered a spontaneous thought. That thought may have led him to think of something else simultaneously. That process could have continued into a transderivational search. The search could have taken him quickly through visual, auditory, and kinesthetic files. You cannot see his invisible thought process; therefore you must keep asking questions. Ultimately, when a party's words and eye accessing cues do not match, you may conclude that the person may not be remembering at all.

Once you document parties' eye patterns, you know where their eyes move most often when they seek information. These accessing cues let you know exactly the representational system they use other-than-consciously. For example, you might ask a person to recall a conversation. That question could send some people directly into an auditory system file where the conversation is stored. Those people are using an auditory representational system. Other parties might look for the same kind of information by using visual accessing. These parties must first run a mental movie. The images show the visual environment in which the conversation happened. Then these parties can tell you about the conversation. These people start their response with an eye pattern demonstrating a visual representational system. They might eventually use auditory accessing to get to an auditory representational system. If they did, however, the auditory system would be secondary.

When you notice eye patterns that seem to accompany retrieving information indirectly, you can be sure that parties are not aware of how they get the information. They just get it. The process occurs outside their awareness. Your job is to recognize the apparent incongruity of words and eye accessing cues. Notice if this is the person's unique pattern. Make a note of it.

Remember that discerning patterns does not give you permission to apprise parties of their eye movements. Rather, I suggest you *verbally* reproduce their eye pattern sequences. That way you can help them communicate. For example, when asking a person to recall a conversation, you might say, "I wonder if you could look back [*visual representational system*] at what happened and then tell me [*auditory representational system*] the conversation that took place." That is, you match the way the person processes information. You invite her to recall it easily. In all cases, I suggest you continue tracking parties' patterns until you are sure about their consistency.

As you build the baseline eye profile, I suggest you look at both eyes of each party. Make sure both eyes demonstrate identical patterns. You will notice many people whose right and left eyes are asymmetrical in shape or positioned slightly differently on their faces. Treat these cosmetically different eyes as identical. These differences are not at issue. Asymmetrical eye *patterns* are noteworthy, however. I have found that a person's two eyes can operate completely or somewhat independently. When they move separately, I must establish which eye is dominant and then track the patterns of that eye to create the person's profile. The secondary eye does follow the dominant pattern at times; however, its movement has little relevance for the party's profile. Tracking the wrong eye can give you misleading information and negatively affect mediation results. If you encounter asymmetrical eye patterns, establish the dominant eye immediately. Use the same method you use for symmetrical pairs. First ask the question that shows nominal dominance (that is, "Do you remember how your first bedroom looked?"). Then ask the follow-up questions. If the party is right-handed, you can generally view the eye moving up and left as the dominant eye. Use the patterns of that dominant eye as your baseline.

Physical Patterns

When I visited Aruba, I was surprised at the novel look of a tree growing there. It is called the divi-divi tree. The trunk grows straight for a few feet. It then bends sharply to form a 90-degree angle. I had never seen one tree like this, let alone a whole island full of them. When I told a local inhabitant I did not know what to make of the tree, he laughed and said it was quite usual to see these trees in all the surrounding islands. The trees could grow straight only to a certain height. Then they were affected by the prevailing wind, which always blew in the same direction. Years later this lesson came back to me. I was flying a small aircraft in Northern Ontario, and I needed to set my Cessna down on a grassy patch where there was no windsock. I needed to know the wind direction so I could land into the wind. As I wondered what to do, I remembered the phenomenon of the divi-divi tree. I spotted the same growth pattern in some nearby pine trees. I had my landing direction.

Today I see this same phenomenon clearly in physical patterns. People usually display their preferred systems in clusters of physical cues. If I want to create a profile, I examine these other-than-conscious clusters of cues. They show me the way the wind usually blows. When you gather information, remember that a single cue or two cues is not a pattern. Look for groups of cues to determine preferred systems and patterns.

Here are some illustrations of clusters of cues that appear in left brain nominally dominant people.

Parties with a visual preference have upward tilted heads. They lean forward. They are compelled to use their hands to illustrate their discussion. For them a picture truly is worth a thousand words. They appreciate images, charts, and graphs. They use their hands to draw pictures in front of themselves or high in the air. If they cannot use their hands while they speak, they become tense and feel restricted because they believe they cannot express themselves adequately. These parties need space in front of them to "see" what you are discussing. They push back their chairs (or themselves) to make the room if they do not have it in front of them. If you force them to look you in the eye, they defocus and look as if they are staring, or they blink slowly. They do this while they make images of what you are saying. These people need you to stay out of their visual space, the place right in front of them. They are happy to have you move beside them, however, and share their "movie screen." People with a visual preference often rest their hands around their eyes or brow when they are not talking. You can usually spot them by their skin tone (the degree of visible blood flow to the face), which is in the pale range for their race. They generally have taut muscle tonicity. Their rapid breathing comes from high in the chest.

Parties with an auditory preference lean their heads to the left or keep them level. They often turn an ear toward the speaker, in order to hear clearly. They also like to read. You can sometimes see their lips moving as they subvocalize the words. Their bodies lean toward the left much of the time. For example, their torsos tend to tip to the left. They cross their legs and ankles toward the left side. They often keep up an external rhythm. One leg or toe often taps continuously as others are speaking. They drum pencils on paper. This continues until they have their turn to speak. Psychologist Dave Dobson has hypothesized that these parties might be listening to internal dialogues while other people speak and might stop tapping only when their internal chatter ceases and their own voices start. Parties with an auditory preference cross their arms over their chests. Their skin tone is medium. Their motions are usually rhythmic. You will see a wealth of cues in their hand movements. These parties interlace their fingers. They also press their fingertips against each other to form a steeple shape. As mentioned, they tap rhythmically or regularly. They jingle keys. When they stir beverages, the spoon hits the cup side in a regular rhythm. They constantly put their hands (especially their left hands) around their mouths or ears. They frequently chew on the ends of pens. They often make a pulling motion on their chins, as if they were smoothing a beard.

Parties with a kinesthetic preference are very right-side oriented. They tilt their heads to the right. They lean their torsos to the right. They cross their legs and ankles toward the right. People with a kinesthetic preference often have deeply flushed skin tones. Their movements are relaxed. Their motions are fluid and expansive. Their breathing is deep and from the abdomen. One hand often mirrors the movement of the other. They move in parallel. You often see these people's hands with the palms up, as if they were balancing a weight in each hand. Their hands tend to hit or make contact with the table or desk as these parties are trying to make their points. You will see people with this preference seek to touch others. For them, contact is communication.

Paralanguage and Language Patterns

The next piece of the profile puzzle comes in the form of para-language and language. Again, I suggest you examine clusters of cues. That way you can get a sense of each party's primary system.

People with a visual preference talk rapidly, from the top of the chest. Their voices tend to be high pitched and their speech jerky. They use visually based expressions, as illustrated earlier. Here are some further examples: "show me the money," "eagle-eyed," "visionary," "myopic," "focused," "rainbow of colors," "apple of their eye," "see right through him," "watchful," and "glaring mistake."

People with an auditory preference talk in monotones or melodically. Their sound comes from midchest. Their vocal pitch is in the midrange, and their speech is fluid. They use sound-based expressions like "sounded like a broken record," "hears a different drummer," "count on me," "twenty-five words or less," "told you so," "it was telling," "telling tales on," "give an account," "read her like a book," and "talk is cheap."

People with a kinesthetic preference speak in low-pitched tones. Their voices are resonant and usually deep because they breathe diaphragmatically. They talk in terms of touch, taste, smell, and emotion. They use expressions like "hold on," "get a grip," "gut level," "tasteless," "walks all over me," "get a whiff of," "spicy," "smells fishy," "smooth operator," and "I feel for him."

Yes and No Cue Chains

Another important part of the puzzle comes in the form of cue chains. You are already aware that a cue chain consists of other-than-conscious signals and that these signals always occur in the same sequence. During mediation, you want to determine each person's respective cue chains for affirmative and negative answers. That is, how does each party indicate yes and no nonverbally? You can then use this knowledge throughout the conflict resolution session. Most important, you must know this information to verify each party's agreement at the time of settlement.

For example, you might see that someone always blushes, clears his throat, and tightens his right fist before he says no. That sequence is at least one of his unique cue chains for indicating no.

Even when circumstances prevent him from talking at a particular time during the mediation process, that other-than-conscious, non-verbal cue chain may appear, indicating a probable negative response to something he is hearing or seeing.

Plan around the other-than-conscious responses of parties. But be careful when you create your strategies. Base your actions on these cue chains only if the subject's response has not been contaminated. Contamination occurs when someone affects another person's verbal or nonverbal answer. Contamination takes place, for example, when a mediator shakes her head back and forth while saying, "You don't want to be a bad neighbor, do you?" In this case, the subject's response is tainted by both the nonverbal head shaking and the choice of words. The uncontaminated question would be asked with the questioner's head held level and immobile. The language structure used would be, "Do you want to be a bad neighbor?" (In fact, the person may want to be a bad neighbor.)

You will find it simple to accurately establish the parties' yes and no cues. At the beginning of mediation, work from the factual information you already have. Tell parties you would like to confirm some information before you begin. Ask them questions for which you already have answers. Make the questions sound as if you are verifying facts. Pose the questions so parties can answer first yes and then no. Consider the following example in which you already know that a mediating party, I'll call her May Smith, lives at 149 Main Street. To elicit an other-than-conscious yes response, first pose questions using accurate information. You might ask, "Is your name May Smith?" or, "Do you live at 149 Main Street?" To bring about an other-than-conscious no response ask questions that you know have inaccurate information. You might ask, "Is your name Mary Smith?" or, "Do you live at 147 Main Street?" Record the other-than-conscious, nonverbal chain of cues for each party's yes and no responses. Once you have the other-than-conscious sequences, you will know during the rest of the session when people's responses are congruent and when they are incongruent.

I suggest you appreciate the responsibility you have once you know these sequences. You are a privileged observer. As I described previously, people are not aware of the other-than-conscious cues they produce. Your job is to track these cues. You can use them productively. Spotting them may help you effect a smoother conflict resolution session. You do not, however, have a license to bring this information into a party's conscious awareness. You may work with it. You can let the mediation benefit by it. But when the information is outside someone's awareness, leave it there.

After you know the parties' unique yes and no cue sequences, watch to see whether the parties' verbal yesses and noes match them. When their words match their other-than-conscious cue chains, their responses are credible. When their words and other-than-conscious cue chains are mismatched, their communication is incongruent. In the latter cases, I suggest the verbal response is the one to investigate. When you encounter this incongruity, ask more questions. Test further for verbal and nonverbal agreement. Refrain from pointing out the inconsistencies to parties. Avoid telling them you do not believe them because their verbal answers do not match their nonverbal responses. Instead, approach people in another way. Ask your questions differently. You may then discover the information you need. You may get congruent verbal and nonverbal responses. If the parties continue to give you incongruent answers, I recommend that you believe the other-than-conscious communication over the conscious communication.

Identifying Action Triggers

As part of your assessment of mediation participants, you need to recognize each party's action triggers. I recommend you follow the PEG, starting with language touchstones and then working through the other triggers. This section focuses on strategies for identifying parties' action trigger characteristics. Refer back to Chapter Three if you wish to review the trigger definitions. Many of the strategies involve asking questions and analyzing the parties' responses. It is of course important for you, and your tracker if you have one, to watch and listen carefully, not just to the meaning of the words but also to word choices, word order, physical patterns, and vocal qualities.

Language Touchstones

To begin eliciting *language touchstones,* ask each party the question, "What's important to you in [this context or this situation]?" For example, you might simply say, "What's important to you in mediation?" Wait for the person's answer. Write down the person's word or phrase, the language touchstone, *exactly* as he has articulated it. Then follow up this answer with another question, "What will having that do for you?" It may be appropriate to replace the word "that" with the person's *exact words* in response to the first question. Again note his *exact* answer.

Parties will give answers that vary from context to context. The questions, however, do not change. They are purposefully neutral. If you were to ask for information in a different way, the question format could contaminate the answers. If there is more than one component in a mediation, ask the same questions for each context. For example, you could ask the question about the context of process and the context of agreement.

When you ask parties these questions, they will use words and phrases in response that express their most highly valued criteria. Take their words at face value. You do not have to know exactly what these language touchstones mean. For example, parties may respond with the words "compensation" or "security." To them "compensation" holds a different meaning than the words "being compensated" or "income." "Security" means something other than "feeling secure" or "feeling safe." That is why you must make a note of the exact words they use rather than what you think their words mean.

What a person articulates in answer to these questions uncovers his standards for how he measures value in a specific context. Once you have established his touchstones, drop exactly those words and phrases into discussions or suggestions. That compels the person to pay attention to you.

Active and Reactive Initiation

You can determine whether someone is an *active* or a *reactive initiator* from her responses to your first two questions ("What's important to you in [this context]?" and "What will having that do for you?"). Active initiators tend to talk about themselves or others performing specific actions. They might say things that express the idea "I make things happen." They use action words like "doing" and "acting." Reactive initiators say things that express the idea that "something occurred and I reacted to it" or "something happened to me." They also tend to use passive constructions. Instead of saying, "I will make a response," they might say, "A response will be made." They talk about hypotheses ("might" and "could") more than certainties. They talk about obligations ("had to"). When parties exhibit both active and reactive initiator components, they combine active and reactive mechanisms in themselves. An example of this is, "I look for new clients (*active*) if I am forced (*reactive*)." When parties demonstrate they have both active and reactive components, note the order, and reflect it in your communication with them.

When you watch and listen to active initiators, you see many changes in body and facial movements. You also hear changes in the volume, tempo, pitch, and timbre of their voice. With reactive initiators, you see few or no changes in body movement and hear little or no variation in voice quality.

Toward and Away Mental Movement

You can discover a party's characteristic mental movement by asking, "What do you want in this mediation?" and, "What will having that do for you?" Many times, however, you do not need to ask the questions. Parties will have already told you about their mental movement in their answers to the similar questions you posed to learn about their touchstones.

Toward mental movers use words that tell what they want to gain or achieve in the mediation. They might say, "getting reimbursement." *Away mental movers* use words that say they want to get away from something. They want to avoid or circumvent a problem. They say things like, "I want to avoid dealing with this ever again." The surface structure of their language may seem to express goals; however, the deep structure will be avoidance oriented. When people use words like "safety," "protection," and security," for instance, to describe their targets, they are, in fact, seeking to avoid some perceived negative. You will also encounter parties with both elements. An example of this duality is, "I want to get reimbursement [*toward*] so I never have to deal with this issue again [*away*]." In these cases, note the order of movement. Then play that order back to the party when you communicate with him. For example, you might say, "Let's start now so we can complete the mediation by 2:00 P.M. [*toward*] and avoid the expense [*away*] of more out-of-town trips."

When you watch toward mental movers, you will often see them shifting physically forward in your direction. You will hear a voice quality whose timbre is definite and direct. It is a quality that some people would interpret as sounding confident. You will see away mental movers often shifting physically away. They also push back. You will hear an unsteady or shaky timbre in their voices. It is a quality that some people would interpret as sounding indecisive or uncertain.

Sometimes I elicit parties' typical mental movement by sketching stick figures on a flip chart or board. The first set of figures runs toward a happy face or dollar signs. The second set runs away from a frowning face or dollar signs. As I draw each set of figures, I turn around frequently. I watch the faces of the parties as I sketch. I notice each person's response when each drawing is done. People nod their heads and smile after I have drawn the picture reflecting their mental direction. I need not say a word. Neither do they.

Inside and Outside Validation

You can assess whom parties rely on to validate their decisions by listening to the parties or by asking them the question, "How do you know if you have [or someone else has] done a good job?" or, "How do you know if someone has conducted a good mediation?"

Inside validators use "I" frequently. They also use expressions like "personal satisfaction," "I decide," and "I make the final decision myself." *Outside validators* look to other people to give them information to make their decisions. They use expressions like "feedback" and "others tell me."

Listen for parties who say, for example, "I talk to all my colleagues, but I make the final decision." On the surface this might sound like a need for outside validation. The words "I make the final decision," however, point to an inside validator. If you have any doubt, ask a follow-up question like this: "What if you think you did a poor job and someone else thinks it was good?" If parties say, "I still think it was poor," they are indicating inside validation. If parties say that the others are correct, they are showing you outside validation. Sometimes you will hear a combination of inside and outside validation. Again, simply note the order. Then you can replay that order during mediation. An example of a combined inside and outside validator is the party who responds to the follow-up question by saying, "I know I've done a good job when I reach my goals [*inside*] and my colleagues tell me [*outside*] I've done a great job."

You will notice no discernable differences between inside and outside validators in nonverbal communication patterns.

Opportunity and Necessity Rationales

You can elicit the rationale parties use by asking the question, "How did you decide on [a particular thing]?" For example, you might ask, "How did you decide on your present job?" "How did you decide on your lawyer?" or, "How did you decide on your current car?" Sometimes you do not even need to ask the question. People will have already revealed their rationale structure in general conversation. They might have disclosed it by answering previous questions too.

People who operate with an *opportunity rationale* indicate that they control their lives. They say things like, "I did [something] because *I wanted to* move up the ladder." They use words like "opportunity," "possibility," and "options." People with a *necessity rationale* tell you that life is routine. They say there are no real choices. They answer, "because *I had to*," or, "*it just happened.*" They use words like "necessary," "needed to," and "obliged." If a person articulates both rationales, note the order. Later, frame your communications with that person in that order. For example, a banker might say, "I saw a chance [*opportunity*] to develop a new client base because I needed [*necessity*] to replace clients who had moved."

As you observe and listen to the parties, people with an opportunity rationale will appear more animated than people with a necessity rationale. This animation often leads some people to a subjective judgment about the two groups. They may consider the people with an opportunity rationale as more upbeat and more optimistic. People with a necessity rationale project an image of being low key. Their lack of animation and use of expressions such as "I had no choice" often lead observers to the subjective judgment that they are fatalistic.

Activity and Time Frame Decision Factors

Within the first hour of every mediation, you should establish the key factors in how each party decides. Do this by listening to opening statements and discussion or by asking each person two questions. The first is, "How do you know when someone is competent [or good] at his or her job?" You may need to explain that the person in question has had the requisite training. Then you follow up the first question with this question, "At what point are you convinced that someone is competent [or good] at his or her job?" In asking these two questions, you are tracking each party's decision-making structure. You are looking, first, for her activity decision factors and, second, for her time frame decision factors.

The term *activity decision factor* refers to an action that has to happen before parties can make a decision. They might have to see, hear, do (that is, experience), or read something. At times, parties need a combination of these activities. Parties who must *see* something in order to make a decision, answer your questions with expressions like "I must see [something]" or "I must watch [something]." Parties who must *hear,* answer with expressions like "I must listen to [something]" or "I must hear [something]." Parties who must *do* something, answer with expressions like "I must work with [something]" or "They must perform [something]." Parties who must *read,* answer with words like "I must peruse [something]" or "I must research [something]."

The *time frame decision factor* addresses how long it takes for parties to be convinced. There are four elements that make up this factor. The first is *reflex acceptance.* Parties having this element are automatically convinced. They need no proof to make a decision. Reflex acceptance is demonstrated by parties who in response to the second question make such statements as "If he was hired, he can do the job." The second element is *number of examples.* Parties in this category must be exposed to a specific number of examples to be convinced about something. They will actually tell you the number they need. These parties might say in answer to the second question, "I know after someone does it a couple of times." The third element is *period of time*. Some parties feel compelled to wait a specific amount of time before they are convinced. They will tell you the specific time period they need. For example, answering the second question they might say, "It usually takes three months for someone to really operate this equipment well." The final element is *constant proof*. Parties with this component advise you that they have to be convinced every time the issue arises. They use words like "ongoing" and "every time." There is no such thing as historical proof for them. Each time is a new time.

You will not observe any particular physical distinctions among parties who have different activity and time frame decision factors.

Identifying Working Frameworks

To continue assessing parties, I suggest you continue to follow the PEG. Look at the parties' working frameworks next. Again, I focus here on the ways you can identify parties' frameworks; framework definitions can be found in Chapter Three.

Micro-Thinking and Macro-Thinking

To distinguish micro-thinkers from macro-thinkers, ask the question, "Can you tell me about a pleasurable family [or work] experience?" Alternatively, you might ask, "If we were going to do a project together, would you want to know the big picture first or the details of what we were going to do?"

Micro-thinkers answering the first question tell you every detail from start to end. They break their answers into little chunks of information. They often use a step-by-step explanation. They use concrete details, labels, proper nouns, names, and years. They use descriptive parts of speech like adjectives and adverbs to make things more precise. For example, when talking about a family reunion, micro-thinkers might say, "I came up with the idea to go to the cottage. It's on an island. The cottage has belonged to my family for years. It was first bought in 1870. When I was a child, my family spent every summer there. When my siblings and I were grown, we decided that each year we would get together at the cottage." *Macro-thinkers* will give you general feedback. They will relay the "big picture." If you were to ask macro-thinkers the same question, they would answer, "My family had our annual reunion at our cottage." When parties respond using both formats, make a note of the order. Later you can communicate with them using their structure.

There is no noticeable physical change in people when they are giving either micro-thinking or macro-thinking answers.

Self-Focus and Others-Focus

In assessing focus, there are no specific questions to ask parties. I gather information about this other-than-conscious pattern through observing and listening to parties. I suggest you do the same. You can start as you track the big picture. You can finalize your conclusions at the table. Notice where the parties' attention is focused.

Parties with *self-focus* talk about themselves and their interests. They use "I," "me," and "my" frequently. They often speak rapidly (although this is also a characteristic of people with a visual system preference and should not be used as the only criterion for self-focus). Much of the time they do not bother to explain to listeners any useful background for what they are saying. They do not check with listeners to ensure understanding. Self-focus parties often have flat voice tones. They are hard to interrupt. They give lackluster or bland answers. When they do respond, their replies tend to be short and impersonal. Parties with *others-focus* talk about others. They include references to listeners. They vary their voice tone. They are easy to interrupt. They stop to check that listeners clearly understand their words.

When assessing parties for this profile component, you will notice that self-focus parties often seem disconnected from the mediator and other parties. They shift away from you by sitting or leaning back. They make minimal eye contact with you. They often show fixed stares. Self-focus parties may appear to be unaware of the world around them. They often seem to "go away" until you give them the next question. After they answer they mentally leave again until the next question. Others-focus parties often lean forward toward parties who are speaking. They frequently nod their heads in the speaker's direction. They tilt their heads to hear more acutely. These parties make eye contact with others in between questions. Their eyes often dart around to check the reactions and responses of other people. Sometimes they smile. Sometimes they touch.

Self-focus parties are inwardly directed. They pay attention only to what is happening within themselves. They are relatively unresponsive to other people. Others-focus parties are outwardly directed. They acknowledge that other people exist. They pay attention to other people's reactions. They rely on others' responses. They view them as vital.

Self-focus people are self-contained. Other people's actions do not generate automatic responses from them. Self-focus people appear not to care about other people in face-to-face environments or on the telephone (that is, they cannot be interrupted). They may be perceived as uncaring. Others-focus people automatically respond to other people's responses. They tend to base their responses primarily on the reactions of others. They pay attention to responses from other people (as opposed to feelings within themselves) when they act. They continue to break away from what they are saying or doing to make sure that others understand them. They stop what they are doing to clarify points. They continue to explain until people are clear. Only then do they move forward.

Loner, Group, and Collaborator Affiliations

In assessing affiliation, I suggest you use the information you have gained from asking the micro-thinking and macro-thinking question, "Can you tell me about a pleasurable work experience?" (If you asked about a family experience rather than a work experience earlier, then reask the question, this time focusing on work.) You might now add, "What is it about that experience that was meaningful for you?"

In answering, *loner affiliators* use self-referenced words constantly. They do not notice other people. In their minds, other people are not necessary to do the task. In fact loner affiliators often consider other people to be a nuisance. They use phrases like "by myself," "on my own," and "I had the responsibility for." Pay particular attention to the grammatical subjects of people's sentences in assessing affiliation. In answer to your questions, loner affiliators might say, "I came up with the idea to create a new product." *Group affiliators* use words that refer to joint effort with others. This effort usually involves some kind of collective participation. They use expressions like "we," "us," "our," "as a team," "together," and "group effort." In answer to your questions they might say, "We ran a company booth in a trade show, and our team connected with seven new clients." If you were to ask *collaborators* about a pleasurable work experience, the subject of their answering sentence would be "I and [someone else]." The someone else might be referred to by name or by job title. Collaborators avoid the words "we" and "us." They do not see themselves as team members. At best, they see themselves as a distinct part of a collective of individuals.

If you want to pinpoint affiliations, I suggest that you make a point to observe parties carefully. Pay close attention to when parties focus on what is most important to them. Watch for visible facial changes that could show emphasis. For example, people might raise the corner or corners of their mouths, pull up an eyebrow, or cock their heads. Also their voice quality might change when they want to stress something. They might raise the volume of their speech or change its tempo or do both.

People, Objects, and Systems Preferences

You can also assess parties' preference for working with people, objects, or systems from their answers to the question, "Can you tell me about a pleasurable work experience?" When you review a response to this question, pay particular attention to the grammatical objects in the respondent's sentences.

Parties with a *people* preference talk about people. They use the words "people" and "person" and they use proper names. They mention specific people and position titles. They might say, "I worked with John Doe to design an office layout." Parties who prefer to work with *objects* refer to things and articles. They use words like "items" and "objects." For example, they might respond, "I liked creating a working model," or, "I like putting up shelving." Parties who prefer *systems* will talk to you about "process" and "systems." They talk about how parts interrelate with each other. For example, they might answer, "I liked revising the auto parts area.

Now we receive a requisition, fill it and have it waiting in the pickup area within thirty minutes." If they talk about people, they are likely to discuss them as parts of an interrelated unit or system. For example, they might say, "I liked organizing staff in human resources. Now they receive a written request, acknowledge receipt by e-mail, and forward it within twenty-four hours to the appropriate area."

Sometimes parties demonstrate more than one preference. Make a note of it so that you may communicate with them later in the mediation by reflecting all their preferences. People do not exhibit any discernable physical patterns related to any of these preferences.

Definite, Variable, and No Operating Codes

A party's operating codes are the rules of conduct within which he operates and the rules of conduct within which he believes others should operate. To elicit the information you need, ask these two questions: "What is the best way for you to ensure your success in mediation?" and, "What is the best way for others to ensure their success in mediation?" Tackle the first question before moving to the second. That is, deal with the operating code of conduct parties have for themselves before going on to determine the code they have for others.

In responding to the first question, parties with a *definite code* use language that identifies one clear structure for themselves. They respond with little or no hesitation. They discuss what they are supposed to do. For example, they may say, "I should work in concert with others." Parties with a *variable code* use language expressing how they can change their rules depending on circumstances. They say things like, "I don't know; it can change." Parties with *no code* do not respond verbally. They just sit there. They sometimes shrug their shoulders. They may look dissociated. They act as if the question did not even register.

The second question asks about the operating code of others. It pinpoints how parties perceive other people's worlds. Parties who believe others should have a *definite code* answer quickly. They know what others should do. Other people's codes may vary from those of the respondents, but there simply must be a definite code of conduct in place. For example, they might say of others, "They should ask their lawyers to help them." Parties who believe others should have a *variable code* also answer the second question with little or no hesitation. They indicate that others' standards may vary from person to person. They say things like, "I don't know," or "It can be different from person to person." For example, they might answer the second question by saying, "Everyone has his own way of doing things. It depends on what he wants." Parties with no concept of operating codes for other people (that is, *no code*) do not answer the second question verbally. Like those who have no code for themselves, they just sit there, and they may seem detached from the questioning activity.

When you put together the responses to both questions, you will see that individuals have different combinations of codes. The following four combinations represent the most common patterns I have found in mediation. The first term in the combination defines the operating code associated with the answer to the first question. The second term defines the operating code associated with the answer to the second question. The first combination is *definite-definite*. Parties with this combination identify a definite operating code of conduct for themselves (that is, "I know mine") and a definite code for others (that is, "others know theirs"). This combination is often seen in successful managers. The second combination is *definite-variable*. Parties with this combination identify a definite code for themselves. They know others have a code of conduct. They would not presume, however, to tell others what that code should be. These parties might say, "Everybody has his own way to arrive at success. It depends. I don't decide for others." This combination is often seen in successful consultants. The third combination is *variable-definite*. Parties with this combination say they are flexible but refrain from identifying a specific code for themselves. They do identify a code for others. For example, they might say of others, "They create a plan, look it over, and do it." This combination is often seen in bureaucrats. The fourth combination is *definite-no code*. Parties with this combination identify a definite code for themselves. Then they say nothing else. This combination is often seen in people who must be ruthless about their jobs. For example, they might answer the first question by saying, "I have to do [a certain thing] to be successful." But they have no verbal answer for the second question because they do not have a mechanism for relating to anyone else's code of conduct. They usually do not know or care about others' standards.

Inside and Outside Pressure Reactions

To recognize how parties react to pressure, ask them about an experience. For example, you might ask, "Can you tell me *briefly* about a work experience that gave you difficulty in the past?" Make sure to emphasize that the response should be short. Refrain from inviting people into a long recounting of a troubling situation. Your goal is to discern parties' typical responses to stress, not to hear all the ins and outs of a particular incident. You want to be able to forecast how people might deal with stress during the mediation.

You will notice that parties with *inside pressure reactions* can usually recall an event easily. They may or may not talk about their feelings. When they do address their feelings, they use words like "feel," "worry," "downhearted," and "crestfallen." Parties with *outside pressure reactions* may not be able to recollect any event. If they do recall one, they seem distant from it. The description sounds impersonal. They might use expressions like "in the past" or "I vaguely remember." For example, they might say, "I remember having a problem getting audited." They do not discuss feelings. People with combined inside and outside reactions can recall an event. They can describe it. They will usually include some reference to feelings. Then they shift out of the experience and the feelings. These people say things like, "I felt bad [*inside pressure reaction*] that I couldn't visit my pal before his surgery, but he recovered just fine [*outside pressure reaction*]."

Listen and look for nonverbal cues. Parties with inside reactions to pressure exhibit strong nonverbal shifts in answering the question. Their voice quality often becomes raspy. Their throats seem to close. Their speech tempo becomes slower. Their timbre and pitch drop. They sigh and breath deeply. Their eyes usually look down and right or left. Sometimes their eyes fill with tears. Sometimes these parties show a skin coloration change. At times they seem to relive the experience. Parties with an outside pressure reaction demonstrate nothing remarkable in their voice quality.

They rarely show any apparent change in physiology. They may shrug and lean back or push away from the table. They may stare as if they were looking at the event in the distance. Parties with inside-outside pressure reactions first exhibit the inside pressure reaction cues. Then, as they shift out of the experience, their nonverbal communication becomes that of parties with outside pressure reactions.

Similarity and Difference Perception

To assess how parties perceive their environment, ask them a question relating to something they are doing now and something they were doing a year ago. For example, you might ask, "What is the relationship between your job now and a year ago?" (Replace "job" with some other word if that seems appropriate.)

People who notice *similarity* in their environment talk only about what is the same in their job now and their job a year ago. For example, they might answer your question by saying, "They're the same," or, "They're alike." People who notice *similarity with exceptions* talk first about the sameness of things. Then they point out the differences and compare them. They use comparative words like "more," "better," "slower," and "worse." They cite exceptions using words like "except" and "but." For example, they might answer, "I'm working in the same area, but I have more responsibility."

People who notice *difference* talk only about what is dissimilar. They use words like "revolutionary," "unique," and "original." They might answer your question by remarking, "The difference is night and day. No relationship." People who notice *difference with exceptions* talk about what is different and then what is similar. They use comparatives: "newer," "older," and so forth. They might answer your question by saying, "I have a brand-new position, but I am still working in marketing." You will notice no discernable physical cues that accompany the characteristics of any of these groups.

As I pointed out earlier, mediators can skew the answer to a question by seeming to signal yes or no with their head movements, by vocally emphasizing certain words, or just by changing a word or two in a question. In this case it is especially important to ask the question as it is shown here. For example, if you say, "Can you tell me about the similarities of your job this year and last year?" you will hear about similarity not difference, and you will not learn the person's usual way of perceiving the environment. Conversely, if you say, "Can you tell me about the differences between your job this year and last year?" you will hear about difference and not similarity. If you ask, "Can you tell me about the relationship of your job *this* year and *last* year?" (emphasizing "this" and "last"), that intonation will encourage the respondent to give you differences only. I suggest you use only neutral terms and avoid emphasizing any words in order to get a response that you can rely on.

Figure 4.1 is a graphic that can be used to determine whether people perceive similarity or difference. If I ask parties, "What is the *relationship* of the triangles?" people who perceive similarity tell me about the sameness of the shapes. That is, they talk about the "three triangles" or the "three geometric objects" and so forth. People who perceive difference talk about the "three separate objects" or "different triangles" and so forth. If people have both types of perception, they might say, "There are three triangles of a similar size, but they don't all face in the same direction." When both types of perception are present, I note the order and communicate with the party in that order.

Figure 4.1. Perception of Similarity and Difference.

What is the relationship of the triangles?

Perfect and Optimized Targets

In assessing parties for this component you may be able to use information from answers to previous questions in which parties described their actions in the context of goals or targets. You can also ask two questions: "Can you tell me about a target or goal you once pursued?" and, "When you did or did not reach it, what did you do?"

Parties who are *perfectionists,* who set perfect targets, express what their target was. They tell you whether they did or did not achieve it. They use expressions like "not good enough" and "dissatisfied." For example, they might respond, "I had to have a report submitted by Thursday at 5:00 P.M. I didn't get it in. I *failed* [that is, I was not good enough] to meet the deadline." *Optimizers,* who set optimized targets, tell you about a goal. Then they tell you the results. They use expressions like "the best I could do" and "good enough." They might respond, "I was supposed to have a report in by Thursday at 5:00 P.M. *I made a real effort* [that is, I did the best I could], but I couldn't do it. Since Friday was a holiday, I submitted it on Monday morning."

When I watch parties who are perfectionists, they often exhibit tight muscles. Their physiology changes when they describe the experience. There is a notable shift when they talk about a goal they missed. Their physical cues are often the same as the cues of people who feel uncomfortable, embarrassed, or angry. Their voices also change in quality when they talk about the experience. Parties who are optimizers rarely show any change in physiology as they talk about the experience. There is no discernable difference in their voice quality.

Starter, Maintainer, and Completer Placements

In assessing this final part of a party's profile, you ask two questions. First, ask the person, "In doing a project, which stage interests you the most: the beginning, middle, or end?" Follow up with this question, "Is there any stage in which you would like not to participate?"

Parties who are *starters* tell you they prefer the beginning. They use words like "inception," "initiation," "start," and "opening."

They might respond, "I like to get things going." *Maintainers* say they like being in the middle of a project. They do not like launching it or shutting it down. They use expressions like "in the middle," "ongoing," "in process," and "already happening." They might answer, "I like it when we are already under way." *Completers* tell you that they like working at the end. They use expressions like "closing down," "completing," "ending," and "finalizing." They might answer, "I like getting people to put pen to paper." There is nothing that physically distinguishes any of these parties from one another.

| Building Rapport

At this point you have profiled your own nonverbal communication patterns, and you have gathered information that you have used to profile the parties, filling out a Profile Element Grid for each one. Everyone is gathered at the mediation table. It is time to begin in earnest the work of building rapport, an effort that will continue throughout the mediation process. There are four major tasks in this step: you must engage the parties in the process, adjust your responsiveness to their communication patterns, change the general pattern of communication in the room if it is less than productive, and configure parties into productive work units.

Engaging the Parties

The verbal processes you are familiar with of making sure people are ready to begin the mediation session, welcoming people, making them comfortable, and setting up some ground rules will be greatly enhanced when you apply nonverbal processes that reinforce these communications.

Getting Parties' Nonverbal Invitation to Start

For several years I taught communication programs for an international management association. During one executive program, I was asked to distill the program's content into simple elements. I did. On a flip chart I wrote:

I   Identify
A   Acknowledge
R   Respond

I explained that this is a formula: I + A + R. It contains the three essential elements for developing rapport. It reflects all three actions that communicators need to do to be successful. All three have to be included. First, communicators have to use their senses to identify one piece of nonverbal communication, one signal sent to them by another person. Then they need to acknowledge the sender's cue with their own nonverbal communication signal. Finally, they have to respond appropriately with a new piece of communication.

This explanation satisfied all but one executive in the class. At the break he asked me for a mnemonic. He said it would be easier for him to remember the steps if he had one. I told him I would let my other-than-consciousness take care of his request. I started to teach again. After an hour, I circled back to the flip chart and spontaneously wrote an "L" at the top of the formula. The formula now looked like this:

L *Leave out any steps and this is what you get*
I Identify
A Acknowledge
R Respond

The executive and the rest of the class had a mnemonic—and a caution. If any element of the original formula is omitted, the second formula will appear. On an other-than-conscious level, LIAR is what people will think of the communicator and his or her communication.

Even when you have done all your advance preparation for mediation, you still need a nonverbal nod from all parties. You cannot expect to develop rapport before you get the go-ahead sign. That is like anticipating a successful marriage without any courtship. If you receive a verbal signal to move ahead, that is a conscious message. A mediating party's conscious yes, however, might be like the answer of a prospective juror. It could be a socially acceptable response but not a reflection of the person's actual other-than-conscious belief.

You must receive every party's nonverbal signal to start. That is the other-than-conscious cue that parties feel safe. This communication also indicates it is appropriate for you to move forward. If you find that a party says yes but nonverbally indicates otherwise, wait. It may take just a moment for the party to feel acclimatized to the mediation environment. Alternatively, you may need to send another signal that invites the party into rapport.

Follow the IAR formula to engage parties. You can develop rapport through this formula in many ways. For example, you can engage parties by identifying, acknowledging, and responding to their unique meeting distances. These distances depend on people's culture, the occasion, and people's preferred representational systems. To pinpoint the unique meeting distance of each person, I recommend you do the following: approach the party at the same pace that he is moving toward you. Then stop at exactly the same time as he stops. You have identified and acknowledged that person's unique meeting distance. You have also created rapport on an other-than-conscious level. Once you observe the unique meeting distance, the person usually responds within moments. The two of you have engaged. If you fail to respect people's meeting distance, people may feel crowded, uncomfortable, or offended.

You can also engage parties by reproducing some of their movements. You have already noted their gross physical movements when you stood across from them and tracked the big picture. Once you are within eyeshot of a party, reproduce at least one of his movements. Your mirroring movement will send an other-than-conscious message, so avoid any action that could signal you are making fun of him or of a disability. For example, replicate his gait, hand motions, or arm or swaying movements. The actual cues that you select are your choice. What is most relevant is that you identify at least one cue, acknowledge it, and respond, so that you develop rapport on an other-than-conscious level. If you can reproduce a chain of two or three physical cues that are outside the person's awareness, you will experience even more profound results.

Finally, I suggest you pay attention to timing. Wait for each party's nonverbal permission to move forward. Think of engagement as being like baseball. The most effective communicators act like great baseball infielders. These players avoid running for the ball. They get themselves into a position to catch it. Then they wait for the ball to hit their glove.

Welcoming Parties Verbally and Nonverbally

The next strategic step I suggest is attending to the breathing patterns of parties and counsel. Matching a breathing rate is like saying "hello" other-than-consciously. You see people's chests and abdomens moving. You hear their breathing rates. Determine whether anyone is exhibiting rapid breathing from high in a tight chest. If so, you may want to treat this physical cue as a potential fight-or-flight fear response. Begin to breathe deeply so the party can other-than-consciously detect your breathing rate and start to match it.

If parties are not demonstrating any fear response, alter your breathing rate to match each party's. This is a profound method of engaging people outside their awareness at the beginning of mediation. Because the party whose breathing you duplicate is the only one who detects your matched breathing, you have to match each party's breathing separately. After you do you can return to your own breathing rate. You have said "hello."

Another way to engage parties is to address each person in the manner that person wishes. I remember presenting a program to the members of a law firm who had been together for many years. During this session I asked each attendee to "write the name you like to be called" on a name tag. I was specific about how I worded the request. I avoided telling them simply to write their names on the badges. Eleven people scribbled some version of their given names onto their tags. The twelfth, I'll call him Frank Anthony, did something different. He wrote, "Tony." During his years at the firm, everyone had called him Frank. No one had ever asked him what he liked to be called. He told me his friends and family called him Tony. He blushed as he invited me to call him that too.

You may want an easy way to encourage people to use each other's names. Here's a tip. If you ask people to wear name tags, request that they place them on their left side. That way people can shake hands with their right hands and see each other's names clearly at the same time. When name tags are worn on the right side, the arm extended for the handshake can obscure the tag. If you want to remember names, here's another tip. After you shake hands, look at the tag, look at the person's face, and immediately move your eyes up and left (to the visual remembered eye position). Visualize the person's face with her name under it. Think of it as her "mug shot." Hold the picture of her face and name in your mind for a moment. Close your eyes briefly. Look up and left again. Make the same picture again. Return to looking at the person. The exercise takes fractions of a second; the results remain. If you ever want to remember that person's name, look at her face then look up and left. The name will be waiting there, in the mug shot file.

Along with verifying how parties like to be addressed, make sure to pronounce their names correctly. Matching articulation is an important paralinguistic acknowledgment. Although some names are daunting, people seem willing to allow mediators to practice until the pronunciation is correct. Some parties are even flattered when mediators take the time to do it. Nail down this component of rapport at the beginning of the session. If you do not, you gamble being regarded as uncaring. You may also look as if you are minimizing the importance of the party with the difficult name. Each inexact articulation could be perceived as an embarrassment or mark of disrespect by the affected party. Often any other parties who recognize your mistake are also influenced negatively.

While you are matching names, you can be matching other nonverbal cues too. This sends a particularly strong message of welcome. Pick one or two low profile cues to match. For example, if you notice that one party raises an eyebrow, do that in response. If someone pulls his mouth into a taut position, reproduce that. If you can replicate a person's tone, do it briefly. The objective is to create an environment in which you send separate, other-than-conscious cues to each party. Each signal says, "Welcome."

Matching systems language also sends a greeting to parties. Rotate through using visual, auditory, and kinesthetic expressions. When you use the preferred system of a party, you engage that party at that point. Along with systems language, also use the physical cues that match preferred systems. Signal with your eyes and hands as well as your breathing and head angle. Match each system as you welcome each party. You will create both verbal and nonverbal rapport.

Finally, remember to use language touchstones and regionalisms if you can. Drop these words and expressions into conversation.

By melding them into the discussion, you make an alien environment start to feel familiar and comfortable.

Creating Parties' Comfort Through Perception

Creating a comfortable working environment is instrumental in fostering rapport. Often parties gauge their degree of comfort through their perceptions of similarity and difference.

Parties who prefer similarity cling to sameness. If you hold more than one mediation session with them, you will see that they want to do things in the same way each time. Often they want exactly the same environment because that makes them comfortable. Even being in a different mediation or caucus room in the same building as before may make them feel uneasy. In new mediation sessions they like to sit in the same relative positions they are used to. For example, some always want to sit close to the front. Some always want to sit at a distance. If you move their positions, they feel disrupted. During mediation these parties prefer that you avoid writing amended points from one flip chart page onto a new page. They prefer that you strike out the old material and insert the revision on the same sheet. People who prefer similarity like lots of repetition. For example, if you put candy on the table during one session, you must put the same candy in the same dish on the table in the next session. If not, they notice that things are not the same and are disappointed. Use green markers when writing on a board or flip chart because green will carry its traditional meaning of "go" for them. It will suggest fresh ideas and forward movement. Avoid using red markers unless you want to signal them to stop. To build momentum with these parties, keep everyone's chair looking the same. Take all breaks for the same length of time. Give everyone the same types of paper and pens to record notes. Make sure these parties perceive that everyone is playing by the same rules.

People who prefer difference seek variety. For them change is refreshing. Just as *perception* of similarity is important to those who prefer sameness, the *perception* of difference—not necessarily actual difference—is key with these parties. To enable these parties to create momentum, provide them with change. I suggest you ask if they want to switch positions with their counsel after breaks. Add some different colored candies to the bowl on the mediation table. Be prepared with an assortment of background or break music to play for them. Use different types of media when explaining points. At times use a flip chart. At other times write on the board. Offer them information on a sheet of paper too. If these people do not perceive difference or change, they get bored and exit mentally. Remember, however, that people who seek only difference make up a minute minority of the general population. Even people who generally prefer difference usually want a bit of similarity too. So feel free to salt your mediation with variety, but to satisfy the majority of the parties provide a substantial amount of similarity.

Empowering Parties Through Guidelines

You can engage people and sustain rapport by empowering them in their own process. You start by sending them a message that you have confidence in them. I suggest that the way to do this is by discussing ground rules. You offer guidelines. They agree to them. They are already used to verbal and nonverbal ground rules in the rest of their lives, so they feel safe with them. Consider how we function in traffic, for example. Many people adhere to the verbal rule that tells them to look both ways before they cross a street. Others also operate with nonverbal ground rules that tell them to honk and wave to a driver signaling that he wants to enter their traffic lane. When you let parties know in advance about mediation ground rules, you help them. They move from an unknown arena into a forum in which they are comfortable.

Again, one of the first items for you to address is names. You want to preclude or neutralize any message of imbalance that might be sent when people mix formal and informal methods of addressing each other. I usually introduce myself by saying, "My name is Barb Madonik." (If someone asks me what I like to be called, even before I ask them that question, I PEG them as possibly others-focus people.) After my introduction, people then call me Barb or Ms. Madonik. Some will not have listened, will not have cared, or will feel more comfortable using my full first name. They will call me Barbara. The form of name with which people respond to me, tells me how they might like to be addressed. Irrespective of my hunches, I always ask them, "What do you prefer to be called?" That is the exact form of the question I use to get an uncontaminated answer. If all parties like to use first names, or first names and nicknames, I ask for everyone's agreement with that. If all prefer surnames, I ask for agreement with that too. If the group has mixed preferences, I arrange for everyone to use the same level of address. That means all parties are addressed formally as "Ms. X," "Mrs. X," and "Mr. X" or all parties are addressed informally by the first names or nicknames they prefer.

I introduce a very subtle nonverbal strategy at this point. While I am talking, I communicate an other-than-conscious message to the parties. I start by explaining how they must allow each other to talk. I explain how they must do this whether they agree or disagree with the other person's point. I suggest they write down points of disagreement on a piece of paper. That way they can remember their ideas and avoid interrupting the speaker. Concurrently with these verbal explanations, I send other-than-conscious cues to the parties. I tap my left thumb once as I talk to them about listening and agreeing. Then I tap the baby finger of my left hand once as I talk about listening and disagreeing. I am setting up an other-than-conscious signal for them. I am showing them how to indicate nonverbal agreement or disagreement. As a result, when they consent or dissent as someone else is making a point, they often reproduce my nonverbal finger cues and send the appropriate signal to me other-than-consciously. That way I often know before they express a word whether they agree or disagree with an issue. I am prepared for their reaction—whether they have verbalized it or not.

You have already made the meta-decisions for the process. You can negotiate the fine points of the ground rules verbally. These remaining issues consist of matters like taking turns talking, confidentiality agreements, and mediator responsibilities. You can add to the parties' sense of empowerment by allowing them to negotiate nonthreatening issues. You will be operating like the parent who tells a child she can pick one of three outfits to wear. The parent has already excluded inappropriate articles. The child feels empowered to make a free choice. When you apply the same technique to mediation, you give parties a sense of choice. This opportunity to choose often communicates a mediator's confidence in parties. People feel they are being seen and heard. They start the mediation by feeling acknowledged. They feel empowered. They engage.

Guidelines also pave the way for introducing the relevancy challenge. In mediation, parties sometimes get off track. When they do, they can get into irrelevant issues. These issues can be time consuming and damaging. Most of all, they can indicate the process is out of the mediator's control. The party carrying the process off track seems in charge. The other party seems to be lacking control and disengaged from the process. There is a major imbalance. To avoid this situation, I explain the concept of the relevancy challenge to parties. I talk about it during the time I explain guidelines. I get agreement from all people to operate using it. When I use this technique, I find I have the option to challenge tangential discussions that are unproductive. I can respectfully bring the mediation back on topic. As a result, all parties feel that the process is under control. With that feeling comes a sense of comfort and engagement.

Adjusting Your Responsiveness

As a mediator you want to create productive communication throughout the conflict resolution process. To be successful you need to adjust your responses to the communication structure of each party at the table. That means you must recognize parties' general communication structures. Then you drop your message into each of those structures. You will be carrying out this simple formula:

PERSON'S COMMUNICATION STRUCTURE
+ YOUR INFORMATION
= YOUR COMMUNICATION OBJECTIVE

Remember that communication structures vary from person to person. As you adjust your responses, also keep in mind that people do not know they are sending other-than-conscious messages. You can adjust your responsiveness in different ways. The methods I describe here are mirroring; responding directly to a person's preferences; asking questions; and working with metaphors, analogies, and humor.

Mirroring Communication

Mirroring can be done consciously. You have often seen this when people wave to each other. You have seen it when people return a thumbs-up gesture to signal "OK." In mediation, I suggest you mirror a piece of physical movement. For example, if a person stands up slightly and reaches across the table to shake your hand, do exactly the same movement. Replicate everything right down to the exact height to which the person rises to greet you. If someone takes off a jacket, consider taking off your jacket too.

You can also use mirroring to respond to cues that parties send outside their awareness. Duplicate voice tone, eye patterns, facial movements, hand movements, breathing cues, and paralanguage cues. For example, you might mirror pursed lips, an outstretched hand, or a tilted head. Use verbal predicates from parties' preferred systems. If each party uses a different preferred system, rotate through the systems. For example, you could say, "I look forward [*visual*] to talking [*auditory*] about reaching [*kinesthetic*] a solution." Also reproduce expressions parties use. Play back their phrases the way you would their language touchstones.

While you are repeating people's expressions, be aware of the rhythm of their conversation. You can reflect that rhythm to develop rapport. When people share a rhythm, or display *synchrony* (are *in sync*), communication flows freely. When there is no shared rhythm among the parties, you must mirror each person's rhythm to build rapport. Listen for the ways parties emphasize their words. Deliver your words to echo that emphasis. Observe when parties use nonverbal signals to accent their words. Note what kind of physical cues they use. Reproduce those movements as you match their beat. Next, observe people's eyes. You can mirror the eye cues described earlier (summarized in Figure 2.1). You may observe incongruities, eye patterns that do not match people's words. For example, parties may talk about feeling sad. This is a verbal kinesthetic cue. If they move their eyes up and to their right that is the usual *visual constructed* position. They may be imagining a situation in which they would feel sad. You do not know what is in their minds. Moreover, what they are thinking is irrelevant to adjusting your responsiveness for the purpose of engaging parties and building rapport. As a result, I suggest you reflect parties' incongruent cues exactly. Match their words by using their preferred representational system and mirror their eye cues too. You are being *congruently incongruent*. You are matching their incongruity exactly.

You will experience this type of incongruity in other areas too. For example, people who sway back and forth may be sending a nonverbal communication. Often this type of movement indicates they are experiencing kinesthesia outside their awareness. They are getting a feeling and reacting to it but are not aware that they are responding to the sensation. If parties move this way when they are talking, I suggest you match their words and reproduce their movement too.

I use both conscious and other-than-conscious mirroring techniques constantly during mediation. I always use other-than-conscious mirroring concurrently with conscious mirroring. The other-than-conscious process has a more profound effect than conscious mirroring because it is the part of communication that takes place outside people's conscious awareness.

Responding Directly to Each Person's Preferences

You have started to adjust your responsiveness by mirroring people's communication cues. Now consider other ways to react. You have already demonstrated flexibility by using words and phrases from each representational system when you welcomed people. The next step is to alert yourself to systems that seem tied together. For example, when you hear parties using an expression like "heated argument," they are combining kinesthetic and auditory references. In the phrase "icy stare," parties link kinesthetic and visual systems.

As soon as you hear this type of combination, I recommend you probe further. When I do, I often find these dual signals tell me the communicator's language pattern loop, the way in which she alternates her primary and secondary systems. So when I come upon a combination, I structure my language to fit the communicator's system sequence. This has a strong effect. The party hears my words and consciously deals with their content. At the same time, other-than-consciously she hears me matching her language loop. This matching language structure that bypasses her conscious filters smoothes the conversation flow, furthers rapport, and reduces tension as she deals consciously with what I have said.

You can build even stronger rapport at this point through your choice of objects and environments. When you interact with people who demonstrate a visual preference, provide a neat and attractive environment. Give them flow charts of the process. Have graphs and maps if the material warrants them. Use colored paper and markers. Allow visual preference parties plenty of space for making mental pictures. Use "before and after" photographs or videotape.

When you work with people with an auditory preference, speak clearly. Have music playing. Provide them with a list or outline of the process; give them structure for the session. Use street or area names rather than landmarks or building descriptions. Give these people reading materials. Have references, citations, and sources available. Provide annual reports. Have testimonials on hand. Use numbers and tables. Provide people with calculations.

When you communicate with people who have a kinesthetic preference give them comfortable environments and furniture. If you are providing an outline of the mediation process, avoid putting that information on a flip chart or board because they cannot associate easily with these objects. Instead, give these people printed sheets they can hold. Give them flow charts that they can trace to follow the process. Allow them to put their belongings, their "stuff," close to them. That brings them comfort. Use working models, miniatures, and tangible objects to make concepts concrete. Realize that these people are sensitive to aromas and to textures of fabrics and paper. They love tear strips. They appreciate appropriate physical contact. They are highly sensitive to feelings.

At various times during the mediation, parties are likely to become distracted. They enter the altered state described in Chapter One. You have to adjust your responsiveness then too. You need subtle and dependable techniques to recapture their attention. There are different ways to do this. Some are more elegant than others. Yelling, "Hey, you!" may be an attention getter but is best left for times when a truck is bearing down on them. That type of communication does not create the rapport you seek.

The most effective method to recapture attention is linked to preferred representational systems. To catch the attention of people with a visual preference, flag them. Flutter something within eyeshot. This strategy can be as simple as picking up a piece of paper and moving it. You can also subtly wave a hand or book in the air. Move to the flip chart from the table. Parties may not consciously see you or the object but other-than-consciously they do, and return from their altered state. They are usually unaware of what caught their attention. They are back though, in the present. To capture the attention of people with an auditory preference use techniques that involve sound. Clear your throat. Crumple rigid paper. Drop a book or pen on the table. Drum your nails on a surface. Rip a sheet noisily off the flip chart. Make any noise. People with an auditory preference will come out of their altered state. Again, they are not necessarily aware of what happened to bring them back into the present moment. To grab the attention of people with a kinesthetic preference, "accidentally" nudge their chairs. Push your papers gently into theirs so the pages move in their hands. Stand up, making sure you jostle the table a bit. Use breathing. Sigh, inhaling and exhaling loudly and deeply. Touch or rub your midline, in the area near your heart. Movement, contact, and sighing brings this group back to the present.

Recapturing attention can occur on an other-than-conscious level because parties are absorbing millions of pieces of information outside their awareness. The key to success in this technique is adjusting your responsiveness to preferred systems. The hidden signals you send to a person with one type of preference are usually not detected by parties with another preference. That means you may have to send separate signals to people with different preferences. Remember, however, that the signals you send to one party can also be picked up by another party with the same preference.

Asking Questions

The more you know about the parties, the better your ability to adapt your responses. I recommend you capitalize on their personal wealth of information by asking questions. The timing and type of

question will vary. Parties' responses allow you to adjust your reactions. Then you can build rapport faster and more effectively.

Earlier in the mediation, when you tracked primary information, you set up a de facto agreement about asking questions. I suggest you continue your inquiries with gentle questioning and avoid
incisive interrogation if you can. Act like Columbo. Fill in information gaps in a relaxed manner. The *Columbo technique* is ideal for
times when parties balk at communication that is too direct. For
example, you might say, "You know, I feel really foolish asking you
this but . . ." or, "I'm sure this is a simple question for you, but it's
really complicated for me. Could you help me understand . . . ?"

In this technique, you back off. You ask questions in an innocu-
ous style. You let parties be the resources. You eliminate feelings
of intimidation and threat. Respondents feel empowered. When
you use the Columbo technique, you preclude any hint of being
"in their face." You want to avoid that because it can produce a
polarity response in parties. This response could be exactly the
opposite reaction from the one you seek. You would shut down
communication.

I find the Columbo technique constantly generates information
I could not bring out using more sophisticated approaches. Parties
relax and lower their guard. After that, I gather high-quality information. Some of the facts I glean would be held back if the parties were more vigilant.

A second questioning technique I recommend is *onionskinning*.
You can use it to determine whether you are responding to the real
issues of concern to the parties. You need to know these core issues
before you can follow the appropriate path to resolution. To skin
the onion successfully, you must be persistent and stay focused. You
need patience. Sometimes you will ask the same type of question
in many ways.

Here is an example of how this technique works. In one of my
cases, parties were ostensibly arguing over their shared driveway
rights. One party had put large flowerpots along the center line of
the mutual driveway. The other party needed the full driveway to
drive his vehicle from the street to the garage in the back. The
mediation started with parties arguing about rights, flowerpots,
access, and egress. Only after onionskinning was the core issue
revealed. My questioning followed this general pattern:

Mediator:	I'm wondering if we could cover this issue about the flowerpots again, Mr. Smith.
Mr. Smith:	OK.
Mediator:	How long have you been putting them in the middle of the driveway?
Mr. Smith:	Two years.
Mediator:	Did you always have them in the driveway during the day?
Mr. Smith:	Yes, I did.
Mediator:	You never had them anywhere else?
Mr. Smith:	No.
Mediator:	Did you ever have them in different spots on the driveway?
Mr. Smith:	Well, yes.
Mediator:	Can you tell me about that?
Mr. Smith:	Well, I did move them from the side of my house to the middle of the driveway during the day.
Mediator:	Can you tell me why you did that?
Mr. Smith:	It gave them more light.
Mediator:	I understand why you would move them into the light in the middle of the driveway, but what was the purpose of moving them back to the side of your house? Wouldn't they need the light the next day?
Mr. Smith:	Yes, they would.
Mediator:	So what prompted you to move them out of the middle of the driveway?
Mr. Smith:	I knew Mr. Jones would be bringing in his car at six o'clock.
Mediator:	What did this mean for you?
Mr. Smith:	I moved the pots right next to my side wall so his car could go through.
Mediator:	That seems pretty thoughtful of you.
Mr. Smith:	Well, yah. It didn't hurt me to do it.
Mediator:	Has the lighting changed at all around the building? I mean, has anyone built a structure that now blocks the way your flowers get their light?
Mr. Smith:	No.
Mediator:	Has Mr. Jones asked if you could resume what you used to do before—I mean, when you left your

	flowerpots in the middle of the driveway and then moved them beside your house at night?
Mr. Smith:	Yes.
Mediator:	And your response was no. Is that correct?
Mr. Smith:	Yes, that's correct.
Mediator:	Has there been any other change that you have made in regard to moving or not moving the flowerpots?
Mr. Smith:	No.
Mediator:	Has there been any other change that anyone else has made in relation to moving the flowerpots?
Mr. Smith:	No.
Mediator:	Has there been any other change that Mr. Jones has made?
Mr. Smith:	Yes.
Mediator:	Has he changed the time he comes home?
Mr. Smith:	No.
Mediator:	Has he made any other change?
Mr. Smith:	He bought a new van.

The onionskinning continued. By the time it was over, the core issue of the conflict became clear. It was Mr. Smith's jealousy over his neighbor's new vehicle. At this point I could adjust my responses to deal with the real concerns.

Introducing Metaphors, Analogies, and Humor

When you use different parts of speech, you appeal to people in fresh ways. *Metaphors* and *analogies* are two methods that foster understanding and rapport. By using them, you can introduce your ideas to parties in a form that lets them extrapolate the ideas to match their past experiences. That way, they understand and are comfortable.

I use metaphors and analogies to help parties make sense of troublesome or complicated concepts. I like them to compare mediation issues to things they already know and understand. I prefer to make my point with metaphors drawn from nature when possible. For example, I might say to parties: "This mediation might have started off looking as if it would be unpleasant. It might have seemed, also, that it was going to gobble up a lot of time and resources. I can assure you, however, that you can make it very worthwhile. Just think of it as a kind of caterpillar. Remember that sometimes a caterpillar isn't the most appealing critter you'll ever see. And does it ever eat those leaves to shreds! But can you take your eyes off that beautiful butterfly that it turns into in the end?"

If I want to work with analogies, I take a similar tack. I tie together things that seem unrelated. I might talk about unnecessary continued conflict as "a well-dressed war zone where no one walks away with a medal."

I trust parties to get creative and arrive at understanding situations. I suggest you trust them too. Instead of explaining every matter in finite linguistic detail, allow parties to appreciate ideas in their own ways. They can make sense of comparisons through their own thought processes. Use metaphors and analogies to introduce painful or distressing ideas. Metaphors and analogies allow you to do this in oblique and gentle ways. As a result you can avoid resistance from the parties more easily.

Humor is another method you may want to use to develop rapport. This technique comes with a warning label. Use it only if you are sure the type of humor and content of the material fit the environment and audience. Mediation is not generally a time that gives rise to comedy; however, there are some moments when humor is ideal. I have found humor an excellent valve for diffusing pressure that is building up in mediation. Before I use humor, though, I always lay a foundation with the parties. I might have chatted with them over the telephone or talked with them before starting the session. I usually have a sense of their backgrounds and ways of thinking that helps me avoid mine-filled areas. Different people find different ideas funny. Ideas that one person finds funny, another will find offensive. My rule of thumb about stories is, if in doubt, leave the story out. If you do think that a short, humorous story illustrates a point, make sure it is apropos to tell it.

If you are not absolutely sure your delivery will be interpreted positively, avoid this technique. Humor must be mastered. It must be expressed as fluidly as breathing. You must be able to weave it in and out of the rest of your communication. If you do not, you risk appearing like a poor stand-up comic. That comportment sends a message of disrespect for the process and parties.

The purpose of humor is to make a point. Stay focused on that point. Avoid sagas. You can lose parties' attention in long stories. People will miss your point. Be as gentle as you can be. Often I find allusions to fairy tales a source of gentle humor. For example, I will say to parties who consistently return late from breaks, "Do me a favor. Would you leave me a trail of bread crumbs, so I can find you if you're not back in ten minutes?" Another source of humorous material can be your own life experiences. Sometimes they are the funniest. They are easy for you to remember and have the greatest resonance with parties. They are true. They make you human too.

Changing Communication in the Room

Sometimes communication among the parties may be shaky at the start of mediation. Once on the right track, it may lose focus. At times parties may have trouble exchanging any kind of productive communication at all. You can use nonverbal strategies to change a poor communication environment and give the parties a better opportunity to reach agreement.

Leading Parties to a More Productive Mentality

When people enter the mediation environment, they bring different attitudes with them. Some may be lawyers who have had positive experiences with mediation. Others may be lawyers who automatically assume adversarial positions when sitting across from other lawyers. Mediating parties may be afraid. At times they may feel angry. Many times they are confused. Some feel strong because they believe they have an air-tight position. Others feel powerless because they are disconcerted or frightened by the process. You want to provide a productive environment for each of them. That way you can create or maintain rapport with the parties and improve their chances of reaching an outcome with which they are satisfied. When the environment is less than productive, I suggest you design one that is more worthwhile. You can do this during caucus periods and in the mediation room.

Start with yourself. Before you begin mediating, use the option circle (Figure 3.3). Remember to inhale and exhale two or three times. Then run the eye square (Figure 3.2). Inhale and exhale deeply one or two more times. Then dig into mediation. By doing this exercise just before starting to mediate, you refresh yourself and give yourself a new perspective. The technique introduces more oxygen into your system. It also sets up a transderivational search. You become more consciously alert. Your other-than-consciousness assembles information outside your awareness. The technique allows you to lead parties with a more fertile approach. You are more mentally flexible.

When you use the option circle, parties sometimes mirror what you do. Even when you perform the mechanics of this technique unobtrusively, parties may notice your pattern either consciously or other-than-consciously. If they notice it consciously, they may ask what you are doing. I suggest you tell them. Say it is a technique you learned for getting really creative and productive in mediation. Question whether they would like to learn it too. If any of them say yes, show them the technique. Let them practice once or twice. After that, they will often reproduce the procedure during the mediation. In particular they will do it each time you cue them by using the technique yourself. Each time they use this technique, they too will become more creative. Their new flexibility will allow them to adjust their responsiveness. They will be more open to suggestions about building or maintaining rapport too.

Parties may not notice or comment on your use of the option circle in the mediation room. If they do not, show the technique to them during a caucus. Parties usually go to a caucus room because they want to discuss issues away from other parties. They often need creativity at this time. They also need new perspectives. This then is an ideal place and time for a demonstration of the option circle. The option circle can give the parties both new perspectives and creativity.

When parties are in an unproductive mind-set, they may be unwilling or unable to cooperate with you and other parties. The mediation may stall. You know how breathing can be used to welcome parties; now consider how you can use it to change the mentality in the room. By altering your breathing rate, you can shift people's frame of mind. You can create or reestablish rapport. To achieve your goal match breathing rates, one after another. If parties breathe quickly, match them. Mirror midspeed rates and slow ones too. If this process assists parties other-than-consciously to match each other's rates, rapport can grow.

Matching breathing patterns is only one way to change communication in the room. I suggest you also consider alternate methods. Sometimes you can invite people to change the representational systems they are using, and that can move them into a more effective mind-set. To lead people from one system to another system, cue them other-than-consciously. For example, if parties are undergoing feelings (pieces of kinesthetic information) that are holding them back, you might lead them to access information visually. That could be more effective for them at this time. If people's heads or bodies are tilted in an auditory position, they might be listening to old, unproductive dialogues and distracted by them. These people might operate in a more worthwhile manner if they accessed a visual or kinesthetic system.

The technique for inviting people to change systems is done in two steps. First, you capture people's attention by using their current system. Then you signal them with a cue from the representational system into which you want them to move. You go through these steps with words, using expressions that evoke each system. You can also move through them nonverbally.

When you read about responding directly to each person's preferences, you learned different techniques to flag people's other-than-conscious attention. Now you can use this same process to accomplish the first step nonverbally. For example, you may notice that people are unresponsive at times when their eye or physical cues signal that they are accessing visual information. If this is an unproductive situation for them, you may want them to access another system. That way, they might be in a more worthwhile mind-set. I suggest you invite them to move to an auditory or kinesthetic system. To achieve this, first match some other-than-conscious cue from their current system. You can do this by using a physical signal like raising your hand, standing up, or stretching. Stretching is an excellent choice. When you stretch, you can use all systems to flag parties. You can raise your arms as a visual cue. Concurrently, you can make a noise that sends an auditory signal. Together with this you can inhale and exhale deeply to send the final kinesthetic message. The action of standing can accomplish the same goals as stretching. As you rise, some parties' eyes follow you. When you make a noise with the chair, you attract auditory attention. By pushing off the table and making it move or shake, you catch the attention of people who are in a kinesthetic accessing state.

Once you have captured everyone's attention, invite everyone into the preferred system you deem most beneficial for them. You can reinforce this system with words. You can also send nonverbal cues that are even more powerful. For example, invite parties into a visual system by looking upward. Draw pictures in the air with your fingers or a pen. Put your hands around your eyes. Lead parties into auditory accessing by moving your eyes from side to side. Draw your eyes down and to the left. Tilt your head or body to the left. Place your hands around your ears or mouth. Drum your fingers or pen on the table. Guide people into kinesthesia by looking down and to the right. Tip your head or body to the right. Inhale and exhale deeply a few times. Touch or tap your chest around the heart area. After any of these nonverbal cues, parties move into new systems in which they can function more effectively for a time. Moreover rapport is strengthened.

Changing the Focus

Sometimes parties get stuck in a thought or issue. A matter or detail becomes contentious. Getting tangled in the point prevents people from interacting in a worthwhile fashion. This is the time you may decide to use the technique of *distraction* to move parties away from the troublesome idea. When you use this technique, you usually do not care where parties' attention will go. You simply want parties to stop dwelling on the idea. Distraction is used on the conscious level. You introduce or point out another idea or event that is happening concurrently with the troublesome one. For example, you can interrupt yourself as you talk. Start by saying, "In discussing this issue—" At that point drop a book, take a drink from a glass of water, or perform some other physical act. You can also distract vocally. Say, "In discussing this issue—" and then cough, clear your throat, or say, "Excuse me" and grab a tissue for your nose. It is that simple. You break the negative communication continuum and have the opportunity to start at a more positive point.

Even when the distraction technique seems called for, it may not always be effective. Because the interruption is perceived consciously, people's filters cease working only temporarily. At the time of distraction there is a momentary state of confusion. Only for that little while are the parties in an altered state. After that they resume combing warily through information on a normal conscious level. They may resist changing their focus when they are addressing an issue important to them. Moreover, on an other-than-conscious level, they may find the distraction disrespectful. They may believe you are not honoring their hierarchy of issues. Rapport is at risk.

As an alternative to distraction, you may elect to use the *redirection* technique. It may be more effective. With it you can more tightly control the communication in the room. You perform this technique in two steps. First, you shift people's conscious awareness as you did in the distraction technique. The difference this time is that you know exactly where you want parties' attention to be focused. You make the end point significant. So, second, you refocus parties' attention on the spot you want. For this technique to work, parties must continue to concentrate on the new focal point. So you must keep referring to the new point. People then stay interested in it because they have limited amounts of conscious awareness. You direct this awareness to the new idea so they lose conscious awareness of their original idea.

During this time, you also have an opportunity to redirect people's other-than-consciousness. People's altered state lasts longer during the redirection technique than it does during the distraction technique. This is an ideal time for you to deliver meaningful messages into parties' other-than-consciousness. The messages can be transferred using the special tone you noted earlier as being effective with the parties. You can slip your messages into the conversation unobtrusively. For example, you could quietly say during the process, "Imagine this happening while we were making headway." You can make the message even more meaningful by touching both parties at the same time. That way you anchor them (that is, link them) to the tone and the positive idea of "making headway." This whole process can be done in split seconds. It is virtually imperceptible. The parties are conscious only of the focal point of the redirection. You are not affecting the con-

tent of the resolution. You are moving parties along the mediation process path. The concealed messages can build rapport.
This rapport allows parties to create their own action plans for successful resolution.

Many times you must deal with the way parties focus on each
other. How people pay attention to each other affects rapport significantly. People tend to focus on themselves (*self-focus*) or others
(*others-focus*). Their physical cues and words give you clues about
their typical focus. You sometimes need to shift this focus.

As I described in Step Four, self-focus parties, among their
other characteristics, are hard to interrupt and frequently use
words that refer to themselves. They give the impression that they
are disconnected from the mediator, other parties, and the
process. They appear as if they do not care about other people.
Parties who are focused on others send messages of interest in
other people, and they check to see that others understand what
they say. You must be the glue that holds these two communication
structures together. You must first capture each party's attention.
Then you can direct that attention. This is somewhat easier when
you work with people who are others-focused. These people intuitively concentrate their attention on those around them. You can
flag that attention. Then you can move it in the direction you want.
You can guide them using verbal and nonverbal cues. You can talk
to them or, literally, point them in a direction. They are receptive
to your communication.

Self-focus parties are more challenging. First, you need to be
clear about what you want to accomplish. Next, you must make use
of their profile information. For example, you can drop their language touchstones into your speech to compel them to listen to
you. You can flag them other-than-consciously in their preferred
system and bring their attention back to the table. For example, if
self-focus parties have a kinesthetic preference, you might open a
stick of spearmint gum so the aroma brings them into the present.
If they have an auditory preference, you could snap off the tab of
a soda pop can. Once you have their attention, match their communication patterns exactly. Push back your chair. Talk in short,
abrupt sentences. Use words like "you" and "your" frequently. Make
sure you talk about them or something that involves them or you
risk losing lose them again instantly.

To change the communication pattern in the room, you may have to become the translator between self-focus and others-focus parties. Let's say that Party A is a self-focus person. After he speaks he will mentally check out. You lean toward Party B, the others-focus person. Look Party B in the eye. Restate Party A's remarks, using longer, more expansive terms than Party A did. This will engage Party B. Party A will not mind. Party A will be withdrawn. After Party B speaks, you turn to Party A, lean back, and replay Party B's statement. Do it in truncated terms. Party B will appreciate your thoughtfulness in recapping the statements. Party B cares that others understand completely. Party A will want only the abbreviated version. In both cases you will be the buffer. Both parties will be satisfied. Moreover, you will have changed the mind-set at the table. Attention will have shifted from style to dealing with issues that need resolution.

Guiding Parties to Communicate with Each Other

Bridging people's communication styles as I have described will allow you to establish a certain amount of rapport. Now I suggest you guide parties to communicate with each other.

If parties already communicate in the same way, you need only direct the process. They do the rest. If parties do not intuitively send and receive messages in the same way, you need to assist them so they can build rapport. Start by laying a foundation that invites parties to cooperate. Find something, other than the mediated issue, that parties have in common. That topic can start the communication flow. If parties hit troublesome issues, I recommend employing the *reframing* technique. First isolate the contentious issue. Then modify the setting or context around it. This change puts a new frame of reference around the original issue for both parties. For example, when some parties say mediation is a waste of money, I ask if they have ever made a payment on a car or piece of furniture. Inevitably they answer yes. Then I ask if they might consider this mediation as "the first payment on a new future." They usually agree and move into the process.

After creating a new, fertile environment like this, you can introduce parties to the *playback* technique. It will allow them to communicate more effectively with each other. I often use this

technique in community-based mediations. I ask the first party to
make an opening statement about the mediation issues. After the
first party is finished, I ask the listening party to repeat what the
speaker just said. The listener does this. I check with the speaker. I
ask if the listener's interpretation was correct. If correction is required, I ask the speaker to correct the playback statement. The listener then repeats the amended statement for the speaker. The
correction and playback sequence may be repeated as often as necessary. Once the information is played back accurately, I ask speaker
and listener to switch roles. The original listener becomes the new
speaker, and the correction and playback process is repeated.

In addition to community-based mediation, other types of conflict resolution benefit from this technique. The procedure encourages parties to understand each other. It also allows them to
acknowledge each other without forcing them to agree. It is an
excellent way to motivate each party to pay attention assiduously
to the other. Moreover, parties often make a discovery. Prior to
playing back these opening statements, parties usually do not
understand the other side's position or interests. They just think
they do. Only when the speaker corrects details, does the listener
realize she may have been mistaken about issues. This clarity goes
a long way toward changing communication in the room.

You can also assist parties to communicate more effectively by
explaining how certain words set up contradictory messages. Pre-
mediation caucus is an ideal place to apprise people of this fact.
Start by alerting them to expressions that send negative signals. For
example, examine the expressions "I'll try" and "I hope." Explicitly, these terms are positive. Implicitly, each carries a message of
failure. Ask parties to replace these expressions with wholly positive messages like "I will do it" and "I'm sure that."

Explain *butting* to parties and tell them how destructive it can
be. Tell them how they can undo positive messages by using words
like "but," "except," and "however." Show how listeners sense,
other-than-consciously, that speakers are nullifying the first part of
the message when they interject one of these words. Explain how
listeners shut down and stop listening. Let parties know that if they
use these words, they risk inadvertently creating tension at the
table. I recommend you give parties an illustration of butting that
does not relate to mediation. For example, ask them how they

would react if someone said, "I really like your suit, but . . ." or, "I really like your new idea, however, . . ." (You do not have to finish these sentences.) Inevitably, parties tell you that they anticipate something unfavorable will follow. Butting undoes the compliment. Suggest that parties avoid these contradictory words. Ask them to use "and" instead or to consider rephrasing the whole message.

Another technique that leads parties to communicate well with each other is *chasing away pink elephants*. Rather than explaining the technique to the parties, just model the concept for them. State what you want. Avoid telling them what you do not want. Point out the value of their talking in concrete terms to you and the other people at the table. Use an illustration. I often tell parties about a colleague who wanted to go on a vacation. He called a travel agent. The agent asked him where he wanted to go. He answered, "Not Barbados. Not Hawaii." The travel agent kept asking where he wanted to go. My colleague kept coming up with "nots." As a result he never did book a trip.

Stay mindful of the distress you yourself could cause if you fail to chase away pink elephants. Consider the counterproductive effects of expressions like "*no* problem" or "*not* to worry." I suggest you replace such expressions with statements like, "You can handle the situation," "That's a simple matter," and, "It's doable."

On the rare times I do choose to introduce the idea of "not," I do it unobtrusively. I manipulate the concept so I can interject a positive idea. For example, I might say to parties, "Don't come up with solutions faster than I can write them on the flip chart." This technique works particularly well with people who have a strong polarity response. I can change the communication in the room by using this technique strategically. I identify the parties with a well-developed polarity response. I do that from their past resistance to suggestions or the diametrically opposite action they take after a suggestion or request. I send these parties a verbal, conscious message. For example, I might say, "I doubt we can come up with more than one or two ways to resolve this point." I know this type of remark acts like a starter pistol for people with a polarity response. Their other-than-conscious response snaps into action, and they start to work to prove they can do something that someone said they could not. Often my comments are acknowledged vocally with laughing or snickering. Sometimes I am met with verbal retorts. Those are my cues that the strategy is working. More-over, the common group reaction often breaks up existing tension. Parties begin a more productive type of communication.

Interjecting Music

In discussing preparation for mediation, I suggested you consider the value of introducing music. The effect on parties is significant. Music changes the rhythm of communication in the room. If you can master the use of music, you can control communication change. That change can build rapport. Have a selection of music available. Know the pieces well. Cue audiotapes to the pieces you want to use. Know which compact disc (CD) tracks you want. Be mindful of your timing in using music and of your selection at those times. These factors have a significant effect on how the music influences the rhythm of the mediation.

Music is a powerful tool. If parties get somewhat dozy, you may want to energize them. Call for a break. Play a lively tune. If medi-ation becomes tense, you may want parties to stretch. You can do this easily. Say *you* need a bit of a break. Invite parties to take one too. Then put on a musical piece. Stretch to it. Invite people to join you. If you want to ease the situation, play gentle New Age sounds. Sometimes that background is very soothing.

The choice is limitless. You can select rock and roll, classical music, ethnic tunes, or New Age music. Have them all available. Parties sometimes joke at first about the music. They do, however, respond positively to it. If parties have a high auditory acuity, keep background music low or the sound will distract them. Initially, all parties will be aware of the sound. Soon they refocus on other issues. Their conscious awareness drops the sound and beat into other-than-consciousness. The rhythm, however, still links parties and assists in building rapport.

Configuring Productive Work Units

Parties come to the table with a variety of skills and backgrounds. They have intuitive ways they like to work. If you fail to recognize these patterns, you could neutralize people's vitality. You could also miss opportunities to create rapport. When you identify people's natural approaches to working, you can allow them to build positive energy. You can then harvest that energy. You can pinpoint at what points of the process parties will be invigorated or lose interest. You can use that energy to solve problems. When you allow people to work the way they naturally need to work, you create an inviting atmosphere. That environment in itself is fertile ground for building rapport.

The information you gather from parties' profiles allows you to recognize how each party functions most productively in a working environment. Then when problem-solving issues arise, you are ready to organize material and people to maximize effectiveness. First, consider the best way to give tasks to each party. Then think of how you can create balanced work units among the parties. Take advantage of the skills and knowledge of all parties. Allow the parties to help create the solutions. To maximize results, work with what you know about parties' affiliations, placements, preferences, and operating codes. The parties will do the rest.

Taking Advantage of Party Affiliation

Start your planning by examining each party's strengths and weaknesses in any process as revealed on the profile. Look at people's interests and energies. Begin by examining affiliation and how assembling work group configurations can ignite or extinguish energy. This structure affects performance inside and outside mediation.

Years ago I met a therapist who doubled as a sports coach. Today this is not an exceptional occurrence. In those days it was. One client was a swim coach. His team had an abysmal record for winning. No one could understand why. The team scout brought in real stars; however, most team members' performance hit rock bottom within two months of donning team colors. My colleague decided to watch the swimmers practice. When the coach was not there, the relay team, as usual, swam well. The platform divers were brilliant. Individual swimmers' times also were outstanding. When the coach appeared, relay swimmers' performance remained stable. However, divers' and individual swimmers' performances bottomed out. When the sports coach analyzed the swim coach's communication with the swimmers and divers, he discovered that the coach was neutralizing performance. He told all swimmers that they were a team. He said they all shared each other's successes and failures. This was an encouraging message for the relay swimmers, who had an affiliation for working as a team. Unfortunately, it extinguished the fire in the belly of individual divers and swimmers, who needed to be stars.

Like this coach, you can fire up creativity in parties. You can also neutralize it. You make the difference by recognizing people's affiliation structures. You can then set up the most effective ways for parties to work as they craft the offer. I look at people's affiliation patterns and then create *loner, group,* or *collaborator* configurations. My focus is on building the most effective environment in which parties can operate and eventually design final agreement terms.

Affiliation relates to two variables: who has the responsibility and who executes the job. As discussed in Step Four, loners like responsibility if it originates with them. They like to execute the job. They must work in isolation to be most effective. They get uneasy and become less productive when they are forced to work with others. Group affiliators seek to share execution of a job. They want to distribute responsibility too. They love being a part of a team or collective that shares. Collaborators want to take on responsibility by themselves. They also prefer to do the job themselves; however, they allow other people to be around who are necessary for the job to exist.

In the case of the swim team, the platform divers were loners. They wanted individual responsibility. They executed the dives themselves. In practice sessions these athletes climbed the stairs, mounted the diving platform, set up the dive, executed it, and swam out of the pool. They repeated this action thousands of times. They did it by themselves. When the coach talked to them in terms of "team," it neutralized these divers. If they had been group affiliators in the first place, they would not have had the innate ability to practice and perform the way they had to to be successful. The swim coach needed to talk to them as individuals. He would have benefited from using the word "you." He should have eliminated any reference to "team," "joint effort," or "us."

Conversely, the relay team swimmers functioned as a team. The relay is an interdependent activity. Everyone had to perform well for the team to win. These swimmers would have flourished being addressed as "group" and "team." The people who gravitate to this sport are likely to be hard-wired to respond as group affiliators.

Swimmers who do individual heats can be loners if they are swimming only to beat their personal best time. Usually this is not the case. They do want to take responsibility and execute the job; however, they also need other swimmers around for competition. In this case, the swim coach should have talked to these collaborative affiliators as "you" or "you and [someone else]." He needed to avoid using the terms "team," "us," and "we."

Now fit these concepts into your planning when you create working units. Loner affiliators do understand social and business hierarchies. They just do not want to be in them. They are not wired for establishing rapport, and they do not make good bosses. In mediation, I suggest you avoid putting these people in charge of a group that must create a solution. Also keep them away from group affiliators. Each of these affiliations frustrates the other. Loners also ignore collaborators. As a result, I suggest you isolate loners as much as possible. Assign them separate tasks. Then bring their contributions to the table and combine these results with the results of others.

Group affiliators do not really understand the boss hierarchy. They have an innate reaction against being a boss or being bossed. They want to share. Let them work together so they can experience the task jointly and then celebrate the success of doing something together. When group affiliators cannot interact with others, they feel lost. However, they annoy loners and collaborators because they always want to share ideas and jobs with them. Loner and collaborator affiliators are unhappy working with group affiliators, and their efforts can be neutralized by this work arrangement.

Collaborators understand social and work hierarchies. They often make the best bosses. They tend to make the most effective managers. If you put them together with either of the other types of affiliators, they want to be in charge. This may cause friction with loners so, again, loners should be allowed to work by themselves. You can also put collaborators together with other collaborators who have individual jobs. Together, their individual totals become the successful solution.

Whether parties are working to find solutions during mediation or crafting a final offer, their affiliation communication structure will influence how well and how quickly the task is completed. When you have a choice about configuring work units, for greatest efficiency and least friction, separate each affiliation group. When you must enlist the efforts of all parties to find a solution or create the final agreement, break down the total job into separate components. Assign some tasks to individual loners who will each work independently. Give other tasks to a collective of people who are group affiliators, so they can work together on them. Give the final set of tasks to a group of collaborative affiliators, who will work with each other to complete the assignment. At a specified time, assemble all the people so their results can be combined to create the final solution.

Maximizing Party Effectiveness

Continue your planning by considering people's placement along the work line. Are they starters, maintainers, or completers? Parties who are *starters* are particularly interested in the initial stage of mediation. During the mediation, they like to start tasks. For example, you can send them a positive message by handing them a quick job to do at the beginning of mediation. The task can be as simple as asking them to close the door so the session can begin. With that task you send an other-than-conscious message acknowledging their starter placement. You can count on starters to be the most productive people in start-up and brainstorming environments. They are the sprinters of mediation. You need also to be aware that they often lose interest quickly once this part of the process is off the drawing board. They sometimes avoid finishing. They have the lowest need for completion of the three placement groups. You may have to nudge them with remarks like, "As soon as we've finished this part, *we can start* [another part]." They need other-than-conscious communication that closing always leads to starting something else.

Maintainers like to be in the position of keeping the status quo. Outside mediation they thrive in jobs that revolve around maintaining a process. They often feel uncomfortable or even overwhelmed if asked to initiate programs. They avoid closing down or terminating processes. In a mediation you might need to light a fire under these parties. You might do this by asking them,

"Would you take over from me to explain [an area]?" With this phrasing, you have inserted them, other-than-consciously, into the middle of a process. Once you have done that, you can rely on them to be the long-distance runners of the process. You need to keep an eye on them toward the end of mediation, however. You might need to prompt them to move to closure. You might do this by saying, "Once we have completed this, you can look forward to an *ongoing* sense of satisfaction."

Completers like closure. They are like the last leg of a relay team. You can count on them to be most productive at times when the mediation or a task needs completion. They have a high need for finishing. They pick up speed at the end. These are the people who do not like starting a crossword puzzle but love filling in the last few words. Your challenge with this group is to move them out of inertia into the completion frame of mind. During your communication with this group you can foster creativity by doing several small things. Always talk in terms of finishing and closing. You can periodically ask them if they would give a flip chart page a "last" look before you turn it. You can hand them something to read so they give it the "final" review before it is approved.

In a multiparty mediation, you can arrange working groups so they contain starters, maintainers, and completers. Balance people's strengths and weaknesses so that the group as a whole can manage all three process stages. If you are working with a limited number of people, you can still balance the work by the way you task parties. Stay aware of parties' intuitive placements. Then call upon each type of placement to bring strength and energy to the process at the time when another type of placement might start to falter or when interest could flag. Use people's strengths effectively. Notice their weaknesses assiduously. Guide the process by balancing placements.

Capitalizing on Working Preferences

Planning for creative problem solving also requires looking at each party's preference for working with people, objects, or systems. This consideration is relevant for putting people in the right jobs during mediation. It relates to how parties organize information mentally. This preference shows where parties focus their attention as they do tasks.

Parties with a preference for working with people, pay attention to others at the table. They make sense out of their worlds according to the communication of the people with whom they are involved. For them, a task is secondary to the people doing it. They are naturals for working with other people. Have them work with each other.

People who prefer to work with objects focus on products, tools, or other items. This preference indicates their deep structure. It relates to how they receive and organize information. If you put this group together with the first group, the first group would perceive the second as detached or unfeeling. Yet this would not be accurate. People by themselves simply hold no fascination for those who prefer to deal with objects. Accordingly, when you plan work groups, consider the tasks. Decide what the various jobs will be by looking at how each party intuitively works. Then give each group separate assignments focusing on the same issue.

Consider the example of a mediation I held with a landlord and tenant. The conflict centered ostensibly around chronically late rent payments. The tenant always deposited the money in the property management box at the end of the second day of each month. The landlord had two choices. He could make two bank deposits, or he could delay depositing all the tenants' checks until the late payment arrived. The landlord was angry because he could not start eviction proceedings until rent was overdue for a much longer period of time. The tenant did not see any problem. The landlord always got his money. Besides, the tenant believed that what he did was reasonable. For months he had been submitting requests for repairs. The landlord always took at least two weeks to do any of them. The tenant was frustrated. He was forced to take time away from his family to do many of the repairs himself. After I listened to the parties and examined their profiles, I isolated their preferences. I saw the solution clearly existing within the parties themselves. The tenant had a preference for working with people. The landlord had a preference for working with objects. As a result, I asked both to come up with a solution. I requested the tenant to focus on finding the part of the solution that would create satisfaction for the landlord. I tasked the landlord to come up with the part of the solution that would get his payments handed in on the first of the month. Eventually they both arrived at a solution. As long as the tenant delivered the rent by the first of the month, the landlord would not have to deal with the tenant. That meant he would not have a job that dealt with people. The landlord committed to repairing the tenant's townhouse, personally, within forty-eight hours of a maintenance request. That meant the landlord could deal with things. That also meant that the tenant would now have his personal time back to spend with his family. He could be with people.

Finally, people who prefer to work with systems like to work with many parts to create a new whole. They pay attention to the elements that have the potential to form parts of their new system. Their preference does not reflect a lack of interest in the well-being of people. Rather, parties who show a preference for systems are simply indicating that they absorb and organize information in a specific way. For example, look at the talent these people bring to a mediation that involves creating child visitation schedules. They have a natural ability to work out timetables. Intuitively, these people are able to absorb all the information about people, times, and places. They also know how to organize it and work it into a smooth process.

Every preference brings valuable qualities to mediation. Together they create a pool of intuitive abilities to create solutions. I suggest you take advantage of the competencies each party brings to the table. Each preference can satisfy a different need. Together they can help form a complete solution.

Working with Operating Codes

The fourth component of work team configuration is operating codes, or codes of conduct. Managing this element is vital to rapport. In Step Four you read how to differentiate these codes. At this stage you put your knowledge to work. How people view operating codes affects how they interact with each other—whether they insist on the same rules for everyone, allow different parties to have their own sets of rules, or have no rules at all. You must pinpoint parties' codes of conduct and their codes for others. Operating codes affect the tasks you give to parties. They tell you whether parties can work well together or whether their communication structures clash. Operating codes also have an impact on how parties view the mediation.

The most common combinations, or structures, of operating codes I identified in Step Four (with the party's own code first and the code of others second) were definite-definite, definite-variable, variable-definite, and definite–no code. The definite-definite structure is valuable in mediation. About 75 to 80 percent of the parties I have encountered in mediation fall into this category. Parties with this structure believe everyone is "playing by the rules." These parties work well with others who have the same structure. They can also work with parties who have a definite-variable combination. Although they can work with people who have a variable-definite combination, they can feel a bit uneasy with them. They cannot work with parties who have a definite–no code combination. The interaction is poor. The two parties are not able to relate to each other. Tensions are heightened. Do your best to keep these parties apart.

Parties with a definite-variable structure have rules for themselves and recognize that other people's operating codes may vary from theirs. They have a "live and let live" mind-set, and they tend to take democratic approaches. Although they can work with anyone, they work best with parties who have the same combination they do. They are a little less productive with parties who have a definite-definite structure because the lack of flexibility of the definite-definite group sometimes slows down people with the definite-variable combination. Definite-variable people can work with variable-definite people. The latter accommodate the former. They can work even with the definite–no code group. A definite-variable structure accommodates everyone else's rules.

Parties with a variable-definite combination make up the most adaptive group of people. They start with a flexible code of conduct for themselves. Although they know that other people have specific operating codes of conduct, they have a deep structure that says, "Other people's code is my code." Accordingly, people in this group accommodate the people or groups they encounter. They assume the codes of others. They go whichever way the wind blows. In business they tend to withstand sweeping corporate terminations because they can be chameleons. They tend to function well as civil servants, persisting through changes in governments. Their attitude is laissez faire. This allows them to work through changes. It allows them to transform their operating codes to fit the different styles of people giving them instructions. In mediation they can assume the structure and set of rules of parties with whom they are working.

Parties with a definite–no code combination identify a clear operating code of conduct for themselves and do not even acknowledge other people's codes. These parties make their own rules. Their concern centers around themselves. In mediation, no other party seems to register. If you can arrange to segregate these parties from other working groups, you may find that most productive. If you do want to create a working unit that includes definite–no code parties, you can match them with parties with a variable code element. Just keep in mind that no code parties do not care. I suggest you pay particular attention during mediation to parties with this combination. They appear to be without conscience. This appearance has the potential to derail working units.

Work gets done if definite–no code parties want it to be done. It does not get done if these parties fight it. You might consider using the polarity response technique here. For this procedure to work well, these parties must react strongly to comments like, "I'm sure you couldn't work with Mr. Jones to come up with a solution." That is, the parties must have a forceful enough polarity response to overcome the response that results from their lack of a code of conduct. My experience is that the polarity response has to be exceptionally powerful to do this.

In addition to prodding the polarity response, you can use a party's view of success to set up a situation in which cooperating appears more attractive than not cooperating. Here is one example of how I execute this in these circumstances. I introduce an idea to Party A, in this example the no code party. I ask her what a successful solution means to her. Her answers will revolve around her perceptions as they relate to her self-interest. I have collected her touchstones, and I now use them. I advise her that success— *as she defines it*—will come only when she and Party B are using a common code of conduct. The code they share can be their choice. I tell her that if there is no common code of conduct, both parties will fail. If both parties fail, clearly that will mean that Party

A has failed. At this point I have attached Party A's achievement to joint success. I have also glued Party A's failure to lack of joint success. Because Party A's self-interest seeks success, she must make a real effort to share a code with Party B. That means including Party B's ideas or the success will not be joint. In this equation, a single party's accomplishment is deemed failure. Therefore, if the success is not joint, Party A is working against herself and her own success. Party A must work constructively with Party B to be successful by her own definition.

Triggering Action

As the mediation proceeds, you can use nonverbal communication to foster exchanges that are critical to a satisfactory process. You can assist the parties to talk about the real issues, to build momentum, to get back on track after derailments, to remain focused, and at the same time to remain flexible, willing to exercise creativity in the interests of resolving the genuine core issues.

Coming Face-to-Face with the Real Issues

Engaging the parties in productive discussion about the real issues that brought the parties to mediation requires an approach that considers parties' sensitivity, their fear, and their true goals. Staying alert to the nonverbal messages parties are sending is vital. Sending fitting messages back and adapting your approach to the parties' needs can mean the difference between a successful and an unsuccessful mediation.

Seeing the Upsides and Downsides of Specificity

When I first entered the field of mediation, I observed many sessions. All were learning experiences. Most were routine. Some stood out. One I remember particularly involved a young woman. She had been injured in a mill accident. The result was a disfiguring, permanent injury. Plastic surgery could not restore her body to its original condition. The injury had affected her mobility considerably. She could no longer do work requiring her to stand. The injury had affected the intimate relationship she had with her fiancé. The mediator in this case was a former judge. She prized herself on being incisive. She believed that "cutting to the chase" was the most effective way to trigger parties to move toward settlement. After both counsels' opening statements, the mediator mildly acknowledged the injured party and the fiancé. She then decided to list key issues on a flip chart. Instead of talking to the young woman and looking at her, she talked directly to the injured party's lawyer and looked at him. She asked, "How do you think we should start? Should we say that this woman can never expect to have a normal life with a man or that she has a permanent disfigurement?"

As a mediator you make judgment calls about communication throughout the conflict resolution process. One thing you must decide is how pointed or oblique to be about approaching issues. On the one hand, specificity allows you to focus in minute detail. If you use the onionskinning technique you can narrow matters down to the smallest element. On the other hand, the Columbo technique gives you the latitude of approaching matters in an indirect way. You take your time circling around issues until both you and the parties are ready to get specific.

Many mediators are often tempted to cut through preliminaries. They want to get to the nugget of the issues as rapidly as possible. They ignore the parties in front of them. They believe that speed equals effectiveness. Isolating issues too quickly, however, may be counterproductive in the long run. Parties need to work at their own rhythm in order to deal with core issues. Moving more slowly at the beginning of mediation may ensure that all parties are still around at the end of the process.

I suggest you start with general questions. Move inward with more and more detailed queries. Keep getting more specific until you meet resistance. When you do, stop. When you encounter opposition, you have probably hit pay dirt. You have struck a core issue. You will recognize resistance through nonverbal cues. This part of the process requires you to pay a great deal of attention to the physical signals parties are sending. Watch people. They display coloration changes. Their breathing changes. They push back from the table. They clench their fists. These are all signals to you to back off that issue. Move to another area. Again ask general questions first and then move inward. Repeat the exercise until you hit resistance. Continue this routine until you have compiled a list of core issues. These are the interests that parties want to deal with at mediation. Let the parties provide the wording of these issues. That way you know exactly how specific or general to be.

Pinpointing the Fear

Sometimes people choose to believe in ideas that bring them comfort. They prefer to ignore things that frighten them. They convince themselves that if they do not acknowledge an issue, it does not really exist. You may have experienced this yourself. Have you ever been in a situation in which people were talking all around a subject? They skirted the issue that was really on their minds. You knew it. They knew it. The matter they did not discuss is sometimes referred to as the *elephant in the middle of the room.* It looms like a large and dangerous creature, but no one wants to admit it is there. Conceding its existence would acknowledge its danger.

Often people come to mediation with a sense of fear. This fear is usually unspoken. It is frequently the underlying force that drives the communication of some parties during mediation. If it is not dealt with effectively, it can stall the session. The fear may relate to the mediation process. It may also relate to an issue within the process. Unless you deal with the fear, the most you can elicit from mediation is *settlement.* You must handle the fear if you have any intention of arriving at *resolution.*

As a mediator you are neutral. This neutrality puts you in an ideal position to notice unusual cues or tension that parties exhibit. The most important indicator of fear is the *absence* of the typical communication that should be taking place. Be particularly alert when normal interactions are not happening. Those missing cues are often a mark of fear. Additionally, you need to sort out cultural mores from signals of fear. For example, you may notice parties who look at each other directly then immediately look away or down. You need to establish whether this pattern is a cultural norm or a signal of fear.

As a mediator you will come up against the signs of fear in many forms. You will see people's muscles stiffen before they talk about a fear. They avoid eye contact. Their breathing comes from high in the chest. Their respiration is shallow and rapid. They often become pale. They also frequently shake. Their voices quiver.

They perspire. They look ready to bolt. Therapists often say that their job is to articulate the patient's fear. You, however, are not a therapist. Your job revolves around facilitating a conflict resolution process. That notwithstanding, there are times when it is in the best interests of the process, as well as the parties, to articulate the fear. You may decide to raise the issue if the parties cannot or will not.

Be careful in flagging a core issue. Fear manifests at many levels. Though you may be able to spot the nonverbal signals, you cannot know which level of fear a person is experiencing. You can, however, begin to change your own breathing to deep diaphragmatic inhalations and exhalations. You can inhale and exhale audibly. Let parties see you drop your shoulders and body in general as you relax your muscles to a greater and greater degree. Relax the muscles in your face. Talk slowly. Speak in a low register. Calm parties by your nonverbal signals. All these other-than-conscious cues mentally assist fearful parties to face real issues.

If you are going to ask people about fear, avoid putting words in their mouths. If you suggest things about which you think they are afraid, you may implant more fear and tension. I recommend you approach the subject cautiously. Look at the example of a medical colleague of mine who works with accident victims. She often says to severely injured patients, "It must be a little scary thinking about what is going to happen after you leave the hospital." She acknowledges the existing fear. She refrains from naming that fear. She allows the patient to name it. All the while, she uses minimizing language to deescalate the fear. In mediation I follow her example to acknowledge and deescalate. For example, once parties have shown nonverbal signals of fear, I might say, "I recognize I'm only the observer here. You are the expert. I certainly haven't gone through your experience. I'm only guessing that if I had been in your position, I would have been scared."

I recommend you practice using statements like, "I'm not sure if I can appreciate your experience fully," and, "I personally have not gone through what you have. I can only search my own experiences for something that I can relate to it. Even then, it may not have been the same for you." I also recommend you avoid lighting the polarity fuse. That could result in parties' telling you that you do not know what they experienced. I suggest you avoid the statements, "I understand," and, "I know what you've gone through."

Such remarks tend to set off an instant negative reaction in many people.

Above all, watch parties for nonverbal signals. After you acknowledge their fear, you should see their muscles become more relaxed. People often sigh, and their breathing changes. If they offer you words that express their fear, use their exact words when you talk about the fear. Avoid substituting your interpretation of their words. The words they use to name their fear are among their linguistic touchstones. These touchstones represent the parties' feelings and experiences relating to the fear. As in dealing with other touchstones, you do not have to know exactly what the words mean. You just have to use the words in the way the parties use them.

Once people have finished expressing their fear, you can begin to deescalate their language. You can use the *match-pace-guide* technique. You have matched their model of fear by acknowledging it. You did this through nonverbal communication and language. You then paced along with them as they expressed the experience in their own terms. You replicated their words. Now you can guide them. Use breathing and muscle relaxation as you also deescalate language. As you move the language down a level, you are not minimizing the importance of the fear or the event. You are simply reducing the level of fear. That assists parties to operate more productively.

Isolating the Real Goal

The next step in facing the real issues is being able to isolate the true objectives of each party. Most parties are consciously aware of their goals. They do not necessarily want to articulate them in the mediation session. Some parties have outcomes that exist outside their awareness. If you do not discern the real issues that concern the parties, two things often happen. The first consequence is that the mediating parties do not reach resolution. The second is that a meditation you thought was completed blows apart as you leave the room.

When most mediators question the parties, they focus on the text of the answers. They do not pay much attention to *how* parties communicate *about* the issues. As a result, many mediators miss people's real goals. To avoid this oversight, I suggest you perform two concurrent activities. Verbally canvass parties for issues. As they articulate them, use either the Columbo or onionskinning technique to get to the core issues and objectives. During this process, pay attention to people's nonverbal communication. Watch for congruency in nonverbal and verbal information.

Two issues can be especially tricky to isolate: *wedding dresses* and *doorknob* issues. The wedding dress is the easier incongruity to detect early. It is a hidden issue, usually an unexplained sum buried in a party's settlement request. The amount does not correlate to any item that has been verified by the party. When you notice an unexplained, isolated amount, I suggest you ask for a caucus. In caucus, I recommend you do some onionskinning. Watch and listen to the party. See whether there is a change as she reviews her method of calculation. I have noticed that parties who explain valid calculations demonstrate congruent verbal and nonverbal messages. All their communication is fluid. They tend to operate in their preferred system. They move through the different segments of figuring easily. As soon as they come to an unaccounted for item—the wedding dress—their communication shifts. The key to noticing the change is hearing the difference in voice rhythm. The cadence is altered, sometimes becoming halting. The party's voice tone changes too. Often the tension of the situation tightens the vocal cords. Pitch often rises slightly. Muscles become tense. Word pace changes. Usually skin coloration becomes either very flushed or very pale. Sometimes perspiration becomes visible.

You have choices to make at this juncture. You might tell the party that other-than-conscious cues alerted you to incongruity. You might also say this type of incongruity often accompanies unfounded claims. Doing either of these, however, is discourteous on conscious and other-than-conscious levels. You might also allow the party to continue to make claims for the unexplained amount. However, that can bring about negative consequences too. I have learned that it is in everyone's best interests for the mediator to resolve a wedding dress issue in caucus. If this is not done, mediations that might have settled may terminate because a party cannot explain a monetary discrepancy.

I use the same approach I use with other nonverbal cues I flag during mediation. I refrain from pointing out other-than-conscious messages to the party. I simply notice the signals and work with them. When I notice a wedding dress, I recognize that the party is the expert about this kind of item. The party already knows she cannot justify it in the same way she can substantiate legitimate claims. My job is to alert her to the consequences of continuing an unfounded request. I tend to use a Columbo approach in talking to the party. I tell her I am neutral. I have no vested interested in her request. I do explain the risk. For example, here is how I approached a group of people with a wedding dress item. This took place during a caucus.

> I recognize that this amount seems important to you. You say you deserve it as part of your settlement from this accident. [*I acknowledged their claim.*]
>
> You have been good enough to show me how all your other financial details fit into your request. I believe it is only right for me to say that I noticed you changed the way you were explaining this amount to me. You accounted for it in a different way than your other expenses. You were really clear about the other expenses. You seemed vague about this. [*I alerted the parties twice that someone noticed a difference between the questionable item and the rest of the claim.*]
>
> I apologize. I guess I'm just a little slow about numbers sometimes. I'm still not sure how you arrived at this amount. [*I used the Columbo technique to give the parties an out if they wanted to say they made a mistake. I gave them an opportunity to change the calculation and put it back on track.*]
>
> Is there something you want to tell me that could help me understand your request? Then I could perhaps help to explain it to the other side. [*I gave the parties the opportunity to tell me about the "wedding dress."*]
>
> I regret to say that if I cannot make sense of it, I cannot do much to help you explain it to the other side. [*I let the parties know that if they continue with this claim, I cannot help them move forward with it.*] More than that, if the other side does not see your point, I have a concern that you may appear uncooperative or unreasonable. [*I used the word "appear" to avoid pointing a finger and saying the parties were in fact uncooperative or unreasonable.*] That would certainly work against your best interests to reach resolution. [*I again alerted the parties. This time I let them know that they must evaluate what they might get against what they might lose.*]

At that point I stopped. I began to breathe slowly and evenly. I matched the body posture of the dominant member of the group. I mirrored his head and finger movements. I matched his eye patterns. Mostly, I left the responsibility of deciding what to do with the parties. They could continue with the unfounded claim and risk the mediation or drop it.

I had done my job. I had noticed these parties' incongruity. I had stopped the mediation session. I had caucused with the group. I had alerted them to a noticeable change when they discussed the issue. I had told them this change could affect them negatively. I had given them the choice to tell me about their wedding dress or not. I waited silently until they spoke. In the end they told me about a business debt they had incurred in the last three months. They thought they could make up the loss out of the mediation proceeds. After a very focused discussion they decided to abandon this part of the claim. They realized it had nothing to do with the mediation. The parties to the mediation settled.

The doorknob issue comes up after you believe all issues have been settled. It is a matter parties have not raised during mediation for various reasons. Sometimes parties are intimidated by the mediation environment. Sometimes they feel afraid to raise the issue. Sometimes they are ashamed to ask about it. Sometimes they want to leave it to the end.

This matter can be the most important mediation issue for the party disclosing it. Because it has the potential to derail settlement if it is dismissed, mediators faced with this situation must reopen mediation. If the issue is not resolved, agreement could fall apart. Parties might suffer buyer's remorse. It must be resolved for settlement to be durable and satisfactory for all parties.

You can minimize doorknob issues by thoroughly questioning parties right at the beginning of mediation. First establish their yes and no nonverbal cue chains as described earlier. Then collect parties' language touchstones, asking, "What issues are important to you in this mediation?" and, "What will having [these things] do for you?" Use the touchstones you gather to canvass each party about his or her issues.

After parties say they have finished giving you all their issues, ask one more time if there are further issues. The parties will answer yes or no verbally and nonverbally. When a party signals congruent verbal and nonverbal agreement, move to the next party. If a party says yes but demonstrates no nonverbally, give the person some leeway. I usually say something like, "That is helpful for now. I'd like to ask you to feel free to come up with other issues later. Sometimes ideas need time to crystalize. You might remember something in a while that you'd like to talk about. Please be comfortable adding something to your list. As a matter of fact, I invite everyone at the table to do the same." At that point, I move on to the next party.

After you have gone around the table, return to the party with the incongruent verbal and nonverbal signals. Ask about issues again. Sometimes parties just need a little time to feel safe enough in the mediation environment to articulate their points. Sometimes they will say that the other side has already raised the issue. At this time, again ask a yes or no question like, "So have I now listed all the issues that you'd like covered?" If you continue to get a nonverbal no, keep checking with the party during mediation and caucus sessions. (Caucus is an especially fertile place to unearth people's concerns.) Keep asking parties about issues until you get congruent agreement. Until then, be aware that there might be a simmering matter that could boil over at any time.

When parties are ready to execute a final agreement, question each party one more time. I do this even if I believe all issues have been addressed. That way I know I have explored as many core issues as possible. If you fail to get a congruent yes from someone at this point, I suggest you make one more effort in caucus to elicit the hidden issue before people put pen to paper.

Enabling the Parties to Build Momentum

After canvassing the parties and examining core issues, you need another set of mechanisms to get parties moving forward to resolution. In an ideal world you could push a button, and parties would move ahead by themselves. In the real world of mediation you must enable the parties to create momentum. When parties believe they have created the environment for resolution, agreement is much easier to reach and retain.

There are four key strategies I suggest you consider. In the first, you create an environment that makes use of parties' tendencies to either act or react. In the second you highlight issue similarities and differences, and in the third you frame discussions as movements toward goals and away from problems. The fourth is helping parties remember events.

Giving Parties a Chance to Act or React

In mediation parties who are *active initiators* talk about "doing," "taking hold of," and "playing at." Their language reflects actions that they undertake. They dig into situations. Their nonverbal communication is animated too. They move their faces and bodies. Their voices sing out different qualities. In contrast, you will hear *reactive initiators* using the passive voice and seeing themselves as the object of events and actions. For example, they say things like, "An idea occurred to me," or, "It happened out of the blue." Their nonverbal cues parallel their verbal patterns. They exhibit few changes in body movement or voice quality. Life happens to them. Their verbal and nonverbal communication reflects that.

Active initiators are the people who typically undertake tasks first. They tend to believe that they make things happen. Reactive initiators usually need something to happen first. That way they can react (against it). When you tell active initiators to brainstorm, they start right away. Reactive initiators need you to supply an idea they can use as a springboard.

This is the way I interact with each type of initiator once I have determined an issue to be resolved. By just identifying it to active initiators, I can mobilize them. I might say to them, "Here's the issue. We're looking for solutions. See what you come up with." As I am using these words, I match their nonverbal cues by being energized. I mobilize my face and body movements. Identifying an issue is not enough to move reactive initiators, however. To enable reactive initiators to build momentum, I slow down. I match their nonverbal signals and become as inanimate as possible. I relax the muscles of my face and body to signal them that a reactive message is coming. I decrease my breathing rate. I take a deep breath and exhale. I also know I need to give parties something verbal against which they can react. I match my lack of physical expression with words like these, "We ended up with this issue [*that is, it happened to us*]." "It landed on our doorstep [*again, it happened to us*]. What can be done about it [*that is, how can we react*]?"

If you are dealing with people who demonstrate both initiator types, notice the order that parties use. Then use both active and reactive messages in the same order. For example, you might say, "Let's get creative [*active*]. Although this wasn't our first choice, we are faced with dealing with these issues [*reactive*]." You would also use the corresponding nonverbal communication concurrently. By creating this environment, you encourage parties to build momentum themselves.

Highlighting Similarity and Difference

In the 1970s, a television network decided to bring on board a new news anchor. The former news anchor was retiring. The new anchor was already known to the public as a newscaster. His appeal was already high. The network's evening national news broadcast was particularly popular in one major U.S. market, and the advertising people promoting the changeover decided to flood one city with these media messages: "A new type of news." "Nothing like it before." "Not your same old news." "It will be unique." In the new anchor's first week, ratings plummeted. The advertising campaign was pulled immediately. On Sunday morning a new campaign began with this message: "The same reliable news. A person you have known and trusted for years." Ratings returned to normal in weeks. The advertising experts had failed miserably in their original campaign. They had not understood how much the population gravitates toward similarity.

In mediation you have to consider people's working frameworks to know what will help them create momentum. One element to consider is their perception of *similarity* and *difference*. Pinpointing this perception is critical. You need to know in which direction parties intuitively move. That direction triggers action. Action builds momentum toward a final resolution.

I have noticed that people who talk about *similarity* see only what fits a pattern. They filter out what does not fit. They cannot recognize subtle change. They want things to remain the same. If they are put in a position in which they are forced to acknowledge some difference, they rebel or resist. People who talk about *similarity with exceptions,* see a basic pattern. Then they notice the exceptions. They like similarity yet still acknowledge differences or variation. They like normalcy and calmness yet they can adapt as changes come along, as long as the changes are not too frequent. Once they have learned to do something, they like to continue to do it for a while.

People who talk about *difference* do not identify a basic pattern. All they see are distinctions. They look for complete change constantly. They need new activities. They like change for change's sake. They must have significant variation all the time. They are bored once they have learned something. They want to move on. People who talk about *difference with exceptions* first see things that do not fit a pattern. Then they notice a pattern in the background. They look for changes accompanied by a few similarities. They need significant change every so often. If they get it, they accept some similarities with it. Once they have learned something, they also start searching for new things.

When mediation discussions are being held, people will home in on similarities or differences from past conversations. The one they recognize depends on their respective perceptions. When you are assisting parties to reach agreements, you must match each person's model of similarity or difference. If you do not, people will feel uncomfortable or reject an idea outright. To assist parties to build momentum, point out information in the discussion that relates to their perception. If they want similarity, point out what is the same. Use expressions like "same," "similar," "just like," "identical to," "matches exactly," "clone," "carbon copy," and "replication." When parties need to see differences, show them what has changed from the last conversation. Use expressions like "different as night and day," "variety," "variation," "exclusive," "unique," "one of a kind," "unparalleled," "in its own class," and "broke the mold." If parties want a little of both, show them what is the same and what is different by using "more" and "less" and other comparatives ("newer," "quicker"). Likewise, later in the mediation you can move parties forward by highlighting the offer's value in terms that parties understand.

Framing Issues as Movement Toward Goals and Away from Problems

The next step you can take is to frame issues in terms of parties' habitual mental movement. Intuitively, people think in terms of either moving *toward* solutions or moving *away* from problems. After you identify mental movement types, interact with toward mental movers by structuring information in terms of reaching a goal. Talk about "attaining the next level," "moving through each point until you are done," and "reaching a satisfactory conclusion." Speak to away mental movers by referring to "eliminating unnecessary work," "pushing away from situations that were not worthwhile," and "getting as far away as possible from this situation." You may want to combine the two elements when you are talking to both types of parties concurrently. You might use an expression like "find a solution that provides protection."

Once you identify each party's framework, you can also forecast how each party will generally approach situations and specifically view the final agreement. You will know that some parties will be motivated to settle because they view resolution as a goal. Others will be propelled to settle because they see resolution as a way to get away from a troublesome issue or to avoid future or additional problems.

Discussing issues effectively invites parties to view ideas as a set of goals or a set of avoidance mechanisms. If you want parties to look at a mediation issue in terms of goals, use terms like "objectives," "what you were shooting for," "hits your target," "meets your needs," and "fulfills your wish list." Structure issues differently for people with an away mental movement, however. In this case, talk about "erasing those charges you didn't want," "getting around the problem of," "avoiding having to deal with," "bypassing the areas of," and "eliminating the situation."

When dealing with both types of parties, remember that toward parties push for solutions. Outwardly they seem to be more positive. Although away parties appear to be deal breakers, they also assist the process. They ensure that all potential problem areas of an issue are covered and resolved so that buyer's remorse is eliminated.

Helping Parties Remember

Another major step in enabling parties to build momentum is assisting them to remember events important to the mediation process as quickly and easily as possible. To accomplish this you need to know how people remember events. Some people are able to recall events in random order. That means they can grab a memory instantly. Others remember sequentially. To remember something specific they must start from the present and inspect every event in order.

When dealing with parties who remember randomly, recognize that they access memories easily. Past events are seen as separate from each other and can be pulled out at will. These parties have the ability to move back and forth to any occurrence that happened at any time. They never seem to forget. If you need these parties to recall information, simply ask them for it.

When you deal with parties who remember sequentially, you must allow them to start in the present and go back in time through every event that seems related to the memory until they reach the specific memory they need. When I work with these parties, I acknowledge that remembering is difficult for them. You might want to do that too. Also stay aware that they may forget many things. You can assist these parties by asking them to break their lives (or business lives or certain series of events) into chunks of time. Then invite them to do a fast rewind of the sequence of events in a given chunk. This process immediately speeds them through many incidents unrelated to the required memory. It moves to the relevant event much more quickly and effortlessly. It is less tiring for other parties too.

When both types of parties are at the table, remain alert for frictions that can arise. Parties who remember sequentially may become frustrated and fatigued. Parties who remember randomly can become annoyed that other parties seem conveniently forgetful.

Dealing with Derailments

When you are in the midst of mediation, some contentious issues are articulated. Some are not. You must stay alert for signals that demonstrate the parties have unspoken issues. Then you must apply techniques to get parties beyond the contentious issues, articulated or unarticulated. This section examines a number of methods for getting people over the hurdles presented by certain issues. It also looks at ways to manage people's different reactions to pressure and maintain their focus and ways to manage time in order to avoid derailments.

Attending to Cues from Systems Outside Awareness

Part of your search for unarticulated issues will involve noticing the nonverbal cues sent outside conscious awareness. These cues are important. Remember that parties send information consciously. They are aware of this communication. Concurrently, they may also be sending nonverbal cues other-than-consciously, using a system they are not employing consciously at that moment. Parties are not aware they are sending these other-than-conscious cues. And, as I have discussed, it is not your job to tell them about cues from that system. Just stay alert for incongruous system signals. Work with those signals. Remember that the other-than-conscious system is less filtered than the conscious system. It is the one that usually can be used most effectively to influence people's communication.

First, look for visual system cues generated outside of awareness. Notice when parties' nonverbal messages do not match their words. For example, watch parties as they talk about something troublesome that they heard. If their eyes go to a visual position (either visual remembered or visual constructed) look more closely. They are giving you a nonverbal cue you should investigate. Although their language indicates awareness only of auditory information, this eye pattern indicates they are accessing visual information. They are being influenced by the visual information outside their conscious awareness. I suggest you trust the nonverbal, other-than-conscious cue as the real influence. As soon as you spot this incongruity, respond appropriately. When the party stops talking, reproduce his eye cues. Concurrently, use a language loop. Start with an auditory expression that matches the party's conscious language. Then move into visual expressions. That way you pace the party. You then continue with visual language. You guide the party into telling you what is on his mind. For example, you might say, "I hear [*auditory*] what you're saying, and I wonder if we can have a look [*visual*] at the situation. Maybe there's another perspective [*visual*] to it. How do you really see [*visual*] things?" You can bring out the real issue and get the mediation back on track.

Auditory influences outside of awareness may threaten the progress of mediation too. When parties are discussing issues, you may see some listening parties consistently move their eyes down and to the left. Often that is a cue that they are not really involved in the current conversation. This eye pattern signals that they are paying more attention to old dialogues or chatter in their minds. This noise may block out the mediation currently underway. These parties are not grounded in the moment. If you spot this pattern, I suggest you immediately get the attention of the party. Make some loud noise. Once you have her attention, talk to her. Have her talk back to you. The party's internal dialogue will cease as soon as she starts to talk. Now shift her focus to a more productive system. Say something like, "I heard [*auditory match*] you say you were OK with this issue. I wonder if we could flesh it out [*kinesthetic lead*] a bit more or look [*visual lead*] at it differently." You match the party's original auditory system. Then you guide her into another system. You may also use kinesthetic or visual cues to lead her into a more productive system for her. Continue to use kinesthetic or visual cues while you are speaking with the party. Be congruent verbally and nonverbally. You want to keep these people out of unproductive internal dialogues by inviting them to operate in another system. Mediation then moves along more productively.

Parties who exhibit kinesthetic system cues outside their consciousness are usually tipped far right in their chairs. Or they rock and sway on their feet. They are experiencing a sensation but are unaware of it. Like the parties who experience the other two systems outside conscious awareness, these people are influenced unknowingly by information they are receiving through the kinesthetic system. Sometimes this effect is useful. Sometimes it is not. When it is not, it can derail the mediation process. When the latter is the case, I suggest that you do the following. First match the party's other-than-conscious cues. For example, you might offer him a cup of coffee. You might put an arm, in an appropriate fashion, on his shoulder. That would connect you other-than-consciously with him. Next, match his linguistic cues. Then lead him into revealing the source of the derailment through another system. That way, the party will not experience any discomfort when dealing with the issue. You might say, "I get a sense [*kinesthetic match*] that we are just scratching the surface [*kinesthetic match*] of this issue. I hear [*auditory lead*] what you say, and I wonder if we could look [*visual lead*] at this a little more. We could highlight [*visual lead*] the events and then talk [*auditory lead*] in detail." You have matched the party's system outside of awareness. You have paced it. Now you have guided the party into a more productive mind-set to move mediation forward.

Using Techniques That Get Beyond Contentious Issues

Milton Erickson was a renown storyteller as well as psychiatrist and founder of the American Society for Clinical Hypnosis. One of his most famous tales is retold by David Gordon and Maribeth Meyers-Anderson in their book *Phoenix*. In this story, Erickson talks about an unbranded runaway horse that trots into a dusty farmyard on a sweltering day. The stray is finally cornered and mounted by a young boy. Within a few minutes the horse and rider disappear down the road. They carry on for quite a distance. Suddenly the animal stops and turns into another farmyard. Standing there is the horse's surprised owner. As the boy dismounts, the owner questions how the boy knew where to stop. The boy responds, "I didn't. I just kept the horse on the road. He knew the way."

In conflict resolution, I have found that parties generally have a sense of where they want to go. Sometimes, however, they get sidetracked. When they do, I usually have to nudge them back on the path to their goals. If a mediation slows down enough, the process can stall. That is a stage you want to avoid. It is easier to speed up a mediation than to restart it.

Sometimes parties are troubled by a matter that is unconnected to the mediation. It interrupts their focus on the process. It distracts them from dealing with the issues. If the distraction continues, the mediation can be derailed. If you spot this type of contentious issue, I suggest you talk to the parties. When the trouble is tied to a specific mediation issue, you need to isolate that matter. If you do not, it can become entangled with other points. Then none of those subjects is available for solution. They are all perceived as attached to each other. If you do not already know what the troublesome subject is, do some onionskinning. Once you have come up with the thorny issue, use one of these techniques.

Crumpled Paper

The easiest way for parties to get rid of the contentious issue is literally to throw it away. I suggest you assist people to do this with the *crumpled paper* technique. Give them pieces of paper and pens. Ask them to "mark on the paper" the thing or things that are bothering them. Sometimes parties are troubled by feelings or things they visualize. When you ask them to commit the niggling issue to paper, you invite them to capture it on paper any way they would like. Avoid using the word "write." Instead, suggest they make any kind of markings they wish. Invite them to tear the paper too if they wish. Wait until they have completed their ideas by writing words, drawing pictures, or tearing the sheet into a shape. When they have finished, ask them to take a good look at the paper. (Each person sees only his or her own paper.) Then request that they all crumple their papers into small wads and toss them into a garbage can. At that point, I recommend you put that trash container outside the room to get the crumpled paper out of sight. When you return, thank the parties for their cooperation and announce that they are ready to move ahead. The vexing matters have been excised from the mediation. They are now relegated to the garbage that has been removed from the room.

I have discovered this technique works well to get mediation back on track. Parties see, hear, and feel their unconnected issues being tossed away. I suggest you use it for a number of reasons. First, it forces parties to separate relevant issues from ideas unconnected to the mediation. Then it encourages parties to jettison those matters that have the potential to undo positive mediation progress. In using this technique you ask the parties to engage in a symbolic and a literal act. You invite parties to materialize abstract thoughts and then discard them.

Marking Out

The technique of *marking out* can also be very useful when parties need to get beyond touchy issues. To set up the environment for this technique, first isolate a physical location in the mediation room. It should be a place in which some positive activity has occurred. Mark out the spot by pointing to it or literally telling parties about it. Reserve a specific tone of voice to use when you are in this positive spot or talking about it. That way, when people hear that tone, they associate it with a positive idea. For example, you might mark out a positive spot by using your selected tone and saying, "Let me just stand here a moment, at the flip chart, and see what good work we've done so far." As a result, each time you use that tone, walk to the flip chart, or refer to the flip chart spot, that spot has been marked out positively on an other-than-conscious level.

Isolate a second area for use when parties hit a contentious issue. It will be the area to which you relegate negative ideas or activities. It will contain all unproductive matters. Mark out that area first on a conscious level. Tell parties, "I always reserve two spots in a mediation room for things that get thrown away. One spot is for garbage. The other is for recyclable substances. Material from the first spot gets tossed out. Items from the second can sometimes be recycled into more useful material." Once you have set up that metaphor, mark out those two spots other-than-consciously. Use a different tone than you used for the positive spot, or use another nonverbal cue. When I use this technique, I use one tone or vocal cue (such as throat clearing) as I refer to the garbage spot. I use another tone or cue (such as pointing with my left hand) to indicate the recycle spot. My words and nonverbal cues separate these negative spots in the minds of parties. You may want to do this too.

Once the positive and negative spots are set up, visit only the positive spot physically. Avoid standing in the garbage or recycle spots. Only point or refer to them. Any time a negative issue comes up, "toss" it into one of the negative locations. When a contentious issue arises, use words, tone, or other nonverbal cues you have already set up to handle the matter, or just point to the garbage or the recycle spots. You might say, "Well, we'll just leave all that stuff over there for now, OK?" If I want to take another, more covert approach, I ask parties how they want to deal with the issue. As I am doing this, *I cue them with the tone or other nonverbal cues I have marked out for garbage or recycle.* This is the most powerful kind of message. Parties receive my other-than-conscious communication clearly. They respond and deposit the issue into the area I direct. The contentious issue is either thrown away or dealt with later more productively.

Backing

When our city was due to experience a total eclipse of the sun, it was a special time. Adults talked about it for days. Children discussed it at school. After dinner one night, a friend's son of nursery school age asked me to explain "how an eclipse worked." Then, as now, I was not much of a scientist. The boy was too little to read. The Internet did not exist. I spotted a penny on the kitchen table and gave it to the boy. I asked him to close his eyes. Then I asked him to bring the penny up to his right eye. I told him to keep his left eye closed, open his right eye, and tell me what he saw. He did all this and then giggled. He said he said he saw just the penny. Next I told him to close both eyes again. I asked him to stretch out the arm holding the penny. Then I asked him to open his right eye again and tell me what he saw. He laughed again and said he saw the whole kitchen. The room was bright, and he saw just about everything in it. Only one small speck of it was blocked "way far away" by the penny. After that, I explained how a total eclipse acted like the penny close to his eye. He could pretend that the penny was the moon. He could imagine the kitchen was the sun. When he did this, he understood how a little moon could block out a big sun.

Parties who are facing derailment or who need to refocus often have one issue blocking their perspective. This issue is like the penny used to simulate an eclipse. The parties have the issue so close that nothing else is visible. When this is the case, I often use the *backing* technique to give people perspective. I ask the parties to stare ahead. I ask if they can see a troublesome issue. They usually respond yes or just nod. Then I ask them if it would be all right if we moved the issue that is distracting them. I explain that it is taking their focus off the mediation. They usually agree. Then I ask them to imagine the issue that is distracting them as an object.

When they nod, I ask if they can pick it up in one hand or two. They usually say one. If they say two, that is fine also. Then I suggest that they slowly move their hand (or hands), picking up the imagined object and then moving it until their hand and the object is behind their heads. I wait until they do it. At that point I ask if they know the issue is there. I wait for a yes. If I do not get it, I tell them we must have dropped the issue along the way. We go back and get it. We do that by repeating the first part of the exercise. Once they acknowledge that the object is behind them, I ask them if they want to place the issue on the napes of their necks or lower. I advise them that they can still reach the issue if they want to. They can see it in the mirror if they look at the backs of their heads. They can even move it back to the front position if they wish. Right now, however, the parties no longer have the issue before their eyes. They can focus on mediation issues.

I recommend this technique when parties lose sight of mediation issues. I believe it is successful because it uses visualization. It also adds a kinesthetic component. Moreover, this technique invites parties to take control of obstacles. It allows them to move a troublesome issue somewhere else without having to abandon it completely. This technique gives parties a new perspective and also lets them retain a feeling of control during mediation.

Magic Button

Continue to invite parties to find their own solutions. When one or more parties cannot see a possible resolution due to an impasse, you can show them how to use the *magic button* technique. This technique invites parties to get creative. It releases them from their preconceived ideas and gives them a license to get beyond their limiting beliefs.

To perform this technique first suggest that the parties take a few deep breaths. Then ask them to relax for a moment. Ask them if it is acceptable to them if you give them a way to get beyond the contentious issue. Wait for their answer. A verbal yes without a nonverbal agreement is not acceptable. Wait another few moments. Sometimes they just need time to feel safe. When you get congruent agreement, move forward. Ask them to continue to breathe evenly. As they are doing that, ask them to imagine a button. Tell them to visualize it as if it were sitting on the table, right in front of them. Have them test the button by pushing on the table. Some will laugh. That is natural.

Next, ask the parties to imagine they can get whatever things they want out of this mediation. All they have to do is push the magic button. They will usually sigh and smile again. They will tell you that is "impossible." Coax them a bit more. Ask them again. As you do this, press down on an imaginary button in front of you. This visual cue is powerful.

I have found that eventually parties actually say what they want. They usually preface their remarks with, "I know I can't have this. What's the use?" Again, I encourage them. They finally verbalize what they want. When they articulate their "impossible" solutions, these thoughts form a basis for moving from an impasse into new stages of resolution. I suggest you do this exercise with all parties. You can do it in caucus. You can do it in the mediation room. Sometimes I find it exceptionally productive for each party to hear the other's wishes. You must judge what is appropriate for the circumstances of each mediation yourself. Once you have the parties' responses, you can begin working with their answers. Their cards are on the table. All parties can now deal with the contentious issues in the context of resolution.

Hanging Balloons

When parties cannot overcome issues by themselves, you can assist them by suspending the contentious issue. You can do this using the *hanging balloon* technique. I suggest you use this approach with a raised issue that is important but not applicable to the material under discussion at the moment. To execute this strategy, I suggest you first acknowledge the broached subject. You must let parties articulating the issue know that you believe the matter has significance. You must also let them appreciate that you want their permission to suspend the issue for a while. I often approach the subject as follows:

> I recognize this is an important point. I also can tell that we are dealing with an important matter right now. If we were to explore the issue you are raising, it might take us off track. [*Saying the "issue you are raising" rather than "your issue" separates the issue from the person.*] Then we would not have a chance to resolve the matter at hand. That wouldn't be satisfactory for either party.

> With your permission [*this phrase is rhetorical here*] I am going to suspend this issue [*saying "this issue" rather than "your issue" reinforces the idea of choosing "something" rather than "someone"*] "up here" for now. [*I hang the issue up as if it were a balloon.*]
>
> When it is appropriate, I will again bring this issue to the table, where it can get the full attention it deserves.

In using this technique, you acknowledge the party raising the issue. You carry parties beyond the contentious issue. And you finish dealing with the matter at hand. On a practical note, I suggest you make a note of the issue you have suspended, to remind yourself to "pull down" the point in question whenever it is most productive to do so. If I have more than one item to put aside for a while, I hang as many balloons as necessary, in a row. Then I choose the most effective time to bring down each balloon and reintroduce the topic. Sometimes the mediation progresses so positively that these troublesome matters become nonissues by the end of the process. In those cases, I just leave balloons to float away on their own.

As If

A related method is the *as if* technique. Ask the parties for permission to do an exercise with them. Tell them that this an activity that allows them to operate temporarily as if the problem has been solved. Explain that they will be able to deal with other points first and then come back to the issue that is holding them at bay. Reassure them. Tell them this technique has helped other parties overcome obstacles and reach resolution. The parties may resist at the beginning. When they become frustrated enough, however, they usually agree to any technique that might get them beyond an impasse.

Once you have their permission to proceed, ask them to close their eyes and breathe deeply a few times. Request that they relax for a few moments. Now ask them to imagine that it is a time in the future. The time could be a long time from now. It could be a short time from now. It does not matter. At the time they are imagining, this part of the mediation is over. The issue that has been stalling the mediation has been resolved. (The way it has been resolved is irrelevant.) They should just imagine that it has been resolved. Ask them to picture what the imagined situation looks like and to listen for what it sounds like. Tell them to experience what it feels and smells like. Let them sense a taste, if there is one. Ask them to breathe deeply a few more times. Tell them to relax. Then ask them to open their eyes slowly. Thank them for their cooperation. Congratulate them on doing a great job.

Let the parties know that they are ready to start the next phase. Disregard the matter that had stalled the mediation. Look at the next issue on the list. Tell parties to deal with this issue as if the preceding troublesome matter has been resolved. Continue to build the momentum that had stopped temporarily. Deal with each point until all are handled. Come back to the contentious issue at the end. By then, there usually is substantially more goodwill between the parties than existed at the time you did the exercise. The parties also feel a sense of accomplishment. The dynamics of the mediation process probably have changed too.

I have used this technique to lift parties out of issues in which they are mired. Parties become free to resolve other dimensions of the conflict. The technique relieves tension and frustration. Moreover, it allows parties to develop confidence in the conflict resolution process. As a result they revisit the challenging issue in a more productive frame of mind.

Relevancy Challenge

One more way to pull parties back from the brink of derailment and keep them concentrating on mediation issues is to use a *relevancy challenge*. If you asked parties to agree on the use of this challenge back when you outlined mediation guidelines, you can now simply call on it to refocus individual people.

You can take advantage of the technique when parties come away from an issue being explored. It is easy to spot when this happens because they seem to disengage from the mediation. They appear to "space out." They are literally focused on something else. Their communication may appear to be driven by an internal dialogue or a feeling. Their physical cues might lead you to believe they are seeing something in their mind's eye. The activity behind the dissociation is not material in this case. What is meaningful is interrupting their process. Challenge them. Then assist them to refocus on the current issue.

I suggest you also use this technique when parties are dwelling on an issue that seems overwhelming to them. Put the parties on notice gently. Advise them that their conversation has shifted away from the point being discussed. Remind them of the agreement all parties made to stay centered on the mediation issues under discussion. Request that they refocus on the original issue. If they are finding it a real challenge to do this, then you can move on to the other techniques that have been described here.

Managing Different Reactions to Pressure

How parties react to pressure affects their concentration. You can keep parties focused by working with their respective reactions to pressure. If you have profiled parties, you already know which parties experience *inside, inside-outside,* or *outside* pressure reactions. Even if you have not had the opportunity to profile this element earlier, you can easily spot it during mediation while parties talk about their experiences.

You will notice that parties with an inside reaction are the most vulnerable to losing focus. They relive experiences. When you ask them to recall an incident, they are inclined to stay in it. They do this as long as they are remembering it. They are totally associated with the memory of the experience. Their bodies and voices shift right back to replicate actions that happened then. Often they do not look at the other parties at the table. They are seeing the experience as they saw it when it happened. They are hearing its sounds. They are reliving the feelings too. They are inside the experience again. The mediation drops away. Although these parties may function well during times of low stress and pressure, they suffer when mediations present them with high stress and high pressure. They tend to react very emotionally. You may need to interrupt their thoughts. I suggest you take advantage of your knowledge to signal to them. Use visual, auditory, and kinesthetic cues to bring them out of the memory. Exiting the experience jars them. You will see physiological shifts, and their voice quality will change back to the way it was before they revivified the memory. They resume the characteristics they displayed before they lost focus. At that point I suggest you remind them about the mediation issue on the table.

You will also see parties who react to pressure by staying outside the experience that might cause stress. They appear to be unaffected when you ask them to recall events. They show almost no physiological change. They demonstrate no vocal shifts. They sometimes sound as though the activity happened to someone else. They may also stare into the distance as if they were watching a movie. When you ask them to describe an incident, they just talk about it. They deal with it as they would any other topic they might discuss. They are dissociated from the experience. These are people who function well in mediations where stress or pressure levels are high. They tend to react unemotionally to stress. They can literally and figuratively shrug it off. They can push away the experience or not even acknowledge it because it occurred in the past. These parties rarely lose focus just because they remember an experience.

Parties who react to pressure by going inside and then outside the experience, combine these two patterns. When you ask them about an incident, they begin by reliving it. Then they choose either to stay in the experience or exit from it. They have the ability to shift in and out of a stressful situation. They may react emotionally to stress or choose to react unemotionally. When you encounter these people at mediation, you may choose to intervene when they lose focus during mediation or you may decide to wait a few moments. Most times, these parties bring themselves out of the experience. If they do it themselves, the transition from the experience to the present is smooth, and the parties refocus by themselves.

Knowing How to Manage Time

When I was in high school, my Latin teacher taught verb tenses the same way in every class. He positioned every event around 9:00 A.M. Every action took place "before 9:00 A.M.," "at 9:00 A.M.," or "after 9:00 A.M." I asked him why he always used that time and never another. He explained that students were used to starting school at nine o'clock. If he used noon, students would think about lunch. If he used three o'clock, their minds would wander as they thought about leaving. If he used 9:00 A.M., he found their minds would always center on school work. The explanation was an interesting lesson. It taught me how time affects the way people formulate thoughts. Today the concept stays with me. Although I know mediation does not involve Latin verbs, I recognize it is influenced by how parties perceive time. Time is a nonverbal factor that can trigger action and derailments in mediation.

Look at the time lines of people in mediation, as discussed in Chapters One and Three. Mediation can go awry when parties with different time lines are at the table. Consider the example of punctual parties who must wait for late arrivals. Prompt people often interpret tardiness as a message of disrespect. Now give some thought to the message received by relationship-oriented people whose discussion is cut off by people on a perceived or real deadline. Both groups see these acts as clear signals of a lack of caring. In both these examples, mediation can suffer. Because both groups interpret messages differently, you have to act as the buffer.

You must manage time and take charge of the process. You do this as much when parties are separated as when they are together. You control time during caucus and breaks. For example, imagine this situation. You are mediating a session with some people who have *off-line* positions in relation to their time lines and some people who have *midline* positions. Communication is finally flowing smoothly. You are approaching the time you had set for a break. You realize you must make a choice to break or continue. You need to balance the results you are achieving and parties' belief systems. On the one hand, people with midline positions do not care about the break. As a matter of fact, they would prefer to keep the conversation moving. They may even be grateful. Like people in polychronic groups, they do not want to risk a relationship for the sake of an intermission. They will actually be impressed if you work through a planned break in order to create a productive outcome. On the other hand, you must also consider parties with off-line positions. They believe that set break times should be honored. When you run into this situation, you must alert the off-line parties before you hit the set time. Tell them that you may run "a bit over." With these parties always avoid using the word "late." Seek permission to continue as long as is needed. Be low key. Refrain from making a fuss. Just acknowledge the parties. Say, for example, "I recognize we agreed to break at about quarter past the hour. With your permission, I'd like to get your agreement to continue.

That way, we can finalize this point. That would be beneficial for both parties." If you fail to acknowledge parties this way, you risk sending a nonverbal message of disrespect.

When you decide to call a caucus with one party, remember, again, that parties who view time from off-line positions are highly sensitive to the time you are absent. Time goes very slowly for them. They watch each minute tick while you are out of the room. They are the people to whom time is money. They may grow resentful of your absence, especially if they are paying your fee. If you must leave to caucus with other people, you must tell them exactly when you will return. Accordingly, you need to be prompt about being back. Meanwhile, arrange to have them do something relevant or to take their rest room break while you are out of the room. This will make them more inclined to believe that they are getting their money's worth.

You need to balance these needs against the needs of people with midline positions. These people care most about what is happening at the moment. They are interested in going to caucus to achieve something. Time is irrelevant. To them the caucus should last as long as necessary to reach the goal. They forget about schedules and deadlines. You need to marshal them to keep them on track.

If both parties agree to caucus independently, you must watch the clock. People with off-line positions are ready to begin again promptly at the specified time. People with midline positions often dawdle. They may arbitrarily decide to take a rest room break or get coffee while they are caucusing or after they are finished. If they return later than the agreed time, they risk sending a negative, nonverbal message to the parties who did return on time. You must be on guard against this situation. Keep midline parties focused. Mind the clock for them if they do not do it. Make sure their positive caucus results are not neutralized by the negative messages they send by returning late.

Treat break time in the same way you do caucusing. Stay alert for the signals sent by parties' actions. A break might be a positive strategic move. It might give parties valuable moments by themselves. During this time, however, you must keep an eye on the clock. That way, the value of the break will not be undermined by lateness that is interpreted as a slight. You, as the mediator, never really get a break because you must always watch the clock. Time is always a factor you must manage, even with yourself. You must be aware of messages that your actions communicate. If you yourself have a midline time line, you must be doubly aware of time. Your lateness can send a substantially negative message to off-line parties. As a result, even your breaks are a time when you must be aware of parties' time needs.

Time is a subtle, nonverbal influence that weaves its way through every mediation. You must know how to use it strategically or it becomes a force that steers mediation. Learn about it. Know how the parties perceive time. That way, you can trigger action. You can also put issues back on track.

Encouraging Physical Movement to Change Mental Positions

In addition to building momentum and dealing with derailments caused largely by an inappropriate focus on a single, untimely issue, the mediator needs to encourage mental flexibility. Getting people on track toward their goals as described in the previous section is one way to promote this flexibility. Another way is to use physical movement to change mental positions.

Using Mental and Physical Prompts

During some mediations you may feel stuck. You may believe you have been doing the appropriate things and still cannot either get parties back on track or get them to change their mental positions and behave more flexibly. When this happens, I suggest you review what you have been doing. Examine whether you have been innovative or just repeating similar types of activities. Communication experts Richard Bandler and John Grinder are specific about what to do in just these cases. In their groundbreaking book *Frogs into Princes,* they advise, "If what you are doing is not working, change it. Do anything else."

Limitations you experience in getting mediation back on track may be self-imposed. I suggest you invite yourself into creativity. Do this through both mental and physical prompts, such as eye cues and props. You will evolve new ideas for yourself and model for others the ability to be flexible and to consider various ways to resolve challenges.

Most mediators usually limit themselves to asking parties to "think about" something or to "analyze" it. This process encourages the distillation and dissection of thoughts in a mechanical way; it uses only words to call on one part of the brain to work at solving a situation. By adding nonverbal cuing, you can stimulate more varied responses. For example, when parties become overly emotional, you can move your eyes to your left side, to the visual and auditory remembered positions. Other-than-consciously, parties mirror the mediator's eye positions easily. You will discover that these positions usually invite parties into less emotional states and encourage them to work through a process. I recommend, however, that you avoiding moving your eyes down and to your left (the position that accesses internal dialogues). If people mirror this eye position, it may distract them from the current issue and take them into memories of unproductive, out-of-date conversations that exacerbate the derailment and have nothing to do with the matter at hand.

In suggesting that parties "analyze" a situation, what mediators often forget is that people have two hemispheres to their brains. I suggest you avoid this mistake. Take advantage of both hemispheres. You can do this by using the *wondering* technique. This procedure invites parties to tap into the right brain. It is the gentlest way to prompt parties to come up with solutions to derailments. It stimulates parties to become creative. You can trigger this inventiveness by moving your eyes to your right side. The most effective position is up and to the right (visual constructed). As you move your eyes, you ask parties to "wonder" or to "become curious" about resolution. You might also ask them to "imagine" or "picture" something. By using visual language you stimulate a part of the brain that does not need words. It works with abstract ideas and images. It collects information without needing to define it. Solutions can then parachute into the parties' awareness through a sense or picture. Parties come up with new ideas. Although many of these concepts may not be practical in their original form, workable solutions often flow out of them.

Using props is another way you can prompt parties to get back on track. Consider a multiparty mediation that addresses automobile damage and personal injuries. All parties may be able to talk generally about incident details. Parties with visual or kinesthetic preferences, however, are significantly limited if they must explain in words alone. Remember, they must translate their sight-based or kinesthetic-based information into language. I suggest you help by drawing a street intersection, for example, and asking parties to show how events occurred. That method is one step along the way to using props to explain. You could take a further step by making miniature vehicles available. Then the parties with a kinesthetic preference could edge the miniatures along the drawing to demonstrate their sense of what happened. This moves mediation toward resolution.

Although mediators may not be entertainers, they can certainly take advantage of entertainers' and trainers' tools. Props can help you stimulate ingenuity. If you give parties oversized implements to hold, the unusual size relationship of the article to the hand stimulates parties' brains to think differently. For example, during caucus you might give parties jumbo-size pencils and request they use them to create three reasonable outcomes for all mediating parties. Parties will become more creative because the physical stimulation replicates a sensation they had during childhood when they were learning and inventive. Moreover, as they concentrate on maneuvering the pencil as adroitly as one of normal size, their conscious awareness is redirected. At that time you can momentarily tap into that less consciously critical state and deliver positive messages about the mediation.

You might bring an overhead projector so you can display cartoons at appropriate or tense moments. You might also carry blank transparencies with you so parties can create plans in caucus sessions and then display them to the others in the mediation room. I know mediators who carry a supply of humorous items that they use to change people's moods. You can use video clips, pictures, whistles, noisemakers, bells, tape recorders, stuffed animals, or battery-operated toys. I always carry a pink elephant. That helps me remember to avoid this creature. It also allows me to explain to parties what happens if they talk about pink elephants. The choice of props is yours. They depend on the messages you want to send. The selection is limitless.

Using Small Movements to Stimulate Change

I have noticed that parties often need some kind of physical movement before they can perform a mental shift. Earlier I suggested
that you set up finger-tapping signals as other-than-conscious cues.
They consisted of small finger movements indicating agreement
or disagreement.

Another technique I recommend is a conscious process. It is
the *switched hand* technique, which merges language associated
with the right brain and physical stimulus. First ask the parties to
place a writing implement in the hand they do not usually use.
Then say to them, in exactly these words: "I'd like to ask you *to get
curious* for a moment. Please *wonder* with me about solutions for
[this issue]." Keep your request general. Then let parties imagine.

The switched hand technique stimulates the right hemisphere
of the brain. That hemisphere often adds a creative element to an
analytical process that is idling parties or taking them off track. You
want parties to make some small physical movements using their
fingers and hands on the page. Using the words "get curious" and
"wonder" can steer them away from deliberating about the issues.
Avoiding words like "think" or "analyze," which ask people to dissect issues, will also encourage creativity.

The switched hand exercise offers a bonus. The unusual feeling of an implement in the hand not used to holding it reproduces
feelings people had as youngsters, back when they were just learning to write. This is an experience similar to the one just described
of writing with a jumbo-size pencil. People get the same sense of
newness and learning to balance something strange in their hands.
The object feels odd. They do not know how to make legible marks
automatically. They must be conscious of every movement. This
feeling often zooms people back to a curious and creative time in
their lives. Right then they usually experience a pleasant sensation
and mental shift as they move their hands.

Rearranging Physical and Mental Territory Links

Gross, or large, physical movement has great benefit too. I suggest
you create an environment in which people get out of their seats
at times. As they move around, they release the counterproductive

muscle tension that builds up during or after negative mediation experiences. This sensation of physical tenseness can remain attached or anchored to the experience. The mind remembers it. So does the body. As the mediator you want to break up that linkage and insert a more positive sensation in its place. Tight muscles are also one component of the fight-or-flight fear response. When parties maintain that physiological response for a protracted period of time, the results are physically and mentally stressful. To avoid this outcome, switch that physical experience with a new, more productive one.

Although general stretching can release some tension, that action does not create a whole new experience. To gain fresh perspectives and flexibility, parties need to move more broadly and gather new physical stimulation. With movement, parties can literally get away from old, ineffective perspectives. They can see things more clearly, hear people in fresh ways, and pick up a variety of other sensations and smells. They experience a brand-new, more positive gestalt. That is the reason I recommend movement in the room.

The easiest way to get people to stir is to call for a general break. If parties are hesitant to come out of their chairs, you might have to create some kind of subterfuge to oust them. This could be as simple as your asking if one of the parties "could please get me a cup of coffee while I make an important note before I forget it." When mediation is progressing, you can sometimes send parties outside for fresh air. They may look at things in a new light when they walk back into the building and mediation room.

Tactics for getting people to move around do not have to be overt or dramatic. I sometimes arrange for natural movement. For example, I "accidentally" drop items so people stoop to pick them up. I purposely leave objects in certain locations before mediation so I can ask someone to get them. I make sure refreshments are outside the room. That way parties must rise and leave, getting a physical change. I ask someone to write on the board. I ask others to tape flip chart sheets on walls. After a break, I might be found sitting in the chair another person occupied before the time-out. This forces that person to sit elsewhere, at least temporarily. The process of nudging parties into physical movement is simple. It is most effective when it is kept that way.

Getting parties to switch chairs is another useful strategy for moving people to action. Even that slight change gives them a fresh outlook. This strategy sounds simple. Sometimes, however, putting it into practice becomes a little daunting, for two reasons. First, some people take a chair in a similar location no matter what the occasion. For example, some like to sit near the front. Some like to sit near the back. This is a habit they have developed. The chosen position gives the person a specific sense of relationship to the other people, furniture, doors, windows, and equipment in the room. The combined feeling, smell, perspective, and sound quality that people sense when they sit in a chair in a particular location is unique for them. It brings a sense of comfort to some people.

Second, in the last twenty-five years I have worked with thousands of people. In most cases a common experience often emerged. I laughingly refer to it as *the rented chair syndrome.* People come into a room and sit in chairs. Although the chairs do not belong to them, they assume ownership of the first chairs in which they sit. They actually seem to stake a claim on the piece of furniture. As an instructor, I have sometimes had to fight pitched battles after I have requested class members to change seats to form new learning groups. Many people act like bulldogs guarding a bone. Their educational level, nationality, and ethnicity are irrelevant. They operate as if they were yielding a part of their identities when someone else sits in "their" seat. To this day, I am amazed by this behavior. However, I also know how it can affect mediation. So I simply work with the information. In a case like this, movement may neutralize action as well as trigger it. If I believe parties have a positive anchor to a particular chair, I avoid forcing them to give it up.

A final consideration for your strategic arsenal should be an appreciation of the value of kinesthetic touch. You already know that parties with a kinesthetic preference have to connect physically. They also move to express themselves. People with a need for kinesthetic touch benefit from moving around the room. They must literally connect with something tangible so they can associate with how others think. Also remember that parties whose primary representational system is visual or auditory rather than kinesthetic may still experience kinesthesia outside their awareness. Moving makes it easier for them too to make a connection with the thoughts of other people.

Touch is powerful. When you invite all parties to move around, you can suggest they touch the chairs of other parties. Have them sit in the chairs of the others too. That way they see what the other side sees and hears. This may have a significant effect. I can remember one mediation that took place in a claustrophobic room that had low artificial light and a small window with a blind. In the break, Party A told me that Party B kept "glaring" at her. I had only seen Party B pulling her eyelids back tautly because the sun was rising and constantly changing positions. At that point I edged over so Party A was forced to sit in Party B's chair as we spoke. I invited her to explain the problem again. As she started to revisit her complaint, she began to squint. Then she flushed with embarrassment as she realized she was "making the face" that Party B had made when the sun was in her eyes. A verbal explanation would not have convinced her. Being in Party B's physical situation did. She said she felt silly about her assumption. More than that, she told me how things looked "really different" sitting in that chair. The move had literally changed her perspective.

Bringing Closure

Even though some action has been triggered, there is still much work for the mediator to do before an offer can be made and a final agreement executed. The mediator must ensure that parties feel confident and clear about what they want so they can make worthwhile decisions. When parties have decided on offer terms and are ready to make an offer the mediator uses information drawn from parties' profiles to help shape offer terms into a network of communication structures that compel listeners to pay attention. After the offer presentation the mediator looks to prevent buyer's remorse by examining parties' views toward resolution and settlement and paying attention to the effects of fear and apology. When the parties have verbally agreed to the offer's terms the mediator then guides the parties to jointly craft the final agreement and ultimately leave the conflict behind.

Helping Parties Make Productive Decisions

Many legends surround the famous artist Michaelangelo. One story describes how he was sculpting one of his most famous works and an admirer questioned him. The devotee wanted to know how the artist conceived of the magnificent pieces he crafted out of solid blocks of stone. Michaelangelo responded he really did little except chisel away excess stone. The sculptures were already there, waiting to be released from within the marble slabs.

I have found that most mediating parties similarly hold a reservoir of potential resolutions within them. The most effective mediator simply moves away the factors that have been hiding these valuable results. You can help to remove these obscuring elements by providing parties with the resources they need to make decisions. You can provide them with validation, raise their conscious awareness, encourage them to avoid bracketing, and teach them how to use the Kelly Decision Wheel.

Providing Validation

Validation is an action trigger for decision making. *Inside validators,* those who determine for themselves whether a decision is acceptable, are self-reliant, often appearing confident about their decisions. They may also exhibit impatience with parties who depend on the judgment of external resources. If you come across this irritation, you need to balance the mediation in regard to this characteristic. One strategy for doing this is to remind parties about the mediation guidelines they agreed on at the outset of mediation. These guidelines oblige the parties to act respectfully toward each other.

Parties who need external people to evaluate situations and decisions must have someone telling them when to start the mediation process, what to do during the session, and even when to stop mediation. You must ensure that these *outside validators* have appropriate people available whom they can reach by telephone, fax, or some other method. If these people are not available, the outside validators will not be able to make a decision. You may not even get the mediation process underway. It certainly cannot come to a satisfactory conclusion. Predictably, these people will turn toward you. When they do, you have to step gingerly because your job is to guide the process. At no point are you to be the mechanism through which a party makes an agreement. Even when outside validators look to you for feedback during mediation, you can only help them operate productively in the process. You must ensure a separate validator is available for decisions. When no one is available, these parties will struggle. There is also a significant chance that if they feel forced to come to an agreement, they will suffer buyer's remorse.

If an external resource for an outside validator is not present or accessible, you may choose another strategy. This strategy has two parts. Take the outside validator into a caucus room. Start by asking, "Is it acceptable to you that I help you find a way to be comfortable making decisions by yourself?" If you ask the question that way, you will get a congruent answer. If the answer is yes move forward. It is likely, however, that the answer will be no. You can expect this conundrum. These parties are not comfortable making decisions by themselves, and they would have to make a decision to answer your question positively. After the party answers, follow up with this statement, "I know you will then be confident about your decisions." Because at this point the party views you as his external validator, he is compelled by his deep structure to accept what you say. With this statement, you are leading him into answering yes when you ask the question again.

The second step of the strategy involves a set of instructions for the party. First, you ask him to take a few deep breaths and relax. Then you ask your original question again, in a slightly different way: "I wonder if it would be OK if I showed you a way to be comfortable making decisions?" Again, wait for a congruent yes. When you get it, proceed. Tell the party to close his eyelids and to relax his eyes under his lids. Tell him to take a few more deep breaths and relax. Then ask him if he remembers a time in which someone he trusted helped him make a decision that turned out well. The party can nod or show you the other-than-conscious left thumb tap you set up earlier to indicate yes. Say that you do not need to know the circumstances. You do not need to know who the person was. Now ask the party to remember how the situation looked, sounded, felt, smelled, and tasted. Give him some time to really savor it. Tell him to breathe deeply as he recalls the situation. Then ask if he felt really comfortable having that person helping him with that decision. Wait until he signals yes. If he does not signal affirmatively, ask him about another experience. Continue until you get an experience that yields a yes. When he does answer yes, ask him to press his right index finger gently on his right leg. Tell him that same confidence in decision making is now being transferred to that spot he is touching. He can have that feeling anytime, without anyone else knowing about it. He just has to take a few deep breaths and then gently press that index finger on that magic spot on his leg. That confident feeling will always return. You might even suggest that he might smile because he now feels so confident about his "secret" outside resource. After you have done this exercise one time, let the party practice it once or twice more. Before he leaves the room, congratulate him on his achievement. That will mean a great deal to him because it comes from an outside source. Now, even though the party's other external sources of validation are not with him in person, at least they will be there in his mind.

Raising Conscious Awareness

Next, help parties to develop clarity about and become grounded in the realities surrounding the settlement. I once saw a T-shirt sporting two cartoons on the front; both showed a parent talking to his teenager. In the first drawing, with the caption "What a parent says," the word balloon above the parent's head read, "Now, son, you be good and drive carefully." In the second drawing, captioned "What your teenager hears," the word balloon above the parent's head read, "Blah. Blah. Blah." What has been said and what is consciously heard are often two different things.

Before parties come to mediation, they often consult with lawyers. Attorneys explain their rights. They also tell them about their responsibilities and the expected range of a settlement. Difficulty often arises when an attorney says things like, "Settlement can range between twenty thousand dollars and five hundred thousand dollars. The usual settlement, however, is twenty thousand dollars. You would have to lose an arm and a leg to get more than that." Unfortunately, parties often react like the teenager in the cartoon. They hear only what they want to hear. They often go into mediation expecting the half million dollars. An offer of less than that is perceived as an insult.

Settlement amounts are one of the most contentious mediation issues. You may know that a party has been given accurate information. However, when it becomes apparent that she heard it only on an other-than-conscious level, you may have to be the one to invite her to consciously consider the realistic amount. You can do this during caucus. There, as a matter of review, you mention the lawyer's conversation. (It is not your job, however, to suggest an actual monetary figure she might get.) Invite the party to acknowledge—even if only on an other-than-conscious level—the situation with which she is dealing. That is, you might see the acknowledgment in a nonverbal cue chain that you know this party uses to signal yes. Then suggest she *play back* to you her understanding of what you explained in reviewing the lawyer's statement. Explain that she does not have to agree with the information. She just has to restate it accurately. Keep asking the party to tell you what you told her. Continue to do this until she does it accurately. Even though she may not like or agree with the information she is playing back, she has consciously processed it. It is not up to you to see that she accepts it. She must take it from that point of consciously playing it back accurately.

Avoiding Bracketing

When parties open discussions with high or low settlement figures, I immediately wonder whether they are bracketing. Bracketing is a tactic some negotiators use. With it they can maneuver to find a middle ground. Bracketing can be constructive or destructive. It may be useful for parties who negotiate with each other all the time. Lawyers who feel comfortable bandying around extremely high or low numbers might employ it successfully. In fact, before mediation, attorneys often predict quite accurately, where the final dollars will settle. I see this often, for example, in cases involving lawyers who mediate regularly with insurance companies.

However, bracketing can be very damaging when used by only one of the mediating parties. If a party asking for monetary settlement uses bracketing and begins with an unrealistically high settlement figure, she may scare off the party who will be expected to pay and who does not realize bracketing is being used. Alternatively, the party who will be making the payment can frighten off the other party by using bracketing to make a low counteroffer. In both examples, only one of the mediating parties knows bracketing is in use. The other believes the offer is a "hard" number.

If I sense a party is using bracketing as a tactic, I investigate. I want to ascertain whether the initiating party is employing this maneuver to get a reaction from the other party or to pinpoint a figure. I handle the situation in one of two ways. My first choice is humor. For example, at one community-based mediation, settlement revolved around compensation for a commemorative china plate that had been destroyed. When the party asking for compensation announced she wanted hundreds of dollars for the plate,

I requested a caucus. In it I asked whether she was looking to replace the memento or intending to get enough money to finance a trip to Europe so she could buy the replacement where she bought the original. This brought a laugh. Then it evoked a second, more serious response. That is the one with which I worked. If parties are serious in making an unrealistic demand, I call a caucus with the parties and their counsel. There I establish whether they are bracketing. I explain that if they continue this way, the mediation could go off track. I ask them to make a decision about how far they are willing to take the bracketing exercise. I advise them of the benefits of pegging a realistic number. I also tell about the risks of scaring away the other party. Finally, I ask them to make a decision about how they would like to proceed. That way I make it their responsibility to get the process going properly again.

Using the Kelly Decision Wheel

Another method I suggest for helping parties make decisions is the Kelly Decision Wheel™© (Figure 7.1). You can use it during mediation or caucus. It is a valuable tool that helps parties decide on their priorities in the mediation. To execute this technique, ask each party to draw a circle. Then ask each party to look at the circle as if it were a clock face and to mark the even-numbered positions (2, 4, 6, 8, 10, 12) with a dot on the edge. Each mark will become the anchor point for an option. Now ask each party to identify six settlement interests or issues important to him or her. For example, in a mediation resulting from a job termination, the issues might be money from a fair settlement, job reinstatement, an apology, a retraining allowance, relocation counseling, and pension and health benefits. Ask the parties to call their interests or issues *options* and to write the names of the options at the anchor points, one option per point, as illustrated in Figure 7.1.

Now take each party through a series of questions that requires them to compare the desirability of the options placed on the decision wheel. Each question asks them which of two of the options they would rather have: for example, "Would you rather have job reinstatement or a retraining allowance?" "Would you rather have relocation counseling or fair settlement money?" "Would you rather have a retraining allowance or pension and health benefits?"

Figure 7.1. Example of Kelly Decision Wheel.

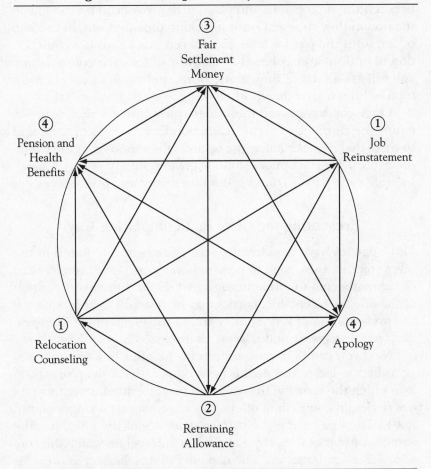

Source: ©1989 Kathleen J. Kelly, 260 Milan Street, Toronto, ON M5A 3Z6
Canada, 416-365-1528, fax: 416-365-1080, e-mail: kellyadr@attcanada.ca.
Reprinted with permission.

Ask parties to answer each question as it is asked by drawing a line between the two options and placing an arrowhead on the line at the option they choose. Continue asking the questions, in random order, until the parties have considered every possible combination of options and assigned an arrowhead for each combination. You will ask a total of fifteen questions, and parties should have a total of fifteen arrowheads when done.

Once you have asked the fifteen questions, ask the parties to count the number of arrowheads pointing to each option, and to write that number above the option (the numbers in the circles on Figure 7.1). The options with the greatest number of arrowheads indicate each party's true and intuitive settlement preferences.

Presenting the Offer in a Compelling Way

Once parties have decided the terms they want included in the offer, you can assist them to present it in a persuasive fashion. Start by remembering the mnemonic LIAR. Even if the overt content of the offer is acceptable, parties may be resistant to accepting it if the presentation of it does not contain the elements of *identification, acknowledgment,* and *response,* as discussed in Step Five.

Next you can help parties present the offer in ways that compel others to listen. You do this by working with the deep structures into which the terms of the offer can be embedded. When you set out to design compelling offers, you are creating messages on two levels. The first level is the surface structure of the offer. It is the text or content of the proposal. This is the level on which the conscious message is carried. The meaning of this message is overt. As I have discussed, people automatically screen communication at this level, and they are aware they are doing this filtering. In mediation, parties examine the contents of the offer to evaluate how it matches their goals. The second level is the deep structure of the offer. This is the communication that is taken in by the receiver's other-than-consciousness and that people do not filter as critically as they do the first level of messages. This is the level on which the packaging of the offer has a profound effect. If a message stacks together a number of deep structures—action triggers and working frameworks—to which the listener is responsive, that creates compelling communication on the other-than-conscious level.

These are the structures that you identified for each party on the Profile Element Grid. The more of these structures that are used, the more compelling the offer.

The following sections examine preferred systems and a number of action triggers and working frameworks from the point of view of creating a network of deep structures. This network allows the mediator to present an offer—or to assist a party to present an offer—in a way that makes sense to the party receiving the offer.

Touchstones and Systems

First, review the terms of the offer to understand them. You can see what parties are willing to give and to take. Second, look over the profile you made for each party. These profiles have documented both the touchstones and systems preferences of all parties. Parties cannot be comfortable accepting offers that do not acknowledge their touchstones and system preferences.

In a relatively informal environment, like that of community-based mediation, parties may create their own offer terms and present them. In other situations, counsel may draw up the documents. In both cases, even when lawyers have cast the entire document in legalese, you can assist in presenting the offer in an inviting way. Start by weaving parties' touchstones into your conversations about the offer. Remember that parties' touchstones articulate their standards for measuring value. At the start of mediation, you collected parties' touchstones for what was important to them in mediation. Before they accept an offer, you should check to see that their touchstones are satisfied so the final agreement will be more compelling.

For example, imagine that at the beginning of the mediation you recorded "fair" and "being heard" as Party A's touchstones for what is important in an offer. You noted "reimbursement" and "satisfaction" as Party B's touchstones. Now, you check with the parties that the offer satisfies these touchstones. You ask Party A, "So if I understand you correctly, Party A, you believe the offer would be *fair* and you would know you were *being heard,* if the offer has covered the issues of X, Y, and Z?" And you ask Party B, "So if I understand you correctly, Party B, you believe the offer will give you *satisfaction* if we consider *reimbursement* for issues X, Y, and Z?"

Offers must also quantify and qualify details satisfactorily. Look at another example, one in which parties start with an offer that is worded one way and then amend that wording. In an offer that covers just quantifiable details, you might see, "Party D agrees to pay Party C one hundred and fifty dollars, in cash, by 5:00 P.M., Eastern standard time, on January 5, 2003." Although those words may satisfy Party C's criteria for content, Party C may still be disinterested because he believes Party D is insincere. Party C's touchstones for an acceptable offer are "happy" and "compensation." Although an offer without those touchstones seems cold to Party C, an offer using only those words for the details would be vague, and this vagueness might lead to further conflict down the road. One solution is to amend the offer so it combines content and touchstones, as in this example from a community-based mediation final agreement: "Party D agrees to pay Party C one hundred and fifty dollars, in cash, by noon, on October 3, 2001. In doing this Party C agrees that he is happy that he is receiving complete compensation for the losses he incurred when Party D's fallen tree damaged the shrubbery in Party C's backyard." Although the wording in this example is certainly not something lawyers would write, parties may agree to any wording they wish.

Even if the wording of an offer has been set by the lawyers and cannot be changed, the offer can still be presented verbally in the context of parties' touchstones. If this step is ignored, a party might reject it on an other-than-conscious level. Look at another example involving Parties C and D. This time, imagine there are lawyers present. Also imagine that the lawyers have set out terms to which all parties have agreed in principle. At that point you know that agreement in principle is a conscious activity. If "happy" and "compensation" are still Party C's touchstones, I suggest you introduce the ideas of being "happy" and receiving "compensation" during a verbal preamble. By configuring a vehicle for presenting the offer's terms in this way, you compel Party C to listen to the offer, irrespective of whether or not he accepts it. You do the same for Party D, using his touchstones, if there is a counteroffer.

A second component of presenting compelling offers consists of using people's preferred systems. This creates an environment in which offer terms are as understandable as possible. It also frees the environment of tension by presenting the offer congruently at both conscious and other-than-conscious levels. When you assist parties to present their offers, use the listeners' preferred systems to explain the terms. If you are constructing the offer wording, include visual, auditory, and kinesthetic expressions. Be prepared to explain the offer in each of the three systems. That way, parties understand offer terms easily and do not become fatigued translating ideas from their secondary or tertiary system into their primary system. If parties do not understand your words, you can choose to do something else. Using more words to explain an idea may be like turning up a radio. The volume changes, but you hear the same song. You need to switch stations to make a difference in what you hear. Similarly, in mediation you can supplement verbal explanation by drawing pictures, using models, or creating lists (using words in a different format). To make offers persuasive, rotate through the representational systems. For example, counsel may create a payment schedule and list it in an offer. If parties have a visual preference, the table may not be as valuable as a small diagram. You could draw a circle that indicates the beginning and end of the payment schedule. Parties may agree more readily if they *see* a start and an end to the payment process. In the case of people with a kinesthetic preference, you can ask them to run their fingers from the top of the schedule to the end. They can literally get a feel for the bottom line.

Macro-Thinking and Micro-Thinking

Creating a compelling offer necessitates breaking down terms to suit the parties receiving the offer. The reason for this is that before parties will accept an offer, they must divide its components into information bits they understand. Ordinarily, they do this themselves automatically, on an other-than-conscious level. At this level, some parties dissect information into small chunks. They are the micro-thinkers. Other parties view the offer in global terms. They are the macro-thinkers. After parties have gotten a sense of the offer through their particular way of interpreting the world, they will consider the terms. This will happen on a conscious level.

Micro-thinkers have a built-in mechanism that divides jobs and incidents into small parts. Their world is focused on specifics. They do not understand large concepts easily. Sometimes they focus so narrowly on tiny aspects of mediation or offers that they fail to see the ultimate target. Micro-thinkers crave minutiae. Their preference for sorting through details appears when a mediation offer is presented to them too. I suggest that you be prepared to walk micro-thinkers through every step of the offer. You must create a path of small, connected steps that they can follow until they reach the last detail. If you fail to do this, they may see offers as unconnected bits or simply an unclear group of ideas. You may even have to take them through every stage of how each element was decided, sequencing the details for them. If you do not, they may become stalled. The more information you can provide, the better for these parties.

Macro-thinkers have a built-in mechanism that synthesizes jobs and incidents into large chunks or patterns. They like to deal in generalities. They work most effectively with overviews and abstracts. These people can become bored when an offer is presented unless they are provided with the whole concept at once. I recommend you allow them to concentrate on the major aspects of the mediation offer. If a macro-thinker has other people with him at the table, suggest that he assign details to these others. Start by explaining the highlights of the offer. Do it as globally as possible. If parties request more information, provide only a little more. Offer additional information only as it is requested.

Stop explaining when parties cease their information requests. You have given them the amount of detail they need. They can agree to an offer comfortably.

When you encounter both micro-thinkers and macro-thinkers at a mediation, it is sometimes beneficial to run through the offer in separate caucuses. That way, you can move quickly with the macro-thinkers, and you eliminate the risk of boring them. Conversely, you can move as slowly as necessary with the micro-thinkers, and you minimize the risk of appearing insensitive to them. You then bring both the parties together in the mediation room when both are ready to craft a final agreement.

Finally, you may have a party who comes to the table with a combination of both micro- and macro-thinking components. She may be either a micro- to macro-thinker or a macro- to micro-thinker. The micro- to macro-thinker asks for details and then wants to know the big picture. Tell her how each step ties into achieving the global goal. Build up to the global perspective once she is filled in on the details. The macro- to micro-thinker wants the big picture first then wants some detail. Give her a global overview then backtrack to show how the details fit into that overview.

Opportunity and Necessity Rationales

In this part of offer presentation, you configure the terms to accommodate people who see opportunity in situations and people who see only necessity. The first group responds positively to an offer built around possibilities. Because their other-than-conscious pattern is to gravitate toward opportunities, they really relish hearing about or seeing options written right into an offer. This group likes choice. You often feel challenged to keep them on track when constructing an offer. They keep coming up with new alternatives even after they have made choices. When you broach the subject of final offers, recognize this preference. Even if there is only one offer on the table, you must say to these parties, "You have *two choices*. You have an *opportunity* to accept the offer. You can also *choose* to decline the offer. You can *pick*." Even though the parties may not fancy the actual terms of the offer, this way of presenting it compels them to consider those terms. They cannot resist the opportunity to choose.

The group that understands situations in terms of necessity likes to deal with one thing at a time. Parties in this group automatically look at an offer as being one part of a process. They think in terms of operating procedurally, not of making choices. Either they *need* to agree to the offer or not. Once matters are discussed and parties are in accord, execution of a final agreement is just the next step in the process. It is routine. There is no option. There is only obligation or responsibility to move forward. When you speak to parties in this group who have accepted an offer, you might say something like, "Now that you have gone through the discussion part of the mediation process and have accepted the terms of the offer, the process is almost complete. The last step is to create and sign a final agreement that reflects the terms." If parties are not in agreement with an offer's terms, you say that it is routine to review declined offers to see where they can be changed to make them acceptable. Then work with the parties to word acceptable terms that can bring them back to the table and move them toward final agreement.

Movement Toward and Away, Similarity and Difference

Yet another factor affecting offer presentation is knowing whether an offer is likely to attract or push away parties. The profile areas to look at here are, first, whether parties move toward solutions or away from problems and, second, whether parties perceive current offers as being similar to or different from past offers.

When you broach the subject of accepting an offer, configure your communication around each party's deep structure in these areas. For example, you might say this to parties who move toward solutions: "When you agree to this offer, you will reach your goal of a reasonable settlement." That phrasing recognizes the party's other-than-conscious mental movement pattern and compels him to consider the offer. If you were to talk about problem avoidance to this person, you would repel him from the offer. When you do talk to parties who intuitively avoid problems, you can say, "I'm glad you are able to complete this today. You can put away any thoughts about ever seeing this situation again." Again, for this latter group, avoidance is the mechanism that propels them. Dangling a goal only forces them away from accepting an offer.

Equipped with the knowledge of which parties recognize similarity in situations and which parties recognize difference, you can point out the parts of the offer that have appeal for each party. When you frame the offer, you say to the group that looks for similarity, "This offer includes the parts of the last offer you liked." To the group seeking difference, you say, "This offer differs from other offers in these ways." You can gain a hearing from parties who see both similarities and differences by saying, "This offer has kept the things you liked [*similarity*] and is even better in many respects [*difference*]."

The other-than-conscious continues to be the element that dictates how forceful offers seem. The content of an offer is secondary to its framework. By setting up the offer in a manner that fits each party's other-than-conscious structures, you launch parties into entertaining the offer.

Activity and Time Frame Decision Factors

Whereas people consciously consider the content of offers, their decision-making criteria usually exist on an other-than-conscious level. In Step Four, I discussed how people decide. They must be satisfied on two levels: activity and time frame. Understanding each party's unique *convincing strategies* is particularly important for presenting offers in a compelling way.

First, people need a particular activity to happen before they can make a decision. This activity consists of seeing, hearing, doing (or experiencing), or reading something. Some people need a combination of two activities instead of just one. A diner at a restaurant, for example, might need only one activity, such as tasting (*experiencing*) the food, to decide the restaurant is a fine one. Another diner might require a combination of activities, such as *seeing* food prepared and then tasting (*experiencing*) it. Similarly, at mediation, parties who need to satisfy only one activity, may need only to hear an offer in order to make a decision. Parties who require a combination of activities may need to see a look on the other party's face and then may need to read the offer.

Second, to be convinced, people need distinct amounts of time to pass or a certain number of examples to happen. Some people are convinced automatically (*reflex acceptance*). They do not need any time or examples to decide. Once their activity level is satisfied they are convinced. For example, these people believe that if their lawyer recommends mediation, they should attend. Other people need to experience a specific number of examples. They might need one (or two or more) disappointing experiences with a lawyer to decide not to retain her again. Some people are convinced over a time period that varies from person to person and circumstance to circumstance. At mediation, these people might need an hour, overnight, a week, or a month to make up their minds. Some people must be convinced constantly. They make each decision as if it were a new consideration. In mediation, these people often read a slightly amended offer as closely as if it were a new offer being tendered. For them, it is.

A conflict resolution session in which I was a co-mediator illustrates how a mediator can work with decision-making factors. The parties in this mediation had been friends at one time. They

agreed to ground rules about talking in turns. The session was progressing well. Party A had told his story. Then I asked Party B to do
the same. As Party B began to talk, Party A's eyes traveled down and
to the left. They stopped at the auditory dialogue position. His face
reddened. His breathing changed. Not two minutes after Party B
began, Party A stood up angrily. He interrupted Party B, saying,
"I was told I could leave at any time. I'm doing it now. I'm not
going to sit here and listen to someone tell lies about me." It
seemed that Party A was a hearing (*activity*) and one example (*time
frame*) decision maker (what I call a *hear-one convincer*). He had to hear
something only one time to be convinced he did not want to stay.
Of course this decision-making process occurred other-than-
consciously. Moreover, he believed that everyone else would be
convinced that he had done "bad things" when these other people
heard what Party B had said even *once* in mediation. When I recognized Party A's convincing strategy, I requested he caucus with me
before he left. He agreed. I used what I recognized about his pattern. I wondered out loud what would happen if he heard Party B
state they both shared responsibility. Would he stay? He said yes. I
called a separate caucus with Party B. I asked him if he would agree
to stating that both parties shared responsibility. He agreed. We all
resumed the mediation. Once Party B had made the requested
statement, Party A relaxed. He listened. The mediation continued.

As a mediator, you are called to assist parties by configuring
information. In this pursuit, you must avoid confusing offer format
with content. If you are conversant in decision-making structures,
you can help parties format offers so that other parties will consider them. Offers with good terms are often rejected out of hand
because their deep structure clashes with structures used by the
decision maker. The decision to decline is made other-than-
consciously. Your assistance is invaluable because you can help parties avoid this unintentional communication conflict.

You can help make offers more viable by ensuring that they
match parties' decision-making criteria. For example, if you recognize that parties need to read something (*activity*) twice (*number of
examples*), you might give them a written offer to read and then say,
"Just a moment, let me have a look. [*You take it back momentarily.
Then you return it to them.*] Thanks. OK. Now have a *second look* at it."
If you recognize a party's structure as seeing (*activity*) and reflex

acceptance (*time frame*), this party might be convinced of good intentions if he sees the faces of the other parties. If you are dealing with parties who have to hear (*activity*) constantly (*time frame*), you might say to them: "I have asked the other party to supply references from people with whom she has done business. Here is a list of their telephone numbers. They've said to feel free *to call* them *anytime* you want to hear about her reputation." When you reproduce parties' decision-making structure, parties are compelled to pay attention to the offer. They still may reject it because of its terms, but they are drawn other-than-consciously to consider it because its structure matches theirs.

I have learned that both activity and time frame factors must be addressed and satisfied for parties to make their decisions. All offers, irrespective of specific content, must be dropped into the parties' decision-making structure. That is the only way parties can say yes and feel comfortable with their decisions.

Guarding Against Buyer's Remorse

Throughout the mediation, the mediator must be prudent about guiding the process in a direction that is most beneficial for all parties. After offers are made the mediator must be particularly circumspect because parties will be affected in different ways. When attorneys attend mediation, they operate in a routine arena. Their clients and also parties attending mediation without counsel enter surroundings that are rarified for them. For some, just the thought of mediation is profoundly altering. For others, it is the act of walking into an alien environment that makes them feel strange. Whatever the proximate source, it can have a significant effect on mediating parties. Some people feel different physically. Some feel different mentally. In the latter case, when their frame of mind is significantly altered, they can be easily distracted. This distraction can allow information to bypass their normal filters. When these filters are not operating in the most effective way, parties can make decisions that they would not ordinarily make. These decisions might be made at the time an offer is presented. These decisions might not be in the parties' best interests.

When you are working with parties in a conflict resolution setting, be aware of predictable altered states. I suggest you stay mindful of the potential results of communication sent on conscious and other-than-conscious levels. Even in routine daily circumstances, we all take in nonverbal communication, including messages sent through time and space and of course the deep structures of verbal messages, that bypass our conscious filters. This latter activity can be greatly magnified during mediation, especially at the time of offer presentation. Even some surface messages, which are ordinarily filtered, are not screened when parties are in altered states.

Because parties are likely to be in altered mental states to at least some degree, the mediator must work to ensure that they are accepting the terms of an offer and acceding to the final agreement with full awareness of what they are doing. That is, the mediator must guard against buyer's remorse. Two ways to do this are to determine whether parties seek resolution or settlement and to recognize parties' feelings, especially those relating to fear and to apologies.

Determining Whether Parties Seek Resolution or Settlement

Once you are cognizant of the effect of altered states, you can assist parties by determining whether they are seeking *resolution* or *settlement*. You can accomplish this most effectively in caucus. There you can have each party define what each term means by asking each one, "What's important to you in resolution?" and, "What will having that do for you?" After each party answers, ask the questions again, replacing "resolution" with "settlement." Parties' answers to these two sets of questions yield touchstones that you can use later to tell you whether parties perceive offers as resolution or settlement. For example, parties might tell you that "resolution" means satisfying a high number of interests that the mediating parties have in common and that "settlement" means maintaining a certain position. Once you know these distinctions, you can determine at the time of offer whether parties are agreeing to settlement when they really want resolution, or vice versa. If you spot this incongruity, you may be able to help parties avoid buyer's remorse at a later date.

The most reliable method for recognizing the potential for buyer's remorse is watching and listening for yes and no cue chains. You have already been doing this during mediation. At the time of the offer presentation, you should continue this process in both the mediation room and the caucus rooms. In the mediation room verbal and nonverbal communication messages often conflict. In the caucus environment parties tend to display more verbal and nonverbal congruity. In either location, however, pay close attention to the nonverbal message and bear in mind each party's criteria for resolution and for settlement.

If parties need to review the offer in macro terms, you have to ask them only whether the offer satisfies their need for either resolution or settlement. If parties have a micro-thinking structure, you need to go over the offer item by item, asking whether each one satisfies their need for either resolution or settlement.

When parties answer yes verbally and demonstrate their unique yes chain of nonverbal cues, invite them to agree to take the offer. When parties say no, stop. You must pick out the unacceptable part or parts of the offer. Keep revising the offer until the parties can give you a congruent yes. If parties say yes and demonstrate their no chain of cues, believe the nonverbal communication. It is an other-than-conscious signal. It indicates that the party does not agree with the offer at that point. However, it might mean only that the party has to review the offer again. Remember that these people are responsive to their decision-making factors and that some people need to review materials more than once before deciding. If the other-than-conscious no persists, you must invite the parties into caucus to elicit the troublesome issue or issues. Ascertain whether the contentious issue arises from content or from communication structure. If lack of agreement arises out of the offer's structure, reconfigure the structure to fit the party. If lack of agreement is tied to content, then adjust what content can be changed. Make every effort to achieve an acceptable format and terms before parties leave caucus. Take the revision back to the mediation room.

Whatever your own evaluation of an offer, guard against contamination of parties' answers. You must be scrupulous about communication around parties because they are vulnerable. Many of their filters are down. They are in a highly altered state. Watch to see whether their lawyers are inadvertently swaying them. Are the parties being influenced to say yes or no when their other-than-conscious cues indicate the opposite? Because their usual protective mechanisms are working differently, parties might be vulnerable to you too. They trust that you are neutral. You, however, may have a belief system that differs from theirs. Your belief system might find an offer's terms acceptable or unacceptable. Accordingly, you might inadvertently send a nonverbal signal that parties should or should not agree to an offer. For example, you might do this with your tone of voice. If you use the tone you usually reserve for saying yes, you communicate other-than-conscious approval. Like other people, you certainly have your own yes and no physical cue chains. You have been learning how to bring people's cue chains into your conscious awareness; however, the parties to the mediation do not do any of this analysis. They simply pick up your cues other-than-consciously. Your cue chains are profound messages for them. As a result, you must make sure parties are giving you *their* yes or no.

Be painstaking about ensuring parties are not just mirroring communication they picked up from you or anyone else. They must demonstrate *their own* unique physical chain of cues for saying yes. If the nonverbal cues they exhibit are not *their* unique chains, disregard these cues. Assume that they are replaying another person's chain. Continue to review the offer or reasons for refusal until you are satisfied that parties either agree or disagree congruently. By doing this you greatly reduce the chances of buyer's remorse.

Handling the Effects of Fear

As discussed earlier, during mediation you often need to handle the effects of fear. Fear also frequently surfaces when offers are made. When parties are afraid, they experience physical changes. They go through mental shifts as well. When people are scared, they are subject to responses they do not ordinarily have. The fear can trigger the fight-or-flight response. That response can change the way parties view offers. Ordinarily parties might see the terms of an offer one way. When fear intervenes, two additional perspectives become possible: a fight dimension and a flight dimension. For example, when an offer is made to people who are afraid, they might reject the offer because they are taking a position of digging in and fighting for their position. Alternatively, they might accept the offer because they are unwilling to confront the other side, and so they flee the confrontation by accepting. In both scenarios the parties are responding to the trigger of fear. The fear usually starts at an other-than-conscious level. It may or may not come into parties' conscious awareness. The initial reaction is the result of a primitive survival mechanism. Often people feel as if they are in a life-or-death situation. Their responses can become extreme and may sometimes bar productive results.

You can assist parties to create worthwhile alternatives to this reaction. Before you say a word, start breathing deeply and evenly. As parties match your breathing it assists them to move out of a nonproductive breathing response caused by fear. Identify their level of fear. Acknowledge it. Then deescalate it. Help parties separate the feeling of fear from their reaction to that feeling. You might suggest that "other people" also experience various feelings during mediation. Tell them that this happens frequently when offers are made. Point out that these feelings lead to responses that are not the people's typical responses, and ask if they might be experiencing something like that. If they say yes, acknowledge them. Deescalate their fear. I sometimes say: "What you're telling me seems to be a pretty typical experience. Many people seem to develop butterflies because accepting an offer is an unusual event for them. They get a fluttering feeling. But it soon goes away once they begin to discuss it." If they say no, keep breathing evenly. Again, you may comment about "other people sometimes feeling and responding" in "interesting" ways during mediation. That way you have acknowledged their experience other-than-consciously. That is enough. Continue to breathe deeply and evenly as you use this strategy. You are letting parties know, on an other-than-conscious level, that it is appropriate to feel afraid. You are just refraining from insisting that they have that feeling consciously.

Complete this technique with parties. Then review the offer with them. When you revisit the issues, you can mention the parties' original responses or not. If you do not refer to their original reactions, remember to keep them in mind as you work forward. If you want to acknowledge and work with the original reactions, you might reframe them. When I raise an original reaction, I sometimes call reactions "nature's way to prime the thought pump for more valuable decisions."

Dealing with the Dynamics of Apology

Offers that are accompanied by apologies have a different effect than do offers that arrive without regrets. Both kinds of offers may be worthwhile. They are just different. The parties are the experts in knowing whether they do or do not want apologies. If you are mindful of each party's reaction to pressure, you can forecast how apologies might be perceived. For example, when people with an *inside pressure reaction* recall an event leading to the conflict, they relive the event. When they make an apology, they tend to be seen as caring or truly empathetic. When people with an *outside pressure reaction* remember an event leading to the conflict, they might seem disconnected from it. They might appear unemotional or uncaring. Their apologies may appear hollow.

Under certain circumstances, an apology can actually undo progress that has been made toward agreement. Consider what happened in a mediation conducted by a colleague of mine. Three women were at odds over a property they had bought as an investment. The women had been friends before investing together. The first woman (I'll call her Party A) apologized for the rift the conflict had made in their friendship. The second woman, Party B, accepted the apology. She said she felt a sense of relief. She said she was not as interested in making a few dollars as she was in keeping old friends. She could see her way to a resolution about the investment. She was ready to move to the stage of finalizing an agreement. The third woman, Party C, rejected the apology outright. She had no interest in Party A's apology. My colleague was surprised at Party C's reaction. He had been lulled into a sense that the mediation was moving toward resolution. He requested a caucus with Party C. In that discussion, Party C said the mediation had nothing to do with personal relationships. She believed that Party A was using the apology as a subterfuge to dodge paying her fair share of a bad business decision. She said Party A was trying to use their past friendship to play on her emotions. She actually resented the apology. She thought it sounded false. She concluded this by the way Party A apologized. Party C had heard Party A use exactly the same tone many times in the past when trying to pacify her headstrong, unruly teenager. Party C thought the apology was inappropriate. She thought this mediation was about a business issue. She wanted a financially acceptable settlement. She was not interested in resuming a personal relationship. Finally, she said she felt that the mediator was "somehow disappointed" in her because she had not accepted Party A's apology.

Many mediators state they are neutral. Yet in the next breath they embrace the idea of apology as a valuable tool. With this expression of belief the mediator is no longer neutral in the area of apology. In view of this, I suggest you deal with your beliefs about apology before you enter a conflict resolution session. Your beliefs may be conveyed through your other-than-conscious communication as well as your verbal remarks. Make sure you are congruent in what you say and in what you indicate other-than-consciously. You must stow away your beliefs about apology at the door. Then you must stay alert for messages that lawyers send their clients. Some attorneys believe that apologies may be an admission of liability. Others believe they are useful as a tactic to "soften up" other parties. Whichever opinion lawyers have, they communicate it, verbally or nonverbally, to clients. If a lawyer believes an apology will be useful, clients may then feel pressured to say or do something that matches their lawyer's belief even though it feels innately wrong or uncomfortable to them. The results may be incongruent messages in the form of ersatz apologies. The sound of insincerity often heightens tension. Listening parties, other-than-consciously, sense the artificial message. Even if an offer is then accepted, parties often come away without a sense of closure. If you believe that you have this kind of situation at hand, I suggest you caucus with the potential apologizers. In private, tell them that making no apology is better than offering one that is feigned. If parties plan to go through only the motions of sincerity, their communication will be incongruous. Other parties will not believe them. Moreover, they themselves will not feel good about the communication. In this case, they might want to consider saying nothing. Or you can ask parties if there is one component of the original problem for which they can sincerely apologize. If they can, they can use that. That is more likely to be productive and credible. I sometimes suggest this compromise. I ask parties if they can say something like this: "I can't really say I regret what I did. I thought it was the right thing to do at the time. What I *can* tell you is that I am sincerely sorry *for the distress that it caused you.*" That strategy acknowledges both parties' positions and feelings.

Guiding the Parties to Craft the Final Agreement Jointly

After parties agree to offer terms, many mediators see creating the final written agreement as their sole responsibility. They shoulder final agreement design as their personal duty. They act as if they alone must put the whole derailed train—or mediation—back on track. This is neither realistic nor advisable. When the mediator is the only one working to blueprint final terms, the parties lack a feeling of ownership of the mediation results. Moreover, the mediator misses opportunities to benefit from the wealth of resources that parties bring to the table.

Putting Parties in Control of the Process

Parties come to mediation with a variety of issues. During the mediation process they sometimes come upon points of agreed mutual interest. You can help them use these agreements as starting points to build a final agreement. If parties have been hesitant to agree, you can give them a starting point now. Invite them onto common ground. Have them work together on a final agreement. If parties are somewhat resistant at first, use a strategy to reframe the environment. Talk about agreement design as the first step toward final resolution. Encourage participation. Invite parties to take ownership of the final product by creating the ultimate terms themselves.

Asking parties to draft an agreement together is a particularly useful technique for the parties in community-based mediations. It also works well in resolving schoolyard conflicts. This strategy is also a powerful tool even when lawyers are present. Through this process the parties can at least take ownership of the ideas of the settlement. Then they can hand over their decisions to be translated into legal terms by their lawyers.

When parties design the final agreement, they choose what is important to them. They also have the opportunity to address matters that the mediator may not have considered relevant. What the mediator believes pertinent is not the issue here. Just listen to what the parties say. You may need simply to sit back and treat party issues the same way you treat language touchstones. The parties are the ones who must appreciate the issues. They must understand them. They must acknowledge them. They must deal with the terms of the offer. They must agree to terms. Your understanding or agreement is secondary. This is the parties' process. Your job is to create the strategies that guide their process.

As the parties start this work, I intervene only once. I ask permission to add one more ground rule to the guidelines they agreed to at the beginning of the mediation, because deciding final terms requires some give and take. I ask them to decide on each issue and then move past it completely. If they dwell on one thing or keep returning to it, they will miss their opportunities to heal the conflict and to let it disappear finally and completely. Here is a typical script I use for this intervention:

> You know, I often look at conflict as a mosquito bite. At first it starts as an irritation. It might go away if someone does not scratch it, but someone usually does scratch it. The scratching continues. The bite gets infected. The scratching increases. The wound festers. No one really attends to it. At first, it is only intermittently annoying. The bitten person thinks it will just go away. Finally, when the skin is red and raised, and the arm is very swollen, the bitten person seeks medical attention. Treatment includes medication for the infection. It also includes letting a scab form. The scab is nature's way of protecting the wound until it heals. Eventually the scab gets smaller and at some point disappears. It may not leave a scar. If the scab is picked, however, the wound is reopened. The infection cycle usually starts all over again. There is also a good chance that the wound will leave a scar that will never disappear.

After parties agree to the new ground rule of deciding on and then moving completely past each issue, they can start working productively.

As the parties make this joint effort, you can encourage their personal contribution and commitment. You may also need to balance the different levels of power among the parties and assist people in creating feasible targets.

Encouraging a Personal Investment in the Process

Parties who draft their own agreement make a personal investment in the process. They cannot sit on the sidelines if they are part of decision making. Moreover, once the mediation is complete, the parties can walk away from the table, but they cannot abandon these agreement terms easily. Parties have made a personal investment in creating or agreeing to these terms. They must honor the final agreement, or they are the ones who fail. They cannot blame the agreement terms for their inability to live up to the terms. If parties fail, they will do so because they should have known better than to agree to certain terms in the first place or because they have not lived up to terms to which they agreed. This gives them a strong motive for abiding by the agreed terms. When they do, everyone wins.

As parties work together, make sure all decided issues are committed to paper. You will need to make discussed issues concrete for some parties. Some parties need to see a final agreement to make it real. Others have to read it. Still others need to hold it in their hands. Putting the agreement on paper accomplishes all this and something else. It gives parties a place to put their signatures. Signing a document holds a special meaning. The act formalizes informal conversation. Some people do not think of verbal commitments as real. Commitments take shape for these people only when they sign their name on a piece of paper that contains the commitments. These parties need the structure of performing an act and seeing their signature. Even reading their name typed on a line does not have the same impact. It is putting pen to paper that signifies commitment and closure. I suggest you use this technique of getting a signature before the final document is produced. Use it with a written draft. It makes that draft real, and you discover whether people are really willing to finalize terms or will balk when the formal document is ready.

Parlaying the Power of Parties

When the parties are feeling empowered and are making a personal investment in creating a final agreement, the mediator can keep the environment productive and invigorate the parties by working with their communication structures. As you read in Step Five, the flame of parties' energies can be fanned or doused depending on how the mediator designs work units. When parties are at the delicate stage of crafting the final agreement, the mediator can facilitate the process and strengthen parties' ability to move forward when he continues to pay particular attention to parties' affiliations, placements, preferences, and operating codes.

Mediators parlay the power of a party by recognizing her communication structure and then matching her with others who have a similar communication structure. This work unit configuration invites the party to put her energy into creating a final agreement rather than to use it other-than-consciously to fight or fit into someone else's communication structure. When a party's thoughts and energy are directed toward the agreement rather than toward mismatched communication structures, the party can become very involved in the decision-making process and can focus on finalizing details.

Creating Feasible Targets

To help the parties work together on the final agreement, you also need to know how each person contends with reaching goals. Then you can predict how that person will create and accept the final agreement.

When you profiled the parties, you noted which parties were likely to be determined to get exactly what they want and which ones were more flexible about their outcomes. You asked them to tell you about one goal they set but did not reach. Some parties talked about pursuing a target again and again. They sounded intense and kept dwelling on the missed goal. These parties have a *perfectionist* pattern. Other parties said they tried their best. Then they "*settled* for the results" and started something new. These parties have an *optimizer* communication structure.

When I want parties to craft an agreement jointly, I look at potential interactions of these different perceptions about targets. Parties who are perfectionists demand precision and getting exactly what they want. They are often difficult to please if results are not precisely what they had in mind. They tend to be heavy-handed with themselves and others about performance. Parties who are optimizers do their best to reach goals, but allow themselves to miss a target if they have made a real effort. They tend to be more satisfied than perfectionists with their performance and that of others.

Make an effort to balance people's structures when you create working units. Put perfectionists with optimizers. If you cannot, anticipate what people will need while crafting the agreement. For example, if all parties are perfectionists, anticipate a relatively high tension level within the group. Each person will insist on exactly the language he or she suggested. Without that language he or she is likely to find the point unacceptable. I suggest you "check in" with them at different times to interrupt this tension. Suggest frequent breaks too, to help them alter their perspectives.

When the parties include both perfectionists and optimizers, anticipate only a minor tug of war. Perfectionists will want to use their own wording. They will often fight for it. Optimizers will usually make an effort to get their points across; however, they will usually yield to a perfectionist's phrasing unless the issue is a critical one for the optimizer. Again, I recommend you drop in periodically to assist in clarification or to suggest breaks.

When all the parties are optimizers, they usually create agreements quickly and require minimal help from the mediator. These parties make suggestions. Sometimes they accept recommendations. At other times they reject them. Frequently they change the recommendations and their suggestions somewhat. Typically, the final agreement reflects an amalgamation of contributions from all the parties. I advise you to review this group's final document most carefully to ensure that the terms really reflect what the parties want to say. This group has a tendency to be the most casual about wording.

Helping Parties Leave the Conflict Behind

When a conflict resolution session ends, parties leave with new experiences under their belts. The process may have taken many twists and turns. In the final analysis, however, the parties' perception of the process depends greatly on how you go about closing it down. No matter what has happened during the day, you have an opportunity to create something productive. Parties need closure after each conflict resolution session. Closure is apparent when the day ends with resolution. In addition, a sense of a positive experience is necessary when mediation is to be carried forward to another day, because parties need a door left open for the continuation of the process. A sense of a positive experience is also essential for parties who must carry on a relationship with each other.

Start your strategy with a nonverbal cue to all parties. Go to the spot you marked out as a positive location, or anchor point. Other-than-consciously the parties will now anticipate constructive ideas. Once you have established this mind-set, give the parties a positive overview of the mediation. Highlight only the worthwhile points of the mediation.

Next get more personal. Make it a point to give each person credit for something. You must do this even if you believe someone seemed uncooperative. You cannot leave any person out of the acknowledgment loop. The silence will be a clear communication that can be perceived as disrespect. It may also be embarrassing and potentially troublesome for the parties who have to deal with the unmentioned party after mediation. You must acknowledge even the most obstreperous person and be truthful when doing it, or your communication will sound hollow and incongruent. Get creative. For example, if you are acknowledging the world's biggest nitpicker you might say, "Frank, I'd like to thank you for keeping us on our toes. I know sometimes your ideas seemed unpopular, but they certainly didn't let us take things for granted. I think that extra challenge really made us comb through each issue more carefully."

Now that you have set up a positive atmosphere, be sure to drop your messages into people's other-than-conscious communication structures. This sends strong, strategic communication. For example, if mediation is concluding you can use the tone you retain for positive messages and say, "I'd like to acknowledge the hard work you all put in. By your efforts we arrived at resolution [*movement toward a solution*] and we didn't have to return to clean up loose ends [*movement away from a problem*]." For an even more profound effect, stack other-than-conscious structures on top of each other. For example, if you are tapping into parties' opportunity and necessity filters at the close of a mediation day and the parties will be meeting again, you might say, "Now that we have had the *opportunity* to resolve basic issues, we can discuss what we *need* to do in the next session." You can add mental movement by saying, "Now that we have had the opportunity to resolve basic issues [*toward*], we can discuss what we need to do in the next session so we avoid [*away*] covering old ground." You can add as many layers to a statement as you wish. Use the structures you gathered from parties' profiles. The more layers you stack, the more powerful the message on an other-than-conscious level.

By using these techniques strategically, you provide closure for a session. You also lay a positive path for parties who will resume mediation or have an ongoing relationship. You have turned the conflict resolution session into a worthwhile experience. You have created new positive anchors. You have acknowledged parties in the most respectful and meaningful way possible.

Another way to help people experience closure about the issues that caused the conflict involves using a physical representation or symbol. My experience has shown that parties often achieve closure when they discard an object after mediation. The item they scrap symbolizes the original conflict. They need to dump it. When I am preparing for a rocky mediation, I often ask parties to wear or bring something they can discard after the session. That way, if the session goes well, positive thoughts are anchored to the item and they keep it. If the session goes poorly, I suggest they jettison the article.

Sometimes the easiest thing for parties to leave behind is the room. If parties are mediating in an facility they will never visit again, you can say to them, "As you close the door on this room, think about it as closing the door on the conflict that brought you here." Parties can then shut away the issues forever. If parties are meeting in a facility in their neighborhood, however, this is not a viable strategy. Parties will pass the location frequently and be reminded constantly of the conflict as they do so. Before using this technique you want to be certain that people have no connection with the building in which the mediation is being held.

You might already have used the crumpled paper technique to assist parties during mediation. You can also use it at the end of mediation. If you have used it once, parties may anticipate being able to toss away troublesome issues. Their other-than-consciousness is primed for your suggestion. Even if you have not used the technique yet, I suggest you ask parties to mark a representation of the conflict on the paper. After they have done that, ask them to crumple the paper and toss it into the garbage. Verbally and tonally reinforce the notion that they are leaving the old conflict in the garbage. Each party can now exit without the old conflict. Each party knows that none of the other parties will ever experience it again either.

Conclusion

When I am tempted to think I know what is best for mediating parties, I remember a story about an executive who mistakenly gives his older boss the impression he wants a romantic liaison with her. He really wants to date her curvaceous niece. The executive does not want to offend his boss, really wants to go out with the niece, and cannot imagine what he can say to solve the situation. He asks his assistant what to do. She tells the executive to approach the boss and just say, "We can't see each other. *You* know *why*." The executive does not have much faith in the advice, but he is desperate. He approaches the enamored boss and blurts out, "We can't see each other. *You* know *why*." There is an excruciating silence. Finally, she says, "I know, I know, you're right. After all . . ." and she lists a string of reasons why they cannot see each other. The executive is stunned. He had not imagined even one of these reasons, and he is off the hook.

Like me, you may sometimes lose sight of the resources right in front of you—the parties to the mediation. There may even be occasions when you begin to believe you have more insight into their decisions than they do. When this happens, I recommend you take a big step back. Remember that, at best, you and I might have some recognition of the parties' verbal and nonverbal patterns. We might even be aware of how to master the structures of their communication. That, however, is just the *how* of communication. Each person is always the expert about what he or she is thinking. The acid test of your expertise and mine is to bend and shape what we know strategically around these thoughts.

Appendix A:
Taking Your Own
Communication Inventory

Instructions. This communication inventory contains eighteen sets of investigation statements. There are three statements in each set.

First, take a blank sheet of paper, and place it over the right-hand column of the inventory. That way you can avoid being influenced in your answers by the words in that column. You will uncover this column later.

Second, read each group of three statements. Identify the statement that best describes you, the statement that next best describes you, and the statement that least describes you. In the score column, enter a number value for each statement, as follows:

300 = the phrase that best describes you

200 = the phrase that next best describes you

100 = the phrase that least describes you

Here's an example:

Description	Your Score
To me:	
seeing is believing	300
hearing the whole story makes it credible	100
feeling something makes it real	200

Be sure to fill in a score for each statement.

Investigation Statements

Description	Your Score	System

1. What I remember most explicitly is:
   - how someone listened to me _____ Auditory
   - how a pal last looked _____ Visual
   - feeling close to a buddy _____ Kinesthetic

2. I prefer to:
   - get a handle on things _____ Kinesthetic
   - focus on detail _____ Visual
   - get feedback on what's happening _____ Auditory

3. My associates can construe how I am by:
   - looking at my appearance _____ Visual
   - touching base with me _____ Kinesthetic
   - asking me to tell them _____ Auditory

4. I am most likely to:
   - take hold of a situation _____ Kinesthetic
   - tune into what folks are saying _____ Auditory
   - get a clear picture of what is being
     outlined _____ Visual

5. When I recall first meeting someone,
   what I remember is:
   - our conversation _____ Auditory
   - his or her appearance _____ Visual
   - a limp or firm handshake _____ Kinesthetic

6. When I decide to act, I tend to do it when:
   - the situation looks right _____ Visual
   - the conditions feel right _____ Kinesthetic
   - the circumstances sound right _____ Auditory

7. I make quickest sense of instructions that are:
   - laid out for me, one after another _____ Kinesthetic
   - told to me in simple language _____ Auditory
   - diagramed or mapped out for me _____ Visual

Description	Your Score	System

8. The most important thing for me at an event is:

   a comfortable seat   _____   Kinesthetic

   seeing the show clearly   _____   Visual

   hearing the performers easily   _____   Auditory

9. I find driving instructions easiest when:

   I look at a city map   _____   Visual

   I read a written guide with street names

      and numbers   _____   Auditory

   I trace the map route with my finger   _____   Kinesthetic

10. When someone is introducing me to a new product, the most important thing for me is:

   to see a sample   _____   Visual

   to read testimonials or references   _____   Auditory

   to have a working model   _____   Kinesthetic

11. The gift I most like to receive is:

   cologne or perfume   _____   Kinesthetic

   a music CD or audiocassette   _____   Auditory

   a framed picture or photograph   _____   Visual

12. I would rather:

   listen to the radio   _____   Auditory

   watch a silent movie   _____   Visual

   build something   _____   Kinesthetic

13. I would rather:

   go to a place where I can work with

      my hands   _____   Kinesthetic

   go to a movie   _____   Visual

   go to a concert   _____   Auditory

14. The worst kind of road has:

   signs that are unreadable   _____   Auditory

   bumps and potholes   _____   Kinesthetic

   nothing interesting to see along the

      route   _____   Visual

Description	Your Score	System

15. A fun day includes:
    chirping birds _____ Auditory
    blue skies _____ Visual
    the sun on my face _____ Kinesthetic

16. My clearest memories of being a youngster include:
    hugs I got and gave _____ Kinesthetic
    kindergarten pictures _____ Visual
    stories read aloud _____ Auditory

17. When I book a vacation hotel, I am interested in:
    how the vacation property looks _____ Visual
    how comfortable the accommodations
      are _____ Kinesthetic
    what people have said about the spot _____ Auditory

18. I know I'm on vacation when I can:
    hear the waves crashing _____ Auditory
    feel the sand under my toes _____ Kinesthetic
    see the swimmers splashing in the water _____ Visual

Scoring. Uncover the right-hand column of the inventory. Transfer your scores to the following scoring chart. You will have eighteen scores that represent the visual system, eighteen scores that represent the auditory system, and eighteen scores that represent the kinesthetic system. Enter these scores in the appropriate columns on the scoring chart.

Then add up the scores in each column, and enter the totals in the bottom row.

Finally, consider the trends your scores reveal. Completing this communication inventory might signal an indication of possible system preferences.

Scoring Chart

	Visual	Auditory	Kinesthetic
1.	_____	_____	_____
2.	_____	_____	_____
3.	_____	_____	_____
4.	_____	_____	_____
5.	_____	_____	_____
6.	_____	_____	_____
7.	_____	_____	_____
8.	_____	_____	_____
9.	_____	_____	_____
10.	_____	_____	_____
11.	_____	_____	_____
12.	_____	_____	_____
13.	_____	_____	_____
14.	_____	_____	_____
15.	_____	_____	_____
16.	_____	_____	_____
17.	_____	_____	_____
18.	_____	_____	_____
Totals	_____	_____	_____

Appendix B: System Expressions

Visual	Auditory	Kinesthetic
sight for sore eyes	I hear you	get in touch
see for yourself	tinkle	heavyweight
panoramic view	utter	in a heartbeat
horse of a different color	whisper	heartfelt
vistas	tell me about it	walks all over him
viewpoint	give voice to	salty
show me	have a calling	spicy
visionary	answer the call	tasteful
dim view	tell a tale	smells rotten
lack of perspective	tattle tale	leave a bad taste
can't see the forest for the trees	speak up	catch-all
transparent	lectures	bring up a point
colorful	voice an opinion	raise an issue
rainbow of color	in twenty-five words or less	lace into someone
look as if	deafening	calms down
appear to be	in an uproar	irritating
luminous	vocalize	move gingerly
visualize	verbalize	dress down
imagine	have your say	uplifting
seeing double	cry out	head toward home
look at it from both sides	asking for it	leave room for
appearance	speak your mind	grasp
watchful eye	discuss it	hot and heavy
see yourself in	argumentative	have a hunch
invisible	debatable	make an impression

Nonsystem (Neutral)

understand
know
learn
believe
comprehend

Resources

Internet Sites

General Interest

http://face-to-face.org/resources.html

www3.usal.es/~nonverbal/miscellany.htm

http://digilander.iol.it/linguaggiodelcorpo/nonverb
(body language)

Publications and Papers

www3.usal.es/~nonverbal/books.htm

www3.usal.es/~nonverbal/varios.htm#journals

www3.usal.es/~nonverbal/papers.htm

www3.usal.es/~nonverbal/publications.htm

www.wkap.nl/journalhome.htm/0191-5886
(*Journal of Nonverbal Behavior*)

www.mediate.com

www3.usal.es/~nonverbal/abstracts.htm

http://digilander.iol.it/linguaggiodelcorpo/biblio
(body language library)

Research Information

www3.usal.es/~nonverbal/researchers.htm

www3.usal.es/~nonverbal/researchcenters.htm

Nonverbal Dictionary

http://members.aol.com/nonverbal2/
diction1.htm (nonverbal dictionary)

Selected Bookshops for Conflict Resolution and Communication Materials

Jossey-Bass
Telephone: 415-433-1740; 800-956-7739
Fax: 415-433-4499; 800-605-2665
E-mail: webperson@jbp.com
Internet: www.josseybass.com

Resolution Bookshop
A Division of MTI-Claremont Press, Inc.
Telephone: 800-967-4555
E-mail: inquiries@resolutionbookshop.com

The Clearinghouse
Program on Negotiation at Harvard Law School
Telephone: 800-258-4406
Fax: 781-933-6750
E-mail: chouse@law.harvard.edu

The Network
Telephone: 519-885-0880, ext. 276
Fax: 519-885-0806
Internet: www.nicr.ca/main.asp?page=3

Audiotapes and Videotapes

The Negotiator, 1998
A Warner Brothers movie, available on videocassette
MPAA Rating "R" (contains profanity and violence)
Internet: http://shopping.warnerbros.com/wbstore.html

Various titles in nonverbal communication and other-than-conscious communication are available from

Anchor Point
259 South 500 East
Salt Lake City, UT 84102-2017 USA
Telephone: 800-544-6480; 801-534-1022
Fax: 801-532-2113
E-mail: information@nlpanchorpoint.com
Internet: www.nlpanchorpoint.com

Dr. D. Dobson
P.O. Box 697
Friday Harbor, WA 98250, USA
Telephone: 800-369-4390
Fax: 360-378-7266
E-mail: information@otcc.com

Georgian Bay NLP Center
92 Parklane Crescent
Meaford, ON N4L 1B1 Canada
Telephone: 519-538-1194; 800-279-1757
Fax: 519-538-1063
E-mail: gbnlp@gb-nlp.com
Internet: www.gb-nlp.com

Audiotapes of presentations by Barbara Madonik at the American Bar Association are available from

Audio Archives
100 West Beaver Creek Road, #18
Richmond Hill, ON L4B 1H4 Canada
Telephone: 905-889-6555
Fax: 905-889-6566
E-mail: archives@idirect.com

Audiotapes of presentations by Barbara Madonik at the Canadian Bar Association (Ontario) are available from

Canadian Bar Association (Ontario)
20 Toronto Street, #200
Toronto, ON M5C 2B8 Canada
Telephone: 416-869-1047
Fax: 416-642-0424
Internet: www.cmcgc.com/cbaoindex/FRAME.HTM

Journals and Magazines

Anchor Point
259 South 500 East
Salt Lake City, UT 84102-2017
Telephone: 800-544-6480; 801-534-1022
Fax: 801-532-2113
E-mail: information@nlpanchorpoint.com

Dispute Resolution Journal
140 East 51st Street
New York, NY 10020-1203 USA
Telephone: 212-484-4011
Fax: 212-541-4841
E-mail: usadrpub@arb.com
Internet: www.adr.org

Psychology Today
49 East 21st Street, 11th Floor
New York, NY 10010 USA
Telephone: 212-260-7210; 800-234-8361 (in the U.S.A.)
Telephone: 303-682-2438 (outside the U.S.A.)
Fax: 303-661-1994
Internet: www.psychologytoday.com

Dispute Resolution Organizations

Association for Conflict Resolution
1527 New Hampshire Avenue NW, 3rd Floor
Washington, DC 20036 USA
Telephone: 202-667-9700
Fax: 202-265-1968
Internet: www.acresolution.org

The Association for Conflict Resolution is an organization formed
by the merger of the Academy of Family Mediators (AFM), the
Conflict Resolution Education Network (CRnet), and the Society
of Professionals in Dispute Resolution (SPIDR).

ADR Institute of Canada, Inc.
Institut d'Arbitrage et de Médiation du Canada
329 March Road, Suite 232
P.O. Box 11
Kanata, ON K2K 2E1 Canada
Telephone: 613-599-0878; 877-475-4353
Fax: 613-599-7027
Internet: www.adrinstitute.ca

The ADR Institute of Canada, Inc./Institut d'Arbitrage et de Médiation du Canada is an organization formed by the merger of the Arbitration and Mediation Institute of Canada (AMIC), and the Canadian Foundation for Dispute Resolution (CFDR).

American Arbitration Association
335 Madison Avenue, 10th Floor
New York, NY 10017-4605 USA
Telephone: 212-716-5800; 800-778-7879
Fax: 212-716-5905
Internet: www.adr.org

American Bar Association
Section of Dispute Resolution
740 Fifteenth Street NW
Washington, DC 20005-1002 USA
Telephone: 202-662-1680; 800-285-2221
Fax: 202-662-1683
E-mail: dispute@abanet.org
Internet: www.abanet.org

Canadian Bar Association
902-50 O'Connor Street
Ottawa, ON K1P 6L2 Canada
Telephone: 613-237-2925; 613-237-1988; 800-267-8860
Fax: 613-237-0185
E-mail: information@cba.org
Internet: www.cba.org

National Association for Community Mediation (NAFCM)
1527 New Hampshire Avenue NW, 3rd Floor
Washington, DC 20036-1206 USA
Telephone: 202-667-9700
Fax: 202-667-8629
E-mail: nafcm@nafcm.org
Internet: www.nafcm.org

National Institute for Dispute Resolution (NIDR)
1726 M Street NW, Suite 500
Washington, D.C. 20036-4502 USA
Telephone: 202-466-4764, ext. 306
Fax: 202-466-4769
E-mail: nidr@crenet.org
Internet: www.ncl.org/anr/partners/nidr.htm

The Network
Institute of Peace and Conflict Studies
Conrad Grebel College
University of Waterloo
Waterloo, ON N2L 3G6 Canada
Telephone: 519-885-0880
Fax: 519-885-0806
E-mail: nicr@nicr.ca
Internet: www.nicr.ca

References

Anderson, V. A. *Training the Speaking Voice.* (3rd ed.) New York: Oxford University Press, 1977.

Andreas, S., and Andreas, C. *Change Your Mind and Keep the Change.* Moab, Utah: Real People Press, 1987.

Andrews, L. B. "You the Jury: Exhibit A: Language." *Psychology Today,* Feb. 1984, pp. 28–33.

Bandler, R. *Using Your Brain for a Change.* Moab, Utah: Real People Press, 1985.

Bandler, R., and Grinder, J. *The Structure of Magic.* Vol. 1. Palo Alto, Calif.: Science and Behavior Books, 1975.

Bandler, R., and Grinder, J. *Frogs into Princes.* Moab, Utah: Real People Press, 1979.

Bandler, R., and Grinder, J. *Reframing.* Moab, Utah: Real People Press, 1982.

Bandler, R., Grinder, J., and DeLozier, J. *Patterns of the Hypnotic Techniques of Milton H. Erickson, M.D.* Vol. 2. Cupertino, Calif.: Meta, 1977.

Barkai, J. L., "Sensory Based Language in Legal Communication." *The Practical Lawyer,* 1981, *27*(1), 41–55.

Bateson, G. *Steps to an Ecology of Mind.* New York: Ballantine, 1972.

Bateson, G. *Ecology of the Mind.* Big Sur, Calif.: Big Sur Tapes, 1978. Audiotape from an Esalen Institute series.

Bateson, G., Jackson, D., Haley, J., and Weakland, J. "Toward a Theory of Schizophrenia." *Behavioral Science,* 1956, *1,* 251–264.

Berry, P. "Effect of Colored Illumination upon Perceived Temperature." *Journal of Applied Psychology,* 1961, *45*(4), 248–250.

Birdwhistell, R. L. *Introduction to Kinesics.* Louisville, Ky.: University of Louisville Press, 1952.

Birdwhistell, R. L. *Kinesics in Context.* Philadelphia: University of Pennsylvania, 1970.

Bush, R.A.B., and Folger, J. P. *The Promise of Mediation.* San Francisco: Jossey-Bass, 1994.

Capacchione, L. *The Power of Your Other Hand.* North Hollywood, Calif.: Newcastle, 1988.

Chomsky, N. *Syntactic Structures.* Hawthorne, N.Y.: Mouton de Gruyter, 1957.

Conn, J. H. *Revised Edition of Braid on Hypnotism: The Beginning of Modern Hypnosis by James Braid, M.D.* New York: Julian Press, 1960.

Covey, S. *The Seven Habits of Highly Effective People.* New York: Simon & Schuster, 1990.

Crawford, M. "Legal Update: Alternative Dispute Resolution." *Canadian Lawyer,* May 1998, pp. 43–44.

Davis, S. M. "The Swish: A Technology for the 'Be Proactive' Habit." *Anchor Point,* 1991, *5*(2), 17–20.

Deutsch, D. "An Auditory Illusion." *Nature,* 1974, *251,* 307–309.

Dilts, R. B. *Roots of Neuro-linguistic Programming.* Cupertino, Calif.: Meta, 1983.

Dilts, R. B. Strategies of Genius: Gregory Bateson." *Anchor Point,* 1990, *4*(9), 1–2.

Dilts, R. B., Grinder, J., Bandler, R., DeLozier, J., and Camerson-Bandler, L. *Neuro-Linguistic Programming.* Vol. 1. Cupertino, Calif.: Meta, 1979.

Dobson, D. *NLP, OTCC & YOU.* Friday Harbor, Wash.: MKM/ULC, 1985. Audiotape of workshop in neuro-linguistic programming and other-than-conscious communication.

Dobson, D. *The Phenomenon of Hypnosis, Other-Than-Conscious Communication, and The Mythical Kingdom of the Mind.* Friday Harbor, Wash: MKM/ULC, 1986. Audiotape of workshop.

Eccles J. (ed.). *Brain and Conscious Experience.* New York: Springer-Verlag, 1966.

Erickson, M. H., and Rossi, E. *The February Man: Evolving Consciousness and Identity in Hypnotherapy.* New York: Brunner/Mazel, 1989.

Erickson, M. H., Rossi, E., and Rossi, S. *Hypnotic Realities.* New York: Irvington, 1976.

Fisher, R. *Getting Together.* New York: Viking Penguin, 1989.

Fisher, R., Ury, W., and Patton, G. *Getting to Yes: Negotiating Agreement Without Giving In.* Boston: Houghton Mifflin, 1981.

Fox, T. "Metaphorical Resource Strategy." *Anchor Point,* 1988, *2*(11), 15–16.

Gazzaniga, M. "The Split Brain in Man." *Scientific American,* Aug. 1967, *27*(2), 24–29.

Gibson, G. *The Senses Considered as Perceptual Systems.* Boston: Houghton-Mifflin, 1966.

Gold, L. "Reframing, Reframing, Reframing: A Mediator's Debt to Virginia Satir." *Anchor Point,* 1993, *7*(6), 34–37.

Goldstone, S., and Lhamon, W. "Auditory-Visual Differences in Human Temporal Judgement." *Perceptual and Motor Skills,* 1972, *34*(2), 623–633.

Goleman, D. "Studies Point to the Power of Non-verbal Signals." *New York Times,* Apr. 8, 1986, pp. C-1, C-6.

Gordon, D. *Therapeutic Metaphors.* Cupertino, Calif.: Meta, 1978.

Gordon, D. "NLP Through Time." *NLP Connection,* 1989, *4*(3), 20.

Gordon, D., and Meyers-Anderson, M. *Phoenix.* Cupertino, Calif.: Meta, 1981.

Gregory, R. L. *Eye and Brain.* New York: World University Press, 1966.

Grinder, J. *On Deletion Phenomena in English.* Hawthorne, N.Y.: Mouton de Gruyter, 1974.

Grinder, J., and Bandler, R. *The Structure of Magic.* Vol. 2. Palo Alto, Calif.: Science and Behavior Books, 1976.

Grinder, J., and Bandler, R. *Trance-Formations.* Moab, Utah: Real People Press, 1981.

Grinder, J., and Elgin, S. *A Guide to Transformational Grammar.* Austin, Tex.: Holt, Rinehart and Winston, 1973.

Groberg, D., Dustman, R., and Beck, E. "The Effect of Body and Head Tilt in the Perception of Vertical." *Neuropsychologia,* 1969, *7,* 89–100.

Gudykunst, W. B, and Ting-Toomey, S. *Culture and Interpersonal Communication.* Thousand Oaks, Calif.: Sage, 1988.

Gudykunst, W. B, and Young, Y. K. *Communicating with Strangers.* (3rd ed.) New York: McGraw-Hill 1997.

Haley, J. (ed.). *Advanced Techniques of Hypnosis and Therapy.* Philadelphia: Grune & Stratton, 1967.

Haley, J. *Problem-Solving Therapy.* San Francisco: Jossey-Bass, 1987.

Hall, D. C. "The Effect of Eye Movement on the Recall of Information with Visual Imagery." *Dissertation Abstracts International,* 1972, *33* (1-B), 461–462.

Hall, E. T. *The Silent Language.* New York: Fawcett, 1959.

Hall, E. T. *Beyond Culture.* New York: Doubleday, 1966.

Hall, E. T. *The Hidden Dimension.* New York: Doubleday, 1966.

Hall, E. T. *The Dance of Life: The Other Dimension of Time.* New York: Doubleday, 1984.

Hall, L. M. "Flashing Back to the Origins of Neuro-Linguistic Training and the Year Is 1933." *Anchor Point,* 1992, *6*(5), 14–18.

Hall, L. M. "Abstracting: How Nervous Systems Create Internal Maps of Reality." *Anchor Point,* 1993a, *7*(1), 25–30.

Hall, L. M. "What Actually Gets Mapped onto the Map?" *Anchor Point,* 1993b, *7*(11), 34–37.

Hall, L. M. "Gregory Bateson on Schizophrenia." *Anchor Point,* 1994a, *8*(2), 40–45

Hall, L. M. "What Are the Steps to an Ecology of Mind?" *Anchor Point,* 1994b, *8*(1), 36–40.

Hall, L. M. *Meta-States: Self-Reflexivity in Human States of Consciousness.* Grand Junction, Colo.: E.T., 1995.

Hall, L. M. *The Secrets of Magic: Communication Excellence for the 21st Century.* Carmarthen, Wales: Anglo-American, 1998.

Haney, W. V. *Communication and Interpersonal Relations.* (6th ed.) Burr Ridge, Ill.: Irwin, 1992.

Harris, T. A. *I'm OK—You're OK: A Practical Guide to Transactional Analysis.* New York: HarperCollins, 1967.

Harvey, J. *The Quiet Mind.* Honesdale, Pa.: Himalayan International Institute of Yoga Science and Philosophy of the U.S.A., 1988.

Hott, R. B. "Back to Basics: Aspects of an Effective Communicator." *Anchor Point,* 1989a, *3*(11), 21–23.

Hott, R. B. "Back to Basics: Models of the World." *Anchor Point,* 1989b, *3*(6), 14–16.

Hott, R. B. "Back to Basics: Anchors Away." *Anchor Point,* 1990a, *4*(1), 24.

Hott, R. B. "Back to Basics: Chunking Animal Vegetable or Mineral?" *Anchor Point,* 1990b, *4*(7), 20–21.

James, T., and Woodsmall, W. *Time Line Therapy and the Basis of Personality.* Cupertino, Calif.: Meta, 1988.

Joseph, N. *Uniforms and Nonuniforms: Communication Through Clothing.* Westport, Conn.: Greenwood, 1986.

Josipovici, G. *Touch.* New Haven, Conn.: Yale University Press, 1996.

Kasai, F. "Reversed Time Lines in 'Converted Lefties.'" *Anchor Point,* 1988, *2*(4), 1–2.

Kluczny, J. W. "The 'As If' Technique." *Anchor Point,* 1989, *3*(10), 20–21.

Knie, P. "Erickson's Oral Tradition: Your Rite of Passage." *Anchor Point,* 1990, *4*(4), 13–14.

Korzybski, A. *Science and Sanity: An Introduction to Non-Aristotelian Systems and General Semantics.* (4th ed.) Lakeville, Conn.: International Non-Aristotelian Library, 1958. [Originally published 1933.]

Kostere, K., and Malatesta, L. Utilizing the Metaphor: An Ericksonian/NLP Approach." *Anchor Point,* 1992, *6*(10), 5–10.

Krauthamer, G. "Form Perception Across Sensory Modalities." *American Psychologist,* 1959, *14,* 396.

Laborde, G. *Influencing with Integrity.* Palo Alto, Calif.: Syntony, 1984.

Lankton, S. R. *Practical Magic.* Cupertino, Calif.: Meta, 1980.

Lankton, S. R., and Lankton, C. H. *The Answer Within: A Clinical Framework of Ericksonian Hypnotherapy.* New York: Brunner/Mazel, 1983.

Lewis, B. A., and Pucelik, T. F. *Magic Demystified.* Lake Oswego, Ore.: Metamorphosis Press, 1982.

Lobel, I. B. "What Mediation Can and Cannot Do." *Dispute Resolution Journal,* May 1998, pp. 44–47.

Madonik, B. G. "Have You Heard What You Have Been Missing?" *The Advocates' Society Journal,* 1989, *8*(3), 9, 12.

Madonik, B. G. "Beyond the Tip of the Iceberg." *The Advocates' Society Journal,* 1990a, *9*(1), 12–15.

Madonik, B. G. "Keeping Them on the Road." *The Advocates' Society Journal,* 1990b, *9*(2), 19–21.

Madonik, B. G. "Dispute Resolution: Not What You Say, But What You Communicate." *Canadian Bar Association (Ontario), Alternative Dispute Resolution Section News,* 1997a, *5*(2), 14–17.

Madonik, B. G. "No Fault Communication Tips." *Canadian Bar Association (Ontario), Alternative Dispute Resolution Section News,* 1997b, *5*(5), 10–12.

Madonik, B. G. "Working at the Level of Irresistible Communication." *Canadian Bar Association (Ontario), Alternative Dispute Resolution Section News,* 1997c, *6*(1), 1–4.

Madonik, B. G. "It's Not Your Birthday Party." *Canadian Bar Association (Ontario), Alternative Dispute Resolution Section News,* 1998a, *6*(6), 11–12.

Madonik, B. G. "Snake Oil, Pigeon Holes, and Crystal Balls: A Practical Look at Dispelling Some Faulty Communication Myths." Paper presented at the Canadian Bar Association (Ontario) Annual Institute of Continuing Legal Education, Toronto, Jan. 1998b.

Maurer, H. *Tao Te Ching.* New York: Schoken Books, 1985.

McCrory, R. H. "Nominalizations for a Change." *Anchor Point,* 1989, *3*(7), 9–13.

Mehrabian, A. *Nonverbal Communication.* Hawthorne, N.Y: Aldine de Gruyter, 1972.

Miller, G. "The Magical Number Seven, Plus or Minus Two: Some Limits on Our Capacity for Processing Information." *Psychological Review,* 1956, *63*(2), 81–97.

Moore, C. W. *The Mediation Process: Practical Strategies for Resolving Conflict.* San Francisco: Jossey-Bass, 1996.

Moravec, H. "When Will Computer Hardware Match the Human Brain?" *Journal of Transhumanism,* 1998, *1* [www.transhumanist.com/#1].

Morgan, G., Goodson, F., and, Jones, T. "Age Differences in the Associations Between Felt Temperatures and Color Choices." *American Journal of Psychology,* 1974, *88*(1), 125–130.

Morris, D. *Bodytalk: The Meaning of Human Gestures.* New York: Crown, 1995.

Morris, D., Collett, P., Marsh, P., and O'Shaughnessy, M. *Gestures.* New York: Stein and Day, 1979.

Nadel, L. "NLP and the Triune Brain: A Contrastive Analysis." *Anchor Point*, 1993, *7*(5) 20–25.

Nierenberg, G. I, *Fundamentals of Negotiating*. New York: Hawthorn/Dutton, 1973.

Nuernberger, P. *Freedom from Stress*. Honesdale, Pa.: Himalayan International Institute of Yoga Science and Philosophy of the U.S.A., 1981.

Perls, F. *The Gestalt Approach & Eye Witness to Therapy*. Palo Alto, Calif.: Science and Behavior Books, 1973.

Podolsky, E. *The Doctor Prescribes Colors*. New York: National Library Press, 1938.

Poyatos, F. *Paralanguage*. Philadelphia: John Benjamins, 1993.

Preusser, D. "The Effect of Structure and Rate on the Recognition and Description of Auditory Temporal Pattern." *Perception and Psychophysics*, 1972, *11*(3), 233–240.

Pribram, K. *Languages of the Brain*. Upper Saddle River, N.J.: Prentice Hall, 1971.

Protas, A., Brown, G., and Smith J., *Dictionary of Symbolism*. [www. umich. edu/~umfandsf/symbolismproject/symbolism.html/index.html], 1987.

Rama, Swami, Ballentine, R., and Hymes, A. *Science of Breath: A Practical Guide*. Honesdale, Pa.: Himalayan International Institute of Yoga Science and Philosophy of the U.S.A., 1979.

Rosen, S. (ed.). *My Voice Will Go with You*. New York: Norton, 1982.

Routier, J. P. "A Sound Approach to the Structure of Experience." *Anchor Point*, 1990, *4*(5), 17–18.

Royer, F., and Garner, W. "Response Uncertainty and Perceptual Difficulty of Auditory Temporal Patterns." *Perception and Psychophysics*, 1966, *1*(2), 41–47.

Scott, I. *The Lüscher Color Test*. New York: Random House, 1969.

Shane, S. "Scientists Explore Our Hemming and Hawing." *Toronto Star*, Oct. 2, 1999, p. L10.

Sommer, R. *Personal Space: The Behavioral Basis of Design*. Upper Saddle River, N.J.: Prentice Hall, 1969.

Toivonen, V.-M., "Using Natural Anchors as Memory Aids." *Anchor Point*, 1990, *4*(2), 17.

Toivonen, V.-M., Kauppi, T., and Murphy, T. "Basic Conjunctions, Part 2: But & And." *Anchor Point*, 1995, *9*(2), 32–35.

Tubbs, S. L., and Moss, S., *Human Communication*. (7th ed.) New York: McGraw-Hill, 1994.

Van der Horst, B. "Edward T. Hall: A Great-Grandfather of NLP." *Anchor Point*, 1993, *7*(2), 23–30.

VandenBerghe, K. "The World According to Eric Oliver." *Anchor Point,* 1994, *8*(10), 13–20.

Weakland, J. H. "The Double-Bind Theory by Self-Reflexive Hindsight." In P. Watzlawick and J. H. Weakland (eds.), *The Interactional View: Studies at the Mental Research Institute, Palo Alto, 1965–1974.* New York: Norton, 1977.

Weber, D. E. "Guidelines for Cross-Cultural Effectiveness." *Anchor Point,* 1990 *4*(3), 1–5.

Weitz, S. (ed.). *Nonverbal Communication: Reading with Commentary.* (2nd ed.) New York: Oxford University Press, 1979.

Wigging, F. K. "Moving Up with Rapport." *Anchor Point,* 1991, *5*(12), 23–25.

Vaihinger, H. *The Philosophy of "As If."* New York: Routledge, 1924.

Zeig, J. K. *A Teaching Seminar with Milton H. Erickson.* New York: Brunner/ Mazel, 1980.

Zeig, J. K. (ed.). *Ericksonian Psychotherapy,* Vol. 2: *Clinical Applications.* New York: Brunner/Mazel, 1985.

About the Author

Barbara G. Madonik is president of Unicom Communication Consultants Inc., a firm specializing in communication consulting and training, and dispute investigation and resolution services. She is a senior communication consultant and mediator. In 1970, she received her B.A. degree from the University of Toronto. In 1987, she pioneered the practical use of nonverbal communication in the Canadian legal system. She has more than twenty-five years of experience working with corporations, associations, governmental agencies, universities, community colleges, and law firms. She also profiles judges, tribunals, and witnesses. She is a director of the Arbitration and Mediation Institute of Ontario, associate member of the American Bar Association, and subscriber of the Canadian Bar Association (Ontario). She has been cited as a jury selection expert by the Professional Marketing Research Society and as a communication expert by Osgoode Hall Law School.

Barbara Madonik has been a charter vice president of the Association for Professional Training Organizations, program consultant for York University and The Advocates' Society Institute, and instructor in both communication and negotiation for the Canadian Management Centre of American Management Association International, Seneca College, York University, and the government of Ontario. She has lectured at the University of Toronto's Dispute Resolution Certificate Program and Osgoode Hall Law School's undergraduate Criminal Law Program and Graduate Law Studies specializing in alternative dispute resolution. She has conducted a variety of workshops focusing on the different strategic uses of nonverbal communication. She has appeared on television and radio. Her articles have been published in law and professional journals and legal association newsletters. She has done programs for the Canadian Bar Association (Ontario) and the American Bar Association. At one American Bar Association program, an executive editor for Jossey-Bass became fascinated by her subject. He wondered if she could write a book telling mediators how to use nonverbal communication strategies for resolving conflict. As a result, she now smiles at the fact that she has, strangely enough, become an interesting channel in the mainstream.

She invites readers to contact her with questions and feedback about their results:

Barbara G. Madonik
Unicom Communication Consultants Inc.
379 Winnett Avenue
Toronto, ON M6C 3M2 Canada
Telephone: 416-652-1867
Fax: 416-652-3143
E-mail: barbara.madonik@utoronto.ca

Index

techniques for gathering, 62–63; questioning techniques to gather, 93–98; representational systems collecting, 4–5; sensory, 15; system words used to express, 12

Initial telephone contact: conversation management during, 86–90; maximizing collected information during, 84–85; maximizing your effectiveness during, 85–86; paralanguage nuances during, 90–93; physical factors in, 83–86

Inside pressure reaction, 57, 144–145, 210–211, 242

Inside validation, 55, 135–136, 222

Inside-outside pressure reaction, 210

Internal dialogues cue, 25

Internal fear cues, 10

Intimate zone, 43

K

Kelly Decision Wheel, 65, 227

Kelly, K. J., 65

Kinesic slip, 7–8

Kinesthetic cue, 25, 26, 28, 129

Kinesthetic representational system: described, 4; moving individual toward, 168–169; offer presentation using, 231; other-than-conscious cues of, 201–202; paralanguage/language patterns of, 130; physical cues/patterns of, 25, 26, 28, 129; using props to aid, 216

L

Language: deescalating speakers,' 89–90; gaining proficiency in system, 75; identifying preferred system using, 10–13, 30; matching, 88–89; used in offer presentation, 229–231; power balance and, 99–101; structures of, 13. *See also* Communication; Paralanguage cues/patterns

Language cues/patterns: butting, 13, 39, 173–174; cultural influences on, 38–39; described, 37; difficulties from individual, 39–40; identifying preferred system using, 10–13, 30; using nonsystem words, 30–31; nonsystem words, 13, 30–31; system words, 12

Language matrix: described, 13; identifying profile of, 51, 54–58

Language models, 13

Language structures: described, 13; high-context, 11, 38–39, 88; low-context, 11, 38, 39, 88

Language touchstones, 55, 132–133, 190, 193, 229–231

Lao-tzu, 42

Lawyer dress codes, 48

Leading process, 12

Left-handed people: assessing physical traits of, 128–129; eye patterns of, 25

LIAR mnemonic, 150, 228

Location issues, 104–105

Loner affiliation, 56, 140–141, 177, 178

Low-contact cultures: described, 20; touching patterns as indication of, 45–46

Low-context communication: described, 11; language patterns and, 38, 39; matching, 88

Lüscher Color Test, 106

M

Macro-thinking, 56, 138–139, 231–233

Madonik, B., 155

Magic button technique, 65, 206–207

Main room preparation, 105–107

Maintainer placement (or maintainers), 58, 147–148, 179–180

Marking out technique, 65–66, 204–205

Match-pace-guide technique, 59, 190